New Cooking
from the
Old West

NEW COOKING

FROM THE

OLD WEST

Greg Patent

Ten Speed Press

Berkeley, California

For Granny, Baba, and Edith Green

Ten Speed Press
Box 7123
Berkeley, California 94707

Distributed in Australia by E. J. Dwyer Pty. Ltd., in Canada by Publishers Group West, in New Zealand by Tandem Press, in South Africa by Real Books, and in the United Kingdom and Europe by Airlift Books.

Cover design by Nancy Austin

Text design by Victor Ichioka

Photos on front and back covers reprinted with permission of the University of Montana, Mansfield Library.

Library of Congress Cataloging-in-Publication Data

Patent, Greg, 1939–
    New cooking from the Old West / Greg Patent.
        p.   cm.
    Includes index.
    ISBN 0-89815-786-2
    1. Cookery, American—Western style.   I. Title.
TX715.2.W47P38   1996
641.5978—dc20   96-16750
                                                                                    CIP

Printed in Canada

First printing, 1996

1 2 3 4 5 6 7 8 9 10 — 00 99 98 97 96

· CONTENTS ·

Acknowledgments

In a project that has taken me three years, there are many people I want to thank.

First and foremost, I want to thank my editor, Lorena Jones. Her invaluable suggestions, guidance, and encouragement, were indispensable in helping this book find its final form.

Much gratitude also goes to: Charles Stewart, for helping convince Phil Wood that the West deserved to have a cookbook of its own; Tony Grace, who spoke so enthusiastically about his days as a chuck wagon cook at the turn of the century; Jo Rainbolt, for introducing me to Tony Grace and arranging a luncheon with him; Chu Chu Pham, for teaching me the rudiments of Vietnamese cooking; Gillian Malone, for bringing me up to date on the Wyoming cooking scene and for introducing me to Sam Western; Sam Western, for expressing his feelings about hunting and for cooking a delicious meal of game with Asian flavors; Sam Arnold, for giving so generously of his time to relate the history of Native American and Western foods; John McCamant, for introducing us to black quinoa; Larry Evans and Kris Love, for generously sharing their wild mushroom harvests with us, and for their friendship; Art and Nancy Callan, for educating me about apple growing in Montana and Idaho and for making available little-known heirloom varieties at our local farmers market; Don Spritzer, resource librarian at the Missoula Public Library, for directing me to historical diaries of emigrants; Rich and Lily Bumbaca, for sharing their enthusiasm for bison with us and introducing their beloved herd up close and personal; Roger, Carla, Leif, and Heidi Cox, for generous supplies of game; Ted and Peggy Christian, also for their generous gift of game; Mike Schwartz, for some of the best elk I've ever eaten; Dale Johnson, archivist at the Mansfield Library at the University of Montana, for opening his photographic files to me; Roland and Marie Smith, for hosting me while I did some research in Portland, Oregon; George Carlberg, chef at Denver's Buckhorn Exchange, for providing many excellent mail-order sources for ingredients; The Washington Apple Commision, for supplying information on apple growing in Washington State; The gardeners, foragers, millers, dairy owners, game purveyors, ranchers, fishermen, and poultry farmers, for caring enough to produce healthful, high-quality food products.

And my darling wife, Dorothy, who not only tasted, evaluated, and commented upon every recipe in this book, but helped me teach my computer to do what I wanted it to do.

I simply could not have done this without all of you.

Preface

The West is not only a place, it is a state of mind—open, receptive, and welcoming. Perhaps the feeling of the West is best expressed by Cole Porter's song, "Don't Fence Me In," which he based on a poem by Bob Fletcher, a Montanan. Although I spent my first eleven years in Shanghai, China, I have lived in the West most of my life—first in San Francisco, then in Missoula, Montana, where my wife and I raised our two sons and continue to live. Over the years, I've come to appreciate the West's natural abundance—wild mushrooms and berries, all kinds of game meat, whole grains, and of course, the hard winter wheat that is essential for making excellent yeast breads.

I began cooking shortly after my family emigrated to San Francisco in 1950. Each day I raced home from school to watch a live afternoon cooking show on KRON-TV hosted by Edith Green, who taught me the basics of baking powder biscuits, pies, cakes, and desserts. As a teenager, I branched out into preparing "real" food and helped my working parents by getting dinner ready before they came home. After I got married, Julia Child's early television shows taught me most of what I know today about cooking.

As I was growing up, it never dawned on me to pursue my passion for cooking as a career. It was just a hobby until 1979, when, at a friend's suggestion, I approached a local television station and proposed a weekly cooking show. At about the same time, I became a finalist in the National Pineapple Cooking Classic and won a trip to Hawaii to compete in a cook-off. That, coupled with my Pillsbury Bake-Off win as a teenager, convinced the management at KECI-TV to make a pilot half-hour show called "Big Sky Cooking"—the beginning of my cooking career. We shot fifty-two episodes, and I published two cookbooks with the recipes. During that time I also wrote a weekly food column for *The Missoulian*, our local paper, while I continued my profession as a zoology professor at the University of Montana.

In 1982 Carl Sontheimer, the president of Cuisinarts, offered me a job I could not refuse. I left the university and began working as his company's national spokesperson. I traveled all over the country and taught food processor cooking classes for many years. Cuisinarts also financed a food processor cooking show broadcast nationally on the Learning Channel. I wrote a food processor cookbook, originally published by Cuisinarts in 1985 as *Patently Easy Food Processor Cooking*, then Ten Speed Press reprinted the book as *Food Processor Cooking Quick and Easy*. For a number of years thereafter, I was a restaurant chef, and I had the good fortune of working with wonderful cooks in Switzerland and Bavaria as part of my training.

I now write about food from my home. Even though I've lived in the United States for more years than not, my early influences have always drawn me to the foods of other lands. My mother's mother, Granny, was Arabic. We lived with her for many years in Shanghai, and she cooked savory Middle Eastern dishes. Baba, my father's mother, cooked foods of her native Russia. I remember especially her superb pastries and desserts. And for a time in Shanghai, we even had a Chinese cook. I can still remember hanging around in the kitchen while she worked, begging for samples of her mouthwatering dishes. Later on after graduate school, my wife and I, along with our two young sons, lived in Naples, Italy, for a year. Our housekeeper there taught us to cook many specialties of the region.

What excites me today are the foods brought by new immigrants to the West. Over the past twenty years, people from Asia, Mexico, Russia, and elsewhere have influenced public tastes by selling their homegrown herbs and vegetables at farmers markets, getting supermarkets to stock ethnic cooking staples, and opening local restaurants. These flavors, when combined with traditional western foods, create wonderful new tastes. For example, Asian-flavored marinades give smoked salmon a new dimension and adding cilantro to a sweet-and-sour sauce for buffalo meatballs brings out the flavor of the meat with newfound clarity. And an exciting variety of fresh herbs, now available in practically every market, add oomph and zest to almost any food.

The ongoing culinary renaissance in the West has motivated me to write this book. In creating these recipes, I have been inspired by innovative chefs and local cooks who continue the tradition of living off the land—they hunt, forage for wild things, and love to try new foods. Cooking is much more than bodily nourishment. Good cooking satisfies the soul, and I am filled with wonder whenever a new flavor combination tells my taste buds that something extraordinary is happening. When I am cooking, I often think of how the character based on the painter Georges Seurat in Stephen Sondheim's musical *Sunday in the Park with George* approaches an empty canvas. "So many possibilities," he says.

~ INTRODUCTION ~

Each advanced step carried us farther and farther
from civilization into a desolate, barbarous country.
But our new home lay beyond all this and was a shining beacon
that beckoned us on…our watchword, Westward Ho!

—Phoebe Goodell Judson, emigrant on the Oregon Trail, 1853

Cooking is a dynamic part of culture and society. Its vitality depends upon a successful union of great ingredients with innovative cooks. The distinctive cuisines of France, Italy, and China, for example, have evolved over hundreds or thousands of years. And it is the precious gift of time that has helped to shape the cuisines into what they are today. Thomas Jefferson believed it would take a thousand years to settle the West. Instead, it happened in just fewer than fifty years, by 1893. Because the history of the West's settlement has been so brief, its culinary potential is just beginning to be appreciated.

I do not believe that the West can claim a truly original cuisine, primarily because the region is so large and was settled by pioneers from so many different backgrounds. However, an extraordinarily wide range of foods, many unique to the region, are grown, farmed, raised, gathered, or hunted in the West. These vital staples, along with the diverse cultures the settlers brought with them, provide the raw materials from which western cooks' imaginations have always taken flight. Buffalo, deer, elk, bear, moose, and all sorts of other game have played a significant role in western cooking, and perhaps no other region in the country offers as many different kinds of edible wild mushrooms. The wild huckleberries that flourish in the mountains of Montana and Idaho are unique. They do not grow anywhere else, and they make the best pies, muffins, and jams imaginable. From the Northwest come highly prized Dungeness crabs, Columbia River sturgeon, Pacific oysters, several species of trout, and Pacific salmon.

The high-altitude western prairies and valleys are prime growing areas for wheat, barley, oats, lentils, and quinoa, one of the newest crops. Large, juicy cherries grow along the shores of Flathead Lake in Montana and in the valleys of northern Oregon and southern Washington.

More familiar plants such as garden-variety rhubarb, strawberries, and raspberries grow in many parts of the country, but they thrive in the cool Rocky Mountain air and along the misty Pacific Coast. The hunting and gathering traditions of the West encompass many independent-minded pursuits, such as digging for clams, a favorite pastime of families on the Pacific Coast. Canning and preserving foods were important traditions, enabling farm families to put up the region's abundant harvest of fruits and vegetables to be savored during the cold winter months. Westerners also smoked meats and fish to preserve them. Typically, the foods were cold-smoked for days, then stored in a cool place for months thereafter. Today, smoking remains popular, but hot-smoking is the preferred method because it is faster and virtually foolproof. All of these aspects of western cooking continue to define and distinguish the cuisine of the region today. This book is filled with recipes and anecdotes that celebrate and chronicle the people and landscape of the old and the new West.

When the first Europeans began settling on the North American continent, they couldn't have known that approximately 10 million Native Americans were already occupying the territory that is now known as Canada and the United States. A multitude of tribes lived on the land, many wandering freely hundreds of miles throughout the year, setting up camps until it was time to move on in search of food, water, or milder weather. These tribes were among the freest people the world has ever known. Tens of millions of bison (also known as American buffalo) roamed the region as well. These powerful, single-minded animals were a vital food source for many of the tribes. Their hides were tanned and used for clothing and shelter, their bones for tools and weapons. The bison sustained many tribes, both spiritually as well as literally.

Over the three centuries after European settlement began, 90 percent of the Native Americans were wiped out by war and disease. By 1840 all of the eastern tribes had been annihilated, subdued, or moved west of the Mississippi for resettlement. Only 360,000 Native Americans were left, practically all living in the West. Meanwhile, the eastern part of the United States filled up fast with settlers. There was only one direction to move, and that was westward. Motivated mostly by the perceived sin of poverty and the promise of abundance and a better life, emigrants staked everything they had to move their families and possessions to the new frontier. Packed into their mobile ox-drawn covered wagon homes, they made their way slowly across the prairies to the Rocky Mountains and beyond, traveling until there was no more land to cross. The arduous trip to Oregon, Washington, or California took four to six months.

Between 1840 and 1860, more than 300,000 pioneers traveled the Oregon Trail. By 1860 the population of Caucasians in the West had swelled from 20,000 to almost 1,000,000. Such rapid expansion was unprecedented in the history of the world, and the inevitable clashes between the new settlers and the Native Americans occurred. There was no way for these cultures to coexist in such a way that the Native Americans could maintain their hunter-gatherer lifestyles. They lived with the earth and took what they needed for survival. They migrated with the seasons in a natural cycle of renewal, and their basic needs were satisfied by a bountiful landscape. The Native Americans owned no property; they didn't believe in the concept.

The Europeans, on the other hand, looked upon the land as something to be tamed, conquered, and possessed. They needed to impose a natural sense of order on what they perceived as chaos. For them, ownership of the land itself was the biggest dream of all. It held the promise of making anything out of anything, and indicated one was worth something. Owning land showed one could provide for his or her family and had escaped the despised poverty. Making a country meant settling the land—dividing it up and parceling it out to private owners.

The West was the place where we Americans became a people unlike the people we were in Europe, a place where we became mythic in our own minds. Mark Twain said he came west out of envy for his brother, who went to the Nevada Territory. Twain imagined his brother "would be hundreds and hundreds of miles away on the great plains and deserts and would see buffaloes and Indians and have all kinds of adventures and maybe get hanged or scalped and have ever such a fine time and write home and tell us all about it and be a hero." Twain hated to miss the fun. So did thousands of others. The lure and appeal of the West proved to be irresistible.

By 1865 stagecoach lines had reached to Denver, Santa Fe, Salt Lake City, and beyond. After the Civil War, expansion quickened as people left the South in pursuit of a prosperous future in the West. The completion of the transcontinental railroad in 1869 sealed the fate of the Native Americans.

The bison also perished in the process. They were hunted by the emigrants for food along the trail, but massive killings took place when commercial enterprises sent professional hunters to shoot the animals for their hides and tongues, considered a delicacy back East. More than 8 million bison were killed in one 3-year period. The carcasses were left to rot on the prairie. The sun-dried bones were crushed and sold as fertilizer for $5 a ton. Some estimates say there were 75 million bison in the eighteenth century. By 1883 only 200 bison remained in the entire West. Ironically, Buffalo Bill's legendary Wild West Show began at the same time, portraying for 30 years an image of the West that even then existed completely in the imagination.

The way West began in Missouri, where the Oregon and Santa Fe trails had their origin. Towns such as Independence, St. Joseph, and Franklin, bustled with commerce as emigrants outfitted wagons with food and other essential supplies for the journey. A covered wagon, fully loaded, weighed about 2,000 to 2,500 pounds. The cost for the endeavor averaged $600, a small fortune.

Trail food was not exciting—salt pork, beans, hardtack, dried fruit, and coffee made up the basic larder. Sacks of flour, sugar, and saleratus (baking soda) were packed for baking. Later, when commercial canned products were available, some wagons transported fruit this way. But the weight was always a consideration, so canned goods were a luxury.

The Santa Fe Trail, which ran from Independence, Missouri, to Santa Fe, New Mexico, was mainly utilized by tradesmen. Because of this, the food available along the Santa Fe Trail was somewhat more sophisticated than on the emigrants' trails. For example, in 1848 Chesapeake Bay oysters were routinely shipped alive during the cool months by rail to Iowa City, the western terminus of the railroad. From there, they were transported by wagon along the Santa Fe Trail to western towns. The live oysters were ingeniously packed in ice-filled barrels with their shell openings facing up so they could be fed. Cornmeal was sprinkled over the top so that as the ice melted, the cornmeal was carried into the oysters. At each stop on the journey, the oyster barrels were repacked with ice from the local icehouse and sprinkled with more cornmeal. Upon arrival at their destination weeks later, the oysters were plump and succulent.

Life on the Oregon Trail was hard and filled with drudgery. Crossing the Rockies before snow made the route impassable was imperative. The trek west ideally began in April or early May and was completed by early October. While there were dozens of daily chores to be done by both men and women, cooking was almost always women's work, performed three times a day. This meant building a fire, brewing coffee, and cooking the main dish, no matter what the weather was.

It is not an exaggeration to say that the daily diet of beans, bacon, and gravy became boring in a hurry. Cooks had to be innovative to keep the bellies they fed satisfied. One woman figured out a way to cook beans to a jelly, which she used as a filling for sandwiches. Women were eager to try their hands at fixing wild dandelions and mustard greens, wild onions, prairie peas, and other wild vegetables that they foraged en route. These foods, besides being a valuable source of vitamin C, were a welcome change to the taste buds. If the emigrants happened to find wild strawberries, and they were traveling with a dairy cow, they feasted on strawberries and cream that night.

The women did a lot of baking on the Oregon Trail. Light bread (a salt-rising bread made with saleratus), sourdough breads, biscuits, and the like were routinely prepared. Fruit and nut cakes, and wild currant or gooseberry pies were baked as special treats. Often women baked far into the night so that their families could enjoy freshly baked bread for breakfast. Men usually did the hunting, and the buffalo, antelope, game birds, rabbits, and fish they brought back to camp, when available, also helped to vary the diet.

Fresh garden vegetables were rare on the trail unless an enterprising settler with produce from his garden met up with the wagon train. Potatoes, a special luxury, sold for $1 a pound. Eggs were as rare as hen's teeth, but pioneers were willing to pay $2 a dozen for them when the opportunity arose. Many families traveled with their own cow, so milk was generally available.

The pioneers faced stormy weather, turbulent river crossings, wagon breakdowns, illness, and occasionally hostile Indians. More pioneers died from cholera than from anything else. Gravestones dotted the Oregon Trail as clearly as Hansel and Gretel's bread crumbs marked their path through the forest. Approximately 10 percent of pioneers perished on their westward journey.

Riding in the covered wagon was so uncomfortable that most people walked the daily 15 to 20 miles. It's been estimated that the pioneers needed to consume about 4,000 calories a day, about twice that recommended for today's diet, so fatty meats and gravies were downed with abandon because of their concentrated energy.

Real cooking, with a home stove and a backyard garden, couldn't begin until the pioneers found a place to settle. When they did, they planted what grew best in the area, raised farm animals, hunted, fished, and gathered wild berries and mushrooms. Pioneers from Europe knew how to identify edible wild mushrooms and were delighted to find these succulent fungi in their new land.

Native Americans also collected wild mushrooms, mostly for ceremonial purposes, but they introduced the settlers to many other techniques and foods, including corn, beans, and squash. They cultivated dozens of crops and utilized over a thousand others that were growing indigenously throughout the continent. Among the methods new settlers learned from the Native American tribes were how to rotate crops efficiently, how to "jerk" meat by drying thin slices in the sun to preserve it, and how to make hominy (an Algonquin word to describe the technique of removing the corn's hard indigestible covering, or hull, in water and ashes to increase its nutritional value). Southern grits, or ground hominy, when boiled in water cooked much faster than the whole kernel, and became a favorite food on the trail.

By the early 1880s, the Pacific Northwest was a well-settled area. In 1885 the San Grael Society in Portland, Oregon, published what may well have been the first Northwest cookbook. In *The Web-Foot Cook Book,* you'll find basic recipes for Beef Loaf, Welsh Rarebit, and Fried Venison. But there are also some recipes that sound contemporary, such as the ones for Raspberry Vinegar, Curried Chicken, Sweetbreads, Pickled Mangos, and Green Corn Cakes. The book ends with a chapter of recipes for the sick room, including one for homemade cough medicine. Keeping in mind that prior to 1845 only about 20,000 Caucasians lived west of the Mississippi, it is extraordinary that within forty years, a cookbook should come from the far western reaches of the migration.

Of course, those of northern European descent weren't the only pioneers. African Americans came to the West after the Civil War. Hispanics were already living in what is now New Mexico and Colorado before the area became states. Chinese came by ship to San Francisco and worked on the railroads and in mining and logging camps throughout the West. All came in search of a better life and all left their culinary mark.

Western cooks are always looking for new ways to prepare familiar ingredients and to experiment with not-so-familiar foods. The ethnic lines have become blurred during the past few years, engendering a more creative use of ingredients and the invention of new flavor combinations. Considering that the old West was the nation's second melting pot, it was only a matter of time before this happened. The only reason it has taken so long is the region is so vast. The eleven western states are the largest in the country, occupying almost half the area of the continental United States. The original pioneers who settled here wanted to recreate the foods of their homelands as best they could with the available resources. We, the new pioneers, create dishes that incorporate the tastes of native and traditional ingredients along with those brought here, grown, and harvested by the newest immigrants. May the parade never end.

~ BASICS ~

When we compare what we consider basic ingredients—sundried tomatoes, specialty cheese, Mediterranean olives, dried wild mushrooms, and shelled nuts—with what the pioneers considered essential when they trekked across the continent 150 years ago, the differences seem staggering. They, of course, relied on enormous quantities of flour, "parched" corn, cornmeal, sugar, bacon, dried beans, rice, dried fruits, and coffee to sustain them on a journey they expected to take several months. Any fresh food they encountered along the way—including game—was a special treat.

Yet, if we look over a list of the emigrants' *basic* food needs, we find many similarities between the items on their lists and those our pantries are always stocked with. Flour, cornmeal, sugar, dried beans, rice, dried fruits, coffee, and nuts are found in just about every American household on any given day. It's just the variety that has broadened over time. Today flour is available in more than a dozen different kinds. For the emigrant, the choice was limited to whatever was in the sack tucked in a corner of the covered wagon. And what about cornmeal? Then it was simply called "Indian meal." Today we have yellow, white, stone ground, water ground, hull-less, and so on. Sometimes we even call it polenta, even though it's still cornmeal.

Whatever you consider the core items in your pantry, take a look at the following ingredient descriptions and instructions for select basics called for throughout this book. With the addition of a few new basics, like cooked wild mushrooms, your pantry will hold the range of ingredients that generations of Western cooks have relied on daily.

IT'S STILL MUSH

Lettice Bryan included a recipe for polenta, or "mush" as she called it, in her 1839 cookbook. Her method does indeed result in the smooth texture she claims.

Sift some fine Indian meal, make a smooth batter of it by stirring in a sufficiency of cold water. Having ready a pot of boiling water, throw in a handful of salt, and stir in your batter till it is like very thick soup. Boil it till of the proper consistence, and stir it frequently to prevent its being lumpy, and to keep it from burning on the bottom. Mush, made in this manner, will never fail to be thoroughly done and clear of lumps, which are two common failures. Cold mush may be sliced and fried brown in butter. They are very good for breakast.

Butter

The recipes in this book call for unsalted butter. In the past, one had to hunt for it in the frozen foods section because it contains no salt and thus has a relatively short shelf life of about 1 month. Because more and more people are using unsalted butter nowadays and the product's turnover is higher, it is commonly available in the refrigerated foods section. If you use salted butter, bear in mind that each stick (½ cup, or 4 ounces) contains the equivalent of about ½ teaspoon salt and adjust accordingly.

Clarified Butter

Using clarified butter, which is butter with the milk solids removed, allows you to fry at high temperatures without much risk of the butter suddenly turning black and burning. Clarified butter is easy to make and keeps well in the freezer. One-half cup of butter makes about 6 tablespoons of clarified butter. To clarify butter, cut a stick into 6 or 8 pieces and place it in a small saucepan over very low heat. As it melts, the butter will bubble gently and foam will rise to the top. When the butter is completely melted, turn off the heat and let the butter stand for several minutes to allow the solids to settle. Carefully spoon off and discard the top foamy layer, then slowly pour the clear golden liquid into a container, and discard the milky white solids. Use as directed in recipes. Clarified butter keeps well in the refrigerator for 4 to 6 weeks.

CLARIFIED BUTTER ON THE TRAIL

Clarified butter has been enjoyed for over a century and was even transported by covered wagon, as evidenced by these instructions, which Randolph Marcy included in his 1859 book:

> Butter may be preserved by boiling it thoroughly, and skimming off the scum as it rises to the top until it is quite clear like oil. It is then placed in tin canisters and soldered up. This mode of preserving butter has been adopted in the hot climate of southern Texas, and it is found to keep sweet for a great length of time, and its flavor is but little impaired by the process.

Cream

Whenever whipping cream is called for, you may substitute heavy cream if you prefer. Although heavy cream contains a bit more fat, the results will be the same with either ingredient.

Duck Fat

Using two ducks, pull away pieces of fat from the body cavity and from under the skin and chop them into 1-inch or smaller pieces. Put the fat in a heavy ovenproof 4-quart pot and add 1 cup water. Place in a 350° oven and stir once after 30 minutes. Cook until the fat is rendered (golden in color) and all of the water has evaporated, about 1 hour. The pieces of remaining fat, "cracklings," should also be golden brown. Strain the fat and cool to room temperature. Reserve the cracklings, which are delicious spread on French bread or chopped and added warm to salads or soup. Store the fat, covered, in airtight containers in the refrigerator for 2 to 3 weeks. It also freezes well and will keep up to 6 months. Small amounts of duck fat make roasted or sautéed potatoes taste sublime. Proper cooking assures that very little of the fat is absorbed. (For a great version of potatoes with duck fat, try Paula Wolfert's recipe for Potatoes in the Style of Quercy, which is in her marvelous *Cooking of Southwest France*.)

Eggs

Unless indicated otherwise, these recipes all use grade AA large eggs.

PRESERVING EGGS

Eggs were so scarce on the trail that pioneer women found various ways to preserve them for future use, especially during the winter months. Here's one technique:

Pack in a clean vessel with small end down, strewing bran between each layer. Then place one or two thicknesses of brown paper on top and cover about one inch thick with salt. Cover close or keep in a cool place.

—Alice Kirk Grierson, *An Army Wife's Cookbook*, circa 1850

Flour

For general cooking I use all-purpose unbleached flour, which is what most of these recipes call for. It is a mixture of hard (high-gluten, high-protein) and soft (low-gluten) wheats and its gluten content is suitable for just about any type of cooking. Whenever I call for "flour" in these recipes, I mean all-purpose unbleached flour.

Cake flour is made from soft wheat and is much less likely to toughen during cake and pastry making; be sure to use it whenever it is specified. Bread flour has a higher gluten content than all-purpose flour and gives breads a pleasant elasticity and chewiness. My favorite bread flour is Guisto's Baker's Choice. It's made from hard organically grown wheat and may be purchased in health food stores or ordered by mail (see page 249). If you can't get bread flour, unbleached all-purpose flour will work quite well.

MEASURING FLOUR
(OR HOW DID THAT FLOUR GET INTO THAT CUP?)

The success of a recipe often depends on how flour is measured and whether it is sifted. The best way to measure flour is to weigh it. If you don't have a scale, however, just follow these simple guidelines. The weights given below apply only to all-purpose or bread flours.

In the old days, flour would sometimes get lumpy during storage, and sifting served two purposes: removing the lumps and aerating the flour. Both these procedures assured that the flour would be easily incorporated into recipes.

Most of the time, you will measure flour by stirring it in its container to aerate it slightly, spooning it into a measuring cup, filling the cup to overflowing, and sweeping off the excess with a metal spatula. A cup of flour measured this way weighs about 4½ ounces. Sifted flour is called for in only a few recipes in this book. You can buy all-purpose presifted flour, but the flour gets packed down during storage and must be sifted for accurate measurement. Sift the flour by placing more than you need in a sifter set over a sheet of waxed paper. Sift and then spoon the flour into a measuring cup, filling the cup to overflowing; do not pack or shake the cup. Sweep off the excess flour with a metal spatula or any straight-sided utensil. Sifted flour measured this way weighs about 4 ounces.

A third way to measure flour is to fill a metal measuring cup by scooping it into the flour container, filling the cup to overflowing, and sweeping off the excess with a metal spatula. This cup of flour will weigh about 5 ounces.

A horse-drawn "binder" (circa 1900),
which cut and bundled grain grasses.

To be sure we're speaking the same language, recipes for baked items specify both the weight of the flour and how to measure it. Cake flour weighs less when measured by any of the three ways described above. Whole wheat flour tends to weigh a bit more. Generally speaking, accurately measuring flour for bread making is not as critical as for making cakes or delicate pastries.

Hazelnuts

Hazelnuts, or filberts as they are sometimes called, grow abundantly in western Oregon. They are usually sold shelled with their skins on. The skins, which taste bitter to some, should be removed before using the nuts by blanching or skinning them as follows. Spread the nuts in a single layer in a shallow baking pan and toast them in a 350° oven for 10 to 15 minutes. Stir the nuts occasionally until they are a toasty brown and have a delicious aroma. Transfer the nuts to a kitchen towel, wrap them up, and let rest. When the nuts are cool, rub them vigorously with the towel to remove the skins. If some skins refuse to come off, just leave them; there is no harm in including a few skins in the recipes.

Stocks

It is well worth making several quarts of chicken, beef, and fish stock and freezing them to have on hand. They keep perfectly for months. It isn't necessary to add salt to stocks while they are cooking. After stocks are degreased, I concentrate them by boiling and reducing, adding the salt at that stage. Whenever a stock is called for in this book, use one of the following recipes.

A roadside picnic (circa 1920).

Chicken Stock

This recipe makes 4 to 6 quarts of stock. The concentration is just right for recipes calling for chicken stock. For a stronger flavor or for use in recipes requiring a rich chicken stock, boil down the defatted and strained liquid until it is reduced by half. To make turkey stock, simply substitute turkey bones—fresh bones for a light-colored stock or bones from a roasted turkey for a brown turkey stock. The ginger adds a refreshing flavor and aroma, without giving the stock a gingery taste.

2 whole frying chickens with giblets (7 to 8 pounds total), or
   7 to 8 pounds any combination chicken backs, necks, and wings

2 large carrots, scrubbed and cut into 2-inch chunks

1 large yellow onion, peeled and cut in half

4 stalks celery with leaves

2 teaspoons black peppercorns

6 sprigs parsley

1 bay leaf

1 (2-inch) length fresh ginger

6 to 8 quarts water

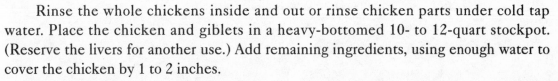

Rinse the whole chickens inside and out or rinse chicken parts under cold tap water. Place the chicken and giblets in a heavy-bottomed 10- to 12-quart stockpot. (Reserve the livers for another use.) Add remaining ingredients, using enough water to cover the chicken by 1 to 2 inches.

Set the stockpot over medium heat. As the water comes to a simmer, skim and discard any scum or foam that rises to the surface. Continue to remove the scum as necessary. Don't allow the liquid to boil. As the stock gets hotter, decrease the heat to very low and cook slowly, partially covered, for 3 to 4 hours. Only a bubble or two should break the surface every now and then. Remove the chicken from the pot and set aside. Strain the stock, discarding the vegetables; cool, cover, and refrigerate overnight. The next day, remove and discard the solidified fat on the surface.

To make a more concentrated (rich) chicken stock, boil a measured amount until it is reduced by half. Cool, cover, and refrigerate. The stock keeps refrigerated for 1 or 2 days or up to 6 months frozen in airtight containers.

Beef Stock

The secret to good-quality beef stock lies in the bones. Oxtail is good because it is high in gelatin and provides a wonderful flavor. Veal bones are also high in gelatin and are good to include. (I tend not to use veal unless I know the animals have not been confined in pens.)

In this recipe, the bones are cooked twice. The first cooking gives you about 10 quarts of strained beef stock. After chilling, remove the fat and taste the stock. It can be used in this form for soups, or you can reduce it by half to concentrate the flavor and intensify richness. A second cooking produces several quarts of liquid that you will further reduce to about 2 cups of a very gelatinous meat glaze, which I use to thicken and enrich sauces. It is a joy to have cubes of meat glaze on hand in the freezer to produce extraordinary sauces in an instant.

15 pounds beef bones, including some shanks,
　　marrow bones, knuckles, or oxtails

2 large leeks, washed thoroughly, and cut into 3-inch pieces

6 to 7 stalks celery with leaves, washed and cut into 3-inch pieces

4 large carrots, washed and cut into 2-inch pieces

3 large yellow onions, with skins on, quartered

Water

½ pound white mushrooms, cut in half if large

1 pound plum tomatoes, cut in half

3 bay leaves

8 sprigs parsley

2 teaspoons black peppercorns

Adjust two oven racks to divide the oven into thirds and preheat the oven to 400°. Arrange the meat and bones in single layers in two large shallow roasting pans and place the pans in the oven. Roast for 1 hour. Place the leeks and celery in a heavy-bottomed 20-quart stockpot. Add the carrots and onions to the roasting pans, dividing them between the two, and roast for 30 minutes. Using tongs, transfer the meat, bones, and vegetables to the stockpot. Pour off and discard the fat from the pans, add about 2 cups water to each, and heat on the stovetop, scraping the browned bits from the pan bottoms. Add the liquid to the stockpot along with the mushrooms, tomatoes, bay leaves, parsley, peppercorns, and enough cold water to cover ingredients by about 2 inches. (The pot will be almost full.)

Set the stockpot over medium-low heat and bring to a simmer. This will take 1 hour or longer. Simmer, uncovered, for 10 to 12 hours. Adjust heat if necessary so that the liquid bubbles very gently. If simmered over low heat, scum will not form. If you bring the stock to a simmer over higher heat, you will need to periodically remove the scum with a slotted spoon.

Remove the meat, bones, and vegetables from the pot and set them aside. Strain the stock through a fine-mesh strainer into another large pot and refrigerate it, uncovered, overnight. The next day, remove and discard the solidified fat on the surface.

Meanwhile, return the meat and bones to the stockpot. (Some vegetables may cling to them and can be included.) Add about 6 quarts of cold water, or enough to cover the bones by 1 to 2 inches. Bring to a simmer as described above and cook slowly for about 10 hours. Strain the stock through a fine-mesh strainer into a 5-quart saucepan, cool, cover, and refrigerate overnight. The next day, remove and discard the solidified fat on the surface.

To make a more concentrated (rich) beef stock from your first batch of degreased stock, boil a measured amount until it is reduced by half. Cool, cover, and refrigerate. The stock keeps refrigerated for 1 to 2 days or up to 6 months frozen in an airtight container.

To make meat glaze, boil the second cooking of the meat and bones stock until the liquid becomes very thick and syrupy, darkens in color, has large bubbles, and measures about 2 cups. (Just estimate this amount, since much of it would stick to a measuring cup, resulting in waste.) Pour the thick liquid into an 8 × 4-inch nonstick loaf pan and let it cool completely at room temperature. It will become solid and have a rubbery texture. Meanwhile, add 1 cup of warm water to the saucepan and dissolve the meat glaze stuck to the sides and bottom by scraping and stirring with a rubber spatula. Reserve this to use as stock.

When the meat glaze is set, cut it into 1-inch cubes and transfer to an airtight bag. The meat glaze keeps frozen for 6 to 8 months.

WIVES, SISTERS, MOTHERS, AND...COWHANDS?

It has been estimated that 250,000 western women owned and ran farms and ranches by 1890. Most, it turns out, were widows or spinsters. These women were called cattle queens. The following verse is from a cowboy ballad called "The Pecos Queen":

She made her start in cattle, yes, made
it with her rope;

Can tie down every maverick before it
can strike a lope.

She can rope and tie and brand it as
quick as any man;

She's voted by all cowboys an A-1 top
cow hand.

Duck Stock

This recipe makes 3 to 4 quarts of wonderful stock.

2 duck carcasses, plus necks, hearts, wings, and gizzards

3 large carrots, scrubbed and cut into 1-inch pieces

2 large yellow onions, unpeeled and cut into quarters

3 stalks celery with leaves, cut into 2-inch pieces

1 large leek, cut into 2-inch pieces

1 head garlic, cut in half crosswise

5 quarts plus 1 cup water

1 cup dry white French vermouth

6 sprigs parsley

6 sprigs oregano

6 sprigs thyme

1 teaspoon black peppercorns

2 bay leaves

Chop the carcasses into 3 or 4 pieces each. Place in a roasting pan along with the necks, hearts, wings, and gizzards. (Reserve the liver for another use.) Roast at 450° for 1 hour. Add the carrots, onions, celery, leek, and garlic. Stir well to coat the vegetables with some of the rendered fat and roast for 30 minutes at 400°. Transfer the duck and the vegetables to a 9-quart stockpot. Add the 5 quarts of water and the remaining ingredients to the stockpot.

Carefully pour off and discard the duck fat in the roasting pan, leaving the browned bits on the bottom. Pour in the remaining 1 cup of water and set the pan over high heat. Scrape the pan with a wooden spoon to release the browned bits. Add the liquid to the stockpot. Over medium-low heat, simmer the stock, partially covered, for 3 to 4 hours, allowing it to bubble gently while cooking. Strain the stock through a fine-mesh strainer. Cool, cover, and refrigerate it overnight. The next day, remove and discard the solidified fat on the surface.

For a more concentrated stock, boil until it reaches the desired strength. If you reduce the stock by half, you will have duck demi glace (a concentrated, gelatinous stock packed with flavor). Both the stock and demi glace keep refrigerated for 1 to 2 days or up to 8 months frozen in an airtight container.

Note: I usually use half the stock as is and boil down the rest to make demi glace.

ONLY THE STRONGEST NEED APPLY

The following entry from Cecelia Adams and Parthenia Blank's *Oregon Trail Diary of Twin Sisters* describes one of the truly awful days they endured while traveling the trail:

Wednesday, June 16

Rainy this morning, very disagreeable getting breakfast. We concluded to go on slowly until we find a better camping place. A man died this morning with the cholera in a company ahead of us…. All the wood we find today is quakins asp[en] which is miserable for fuel. Have no wild game yet, altho our boys are on the chase most of the time. Passed 11 new graves. Crossed Weed Creek, encamped 1 mile from the Platte. Poor wood and miserable water [but] good grass. Made 13 miles.

Form 1804

THE WESTERN UNION TELEGRAPH COMPANY
INCORPORATED
25,000 OFFICES IN AMERICA.   CABLE SERVICE TO ALL THE WORLD

This Company TRANSMITS and DELIVERS messages only on conditions limiting its liability, which have been assented to by the sender of the following message. Errors can be guarded against only by repeating a message back to the sending station for comparison, and the Company will not hold itself liable for errors or delays in transmission or delivery of Unrepeated Messages, beyond the amount of tolls paid thereon, nor in any case beyond the sum of Fifty Dollars, at which, unless otherwise stated below, this message has been valued by the sender thereof, nor in any case where the claim is not presented in writing within sixty days after the message is filed with the Company for transmission. This is an UNREPEATED MESSAGE, and is delivered by request of the sender, under the conditions named above.

THEO. N. VAIL, PRESIDENT   BELVIDERE BROOKS, GENERAL MANAGER

RECEIVED AT

4 WU F 10 FILED 11 45 RM

WINNEMUCCA NEVADA APRIL 10 TH 1913

RAY DRUCKENMILLER

TRY P O ELKO NEVADA

CAN USE YOU ALL COME IMMEDIATELY BRING SADDLES AND BEDS

MILLER AND LUX

12 10 P M

As the cattle industry took root in the West, telegrams like this one spurred cowhands to take up life on the range.

Fish Stock

Unlike meat stocks, fish stocks cook for only 30 minutes. Be sure to use bones from non-oily fish, such as halibut, flat fish, or sturgeon. Unless you live near the sea or have a large fish market in your city, it can be difficult to find fish bones. Your best bet is to ask your fish market to save the frames (skeletons) from any whole fish they buy and fillet. Fish bones can be stored frozen until you have enough to work with. This recipe makes 4 to 6 quarts of stock.

6 pounds fish bones from lean fish, including heads and trimmings

1 large carrot, scrubbed and thinly sliced

1 large leek, thinly sliced

1 large yellow onion, peeled and thinly sliced

12 sprigs parsley

1 cup thinly sliced fresh white mushrooms

1 teaspoon black peppercorns

2 cups dry white French vermouth

Cold water

Salt and pepper

Chop the fish bones into large chunks. Place all of the ingredients in a heavy-bottomed 10- to 12-quart pot, adding enough cold water to just cover. Bring to a simmer over medium heat, removing any scum that rises to the surface. Lower heat to a gentle simmer and cook for 30 minutes. Strain through a fine-mesh strainer and discard solids. Season with salt and pepper and use as directed.

For a more concentrated stock, boil a measured amount of unseasoned stock until it is reduced by half. Cool, cover, and refrigerate. The stock keeps refrigerated for 1 to 2 days or up to 2 months frozen in an airtight container.

Wild Mushrooms

Hundreds of species of wild mushrooms grow in the Pacific Northwest and in the Rocky Mountain West. Late spring rains bring up the first mushrooms of the season. If there is a warm, wet June, more varieties pop up all over the hillsides. Early fall rains bring even more.

Many kinds of wild mushrooms are available in well-stocked markets all over the country at different times of the year. Or you may find there's a mycologist leading mushroom hunting expeditions in your area. (Check with local colleges and natural food stores.) Whether you buy your wild mushrooms at the market or forage for them with the guidance of a professional, *Mushrooms Demystified* by David Arora will help you identify hundreds of mushrooms. I suggest you buy wild mushrooms as they appear in your markets and cook them even if you have no immediate plans for them. You will be glad you did. The cooked mushrooms can be frozen for future use; here are general instructions for doing so.

HUNTING WILD MUSHROOMS

The first wild mushrooms I ever foraged were inky caps on San Juan Island in the Puget Sound. Then I found *Aleuria aurantia*, a beautiful orange-colored disc-shaped fungus, closely related to truffles, growing on the fallen trees in the forest. They were delicious sautéed in butter, as are many kinds of edible wild fungi. That was the extent of my wild mushroom knowledge until I met Larry Evans, a mycologist living in Missoula. Larry publishes his own newsletter (*The Fungal Jungal*), leads forays into the nearby hills searching out edible wild mushrooms, and teaches courses on mushroom identification. His wife, Kris Love, is an outstanding cook and has created all sorts of delicious recipes using wild mushrooms. Larry and Kris have included me and my wife, Dorothy, in several wild mushroom tastings. In the process, I've learned that there is much more to delicious wild mushroom eating than the well-known morels, chanterelles, porcini, and oyster mushrooms. For example, the "gypsy" mushroom, *Rozites caperata*, has a nutty, toasty taste that some mushroom enthusiasts consider superior to morels. The royal bolete, *Boletus abieticola*, is tender and has a meaty taste that is so addictive I could not stop eating them until they were all gone. Then I'd call Larry and ask him when he was going to look for more.

Characteristics of Mushrooms

Wild mushrooms have distinct characteristics. Most spring up from the soil; some grow on tree trunks. Regardless of their different growth habits, the flavor and texture of each species is unique. Golden trumpet-shaped chanterelles have a subtle flavor. They are aristocratic and royal, and deserve to be treated that way. Pair them with cream, butter, and noble spirits such as cognac. The morel, on the other hand, is the king of the forest with its big, earthy taste. Even when morels are not the dominant ingredient, they lift the flavors of any dish. Oyster mushrooms grow in clumps on trees and are grayish, which gives them an oysterlike appearance. They have a firm, somewhat chewy texture and a lusty, full taste. Shaggy manes stand alone, both in flavor and their growth habits. They inspire expediency because they remain in pristine condition for only a few hours before dissolving into an inky black mess. They are the blandest tasting of the four types described here, but cooking them in a healthy dose of butter imparts seductive flavor nuances that are difficult to beat.

CHANTERELLES

Carefully remove any dirt from ¾ pound of chanterelles with a soft-bristled brush. Melt 4 tablespoons butter in a 12-inch skillet over low heat. Add the mushrooms, ½ teaspoon salt, and a few grindings of black pepper. Toss to coat the mushrooms with the butter, and cover the pan. Cook slowly, stirring occasionally, until the mushrooms are tender but have a slight firmness, about 15 minutes. Stir in 1 large minced shallot and 1 teaspoon chopped fresh tarragon. Cook, covered, 5 more minutes. The mushrooms should be lightly browned with no juice remaining in the pan. If there is juice, raise the heat and cook rapidly until the liquid has evaporated. Set aside to cool for use in recipes, or cool, cover, and refrigerate for a day or two. For longer storage, freeze in airtight bags for up to 6 months. Makes 2 to 2½ cups cooked chanterelles.

MORELS

Carefully brush away dirt from 1 pound of morels and trim away the stem tips if they are gritty. If the mushrooms are small (up to 1½ inches long), leave them whole. If larger, cut them into 1-inch pieces. Cook no more than 1 pound at a time. Melt 4 tablespoons butter in a 12-inch skillet over medium-low heat. When the butter is hot and foamy and begins to turn a light nut brown, add the morels. Stir well to coat the mushrooms with the butter. Cover the pan and cook about 5 minutes, shaking the pan once or twice, until the morels are tender but slightly firm. Turn the mushrooms into a large wire strainer set over a bowl and let stand until they are completely cool and well drained. Store, covered, in the refrigerator for a day or two, or freeze in airtight bags and store for up to 6 months. The morel liquid may be frozen and used to flavor soups or stocks. Makes about 3 cups cooked morels.

OYSTER MUSHROOMS

Brush away any dirt clinging to 1 pound of oyster mushrooms and trim off tough ends. Cut the mushrooms into 1-inch pieces. For each pound of trimmed oyster mushrooms, melt 4 tablespoons butter in a 12-inch skillet over medium heat. When the butter foam begins to subside, stir in the mushrooms and season with ½ teaspoon salt and ¼ teaspoon freshly ground black pepper. Cover the pan and cook, stirring once or twice, for about 5 minutes, or until the mushrooms are tender but slightly firm. Cool and refrigerate, covered, for up to 2 days, or freeze in airtight bags and store up to 6 months. Makes about 3 cups.

SHAGGY MANES OR INKY CAPS

These mushrooms have tall, domed white caps and white stems. They get their name from the fringes adorning the caps, giving them a shaggy, unkempt look. They appear along country roadsides right after a rainfall in spring and fall and have a life expectancy of less than 1 day. Within 24 hours, they literally dissolve into a black liquid, so you cannot delay in using them. Shaggy manes have a very high water content; 1 pound will yield only 1 packed cup when cooked.

Rinse 1 pound shaggy manes in a large basin of water as rapidly as you can, gently swishing them around to remove the dirt. Quickly transfer to a large colander. Squeeze a handful of mushrooms gently between your hands to remove excess water. Don't worry if the caps or stems crack. Cut off and discard the knobby stem ends and slice the mushrooms crosswise about ½ inch thick. Place them in an ungreased 12-inch-wide, 2-inch-deep pan (a 5-quart sauté pan is ideal). Cook over high heat, stirring occasionally at first, until the liquid released by the mushrooms has almost evaporated. Stir continuously during the last minute of cooking to prevent them from burning. Turn the mushrooms into a large wire strainer set over a bowl and allow to drain and cool completely. Freeze the liquid to flavor soups or stocks. Refrigerate the cooked mushrooms for 1 to 2 days or freeze in airtight bags for up to 6 months.

CRAZY FOR FUNGI IN COLORADO

On the Saturday before Labor Day, people from all over the country rush to the historic mining town of Telluride, Colorado, to pay homage to the mushroom. At the Telluride Mushroom Festival adults and children dress up as their favorite mushrooms, march in the parade, and then head off to the annual dance. The festival culminates with a wild mushroom feast, featuring the fungi that the 200 participants have collected during the previous two days. At Telluride's 7,500-foot elevation, the mushroom all fruit at the same time, in late August. The climate and soil isn't right for a lot of mushroom varieties, but those that do grow there thrive. Entire hillsides may be covered with chanterelles. One writer gathered enough king Boletes in an hour to fill the trunk of his car. What makes Telluride's mushroom ecosystem so special is the abundance of healthy coniferous forests, which provide the ideal environment for the mushrooms.

APPETIZERS

In the Old West, appetizers were served mainly in the homes of the wealthy and in fancy hotels. Those appetizers were commonly modeled on French foods because so many of the settlers were European emigrants who continued to value the principles and traditions of French cuisine when they came to the region.

The recipes in this chapter summarize my approach to the West's new cuisine, with an emphasis on using traditional foods of the region with fresh, ethnic twists. Were it not for the large numbers of Southeast Asians now living in Missoula, I doubt that Gingered Buffalo Meatballs with Jicama in Sweet and Sour Sauce would have been created. Similarly, the flavors of Greece have influenced my cooking, thanks to the large Greek population residing here. The natural pairing of wild agaric mushrooms and feta cheese inspired the delicious and easy-to-prepare Greek-Style Stuffed Portobello Mushrooms. With the exception of the Vietnamese Seafood Imperial Rolls, none of these recipes is difficult or complicated to prepare.

Follow-the-Sun Kosher Dill Pickles

• Yield: 3 quarts •

This recipe was given to me many years ago by Avis Olsen of Pinesdale, Montana, when I had a weekly cooking show on local television. I have made these pickles almost every summer since then. Wait for a warm, sunny day to make them. I start them in the morning on the front porch, with direct sun shining on the jars. As the sun moves in its arc across the late summer sky, I move the jars accordingly, putting them on the bedroom porch at midday, moving them to the greenhouse in the late afternoon, and finally transferring them to the back porch, where the jars soak up the sun's last warming rays. If you like your pickles less sour, cut back a bit on the vinegar. But do try them this way first.

24 to 30 small, firm pickling cucumbers

3 tablespoons salt

3 teaspoons pickling spices

6 tops fresh dill plants

3 to 6 cloves garlic, peeled

2 to 3 cups distilled white vinegar

Water

Alum

Wash three wide-mouthed, quart-sized Mason jars in hot soapy water, rinse thoroughly, and drain. Wash the cucumbers and pack them into the jars, leaving a bit of room at the top. Add 1 tablespoon of the salt, 1 teaspoon of the pickling spices, 2 tops of the fresh dill, and 1 or 2 of the garlic cloves to each jar. Fill the jars halfway with vinegar and add water up to the jars' necks. Put the lids and bands on the jars, but don't seal them tightly.

Place the jars in the sun for 8 hours or more, moving them during the day to follow the sun and turning them from time to time. The cucumbers will change from a bright green color to an olive green color by the end of the day. If there isn't enough sun in one day to do the job, or if you started the process late in the day, you can return the jars to the sun the next day and follow the procedure again.

After 8 hours of sun, bring the jars in, uncap them, and add a pea-sized bit of alum to each jar. (If the alum is powdered and not in a chunk, use a scant ¼ teaspoon.) Once the alum is added, replace the lids and seal tightly with the bands. Invert the jars 2 or 3 times to mix in the alum. Set the jars in a cool place for 3 days, at which point you can eat the pickles or store them in the refrigerator. They keep well for 3 to 4 months. Sometimes the lids seal all by themselves, creating a vacuum. Those that do should ensure that the pickles inside will keep even longer.

Gingered Buffalo Meatballs
with Jicama in Sweet and Sour Sauce

· Yield: 40 meatballs ·

Lean and mild-tasting ground buffalo lends itself to all sorts of seasonings. But any sauce you serve with the buffalo must not overwhelm the meat's mild taste. Ginger helps bring out the sweetness of the meat, and the slightly sour sauce makes you want to eat one after the other. Incidentally, the light soy is not a low-sodium product, it is simply lighter in color than regular or black soy sauce.

Buffalo Meatballs

1½ pounds ground buffalo

1½ tablespoons peeled, minced fresh ginger

½ cup (2 ½ ounces) finely diced, peeled jicama

2 cloves garlic, minced

1 tablespoon dry sherry

2 tablespoons light soy sauce

1 teaspoon salt

¼ teaspoon freshly ground black pepper

1 egg

2 tablespoons water

1 tablespoon cornstarch

2 tablespoons vegetable oil

Nonstick cooking spray

Sweet and Sour Sauce

1 cup sugar

1½ teaspoons salt

⅓ cup dry sherry

½ cup light soy sauce

1 tablespoon dark soy sauce

1 teaspoon chili paste with garlic (such as Lan Chi)

1 cup water

½ cup distilled white vinegar

½ cup ketchup

3 tablespoons cornstarch

2 tablespoons dark sesame oil

½ cup chopped fresh cilantro leaves

Place the ground buffalo in a large bowl. Add the ginger, jicama, garlic, sherry, light soy, salt, and pepper. Mix well with a fork. In a separate bowl, beat together the egg, water, and cornstarch with a fork to combine well. Mix in the oil. Add to the buffalo mixture and beat well with a fork until thoroughly combined.

Adjust the oven rack to the center position and preheat the oven to 350°. Lightly coat a large, rimmed 18 × 12 × 1-inch baking sheet with cooking spray. Using the palms of your hands, shape the buffalo mixture into 1-inch balls. Place the meatballs 1 inch apart on the prepared sheet. Bake for 20 minutes. Remove the pan from the oven and set aside while you make the sauce.

For the sauce, combine the sugar, salt, sherry, light soy sauce, dark soy sauce, chili paste with garlic, ½ cup of the water, vinegar, and ketchup in a 4-quart saucepan. In a small bowl, combine the remaining ½ cup water with the cornstarch and set aside. Bring the mixture in the saucepan to a boil over medium-high heat, stirring occasionally. Stir the cornstarch mixture well and quickly add it to the saucepan while stirring continuously but gently with a rubber spatula. Boil the mixture 1 to 2 minutes, or until it is clear and slightly thickened. Remove the pan from the heat and stir in the sesame oil. Drop the meatballs into the hot sauce and set aside until serving time. (The meatballs may be made hours ahead up to this point. Cover and refrigerate when cool.)

To serve, set the uncovered saucepan over low to medium heat and bring to a simmer slowly, stirring occasionally. When piping hot, add the cilantro and transfer the mixture to a serving dish. Serve with toothpicks.

THEIR WORK WAS NEVER DONE

After an exhausting and dirty day of travel, pioneer women were still faced with long hours of work at the campsite.

Although there is not much to cook, the difficulty and inconvenience in doing it amounts to a great deal—so by the time one has squatted around the fire and cooked bread and bacon, and made several dozen trips to and from the wagon—washed the dishes (with no place to drain them) . . . and gotten things ready for an early breakfast, some of the others already have their night caps on.

—Helen Carpenter, 1857

Dungeness Crab~Stuffed Morel Mushrooms

• Yield: 6 servings •

This is a very special dish. Make it when you can get top-quality Dungeness crab and large morel mushrooms. One late spring, my friends Kris Love and Larry Evans presented me with the biggest, most beautiful morels I'd ever seen, and they inspired this recipe. I had just bought some fresh crab, and the pairing seemed natural to me. The perfect cap size is about 3 inches, not including the stems. The mushrooms should be served as a sit-down appetizer or first course.

6 to 10 large fresh morel mushrooms

1 ounce small fresh morel mushrooms

2 tablespoons butter

¼ cup finely minced shallots

¼ pound Dungeness crabmeat

2 tablespoons dry sherry

½ cup fresh fine bread crumbs made from day-old
    crustless French or Italian bread

½ teaspoon salt

¼ teaspoon freshly ground black pepper

Pinch of ground cayenne pepper

2 tablespoons finely chopped fresh tarragon

¼ cup whipping cream

Drops of lemon juice (optional)

Butter-flavored cooking spray

2 tablespoons grated Parmesan cheese

Carefully look over the large mushrooms and brush away any dirt. Cut them in half lengthwise and set aside. Finely chop the smaller morels (you should have about ½ cup) and set them aside. Melt the butter in a 10-inch skillet over medium heat. Add the shallots and chopped mushrooms. Stir and cook for 2 minutes. Add the crabmeat and sherry. Stir and cook another 2 minutes on medium-high to heat the crab and reduce the wine. Add the bread crumbs, salt, pepper, and cayenne. Cook, stirring, 1 minute. Remove from the heat and stir in the tarragon and cream. Taste carefully, adding salt, pepper, or lemon juice if needed.

Spray a large, heavy baking sheet lightly with butter-flavored spray. Place mushrooms cut side down on the sheet and coat them with the spray. Turn them over, and spray the mushroom cavities. (This method may seem unconventional, but I've found it's the easiest way to butter the mushroom caps.) Space the caps about 1 inch apart. Spoon the filling into the caps, mounding it in the center. Sprinkle with the Parmesan. The caps can be prepared hours ahead up to this point; just cover loosely with plastic wrap and refrigerate.

When ready to bake, adjust an oven rack to the center position and preheat the oven to 375°. Bake 15 to 20 minutes, or until the filling is lightly browned. Serve hot.

Greek-Style Stuffed
Portobello Mushrooms

• Yield: 6 servings •

Field agarics, which are close relatives of the commercially available portobello mushrooms, grow abundantly in spring and summer in the Mountain West. The agarics and the portobello mushrooms look identical and have similar tastes and textures. I use the agarics whenever I can get them, but the portobellos do not suffer by comparison. The saltiness of the feta cheese and olives contrasts nicely with the mushrooms' sweetness. A good accompaniment is a salad of arugula or mixed baby lettuces dressed with olive oil and balsamic vinegar.

6 portobello mushrooms caps (4 inches in diameter), stems removed

Marinade

2 cups chicken stock (see page 11)

½ teaspoon salt, if using unsalted chicken broth

½ teaspoon freshly ground black pepper

½ teaspoon dried oregano leaves, crumbled

⅓ cup extra virgin olive oil

Stuffing

¾ cup fresh fine bread crumbs, made from day-old
    crustless French or Italian bread or an English muffin

1½ tablespoons finely chopped fresh oregano

¼ teaspoon freshly ground black pepper

8 kalamata olives in brine, drained, pitted, and chopped

¼ cup (1 ounce) crumbled feta cheese

2 tablespoons extra virgin olive oil

Salt to taste

Carefully look over the mushrooms and brush away any dirt. Combine the marinade ingredients in a 13 × 9 × 2-inch baking dish. Add the mushroom caps, turning to coat them well. Cover the pan tightly with aluminum foil and set aside to marinate for 2 to 3 hours or longer in a cool place. (This may be kept overnight in the refrigerator.) Turn the caps 3 or 4 times while marinating. Bake, covered, in the center of a preheated 400° oven for 30 to 40 minutes, or until the caps are tender. Cool, covered, in the pan. To stuff the mushrooms, remove them from the marinade and set them aside on paper towels to drain well.

To make the stuffing, use a fork to combine the bread crumbs, oregano, pepper, olives, feta cheese, and olive oil in a small bowl. The mixture will be moist but should not stick together. Add salt to taste if necessary. Place the caps upside down on a lightly oiled baking sheet. Sprinkle 3 to 4 tablespoons of the filling loosely and evenly over each cap. Pat in place very gently with your fingers, without packing the filling down. The mushrooms may be prepared hours ahead up to this point; just cover and refrigerate until ready to bake.

Preheat the oven to 375°. Bake on the center rack for 15 to 20 minutes, or until the filling is lightly browned in spots. Serve warm.

Indulging in a fancy picnic near Missoula, MT, 1903.

Chanterelle Mushroom and Asparagus Tart

· *Yield: 12 servings* ·

This is a special appetizer to make in spring, when both asparagus and chanterelles are plentiful. Serve it with a small salad of mixed baby greens. You can prepare this dish as a single tart or as individual tartlets in miniature muffin pans.

Pastry

1½ cups (6¾ ounces) unbleached all-purpose flour

½ cup (1¾ ounces) cake flour

½ teaspoon salt

¾ cup chilled unsalted butter

⅓ cup ice water

Filling

18 to 20 asparagus tips, 2 inches long

3 large eggs plus 1 egg yolk

1 cup heavy cream

⅓ cup milk

½ teaspoon salt

⅛ teaspoon freshly ground black pepper

Pinch of freshly grated nutmeg

1 cup cooked chanterelles (page 18)

2 tablespoons grated Parmesan cheese

Measure the flours by spooning them into measuring cups, filling the cups to overflowing, and sweeping off the excess with a metal spatula. To make the dough using a food processor, place both flours and the salt in the work bowl with the metal blade in place. Cut the butter into 6 equal pieces and add it to the bowl. Pulse quickly 3 or 4 times to cut the butter into the flour. While pulsing very rapidly, add the water through the feed tube in a steady stream and pulse 20 to 30 times, or until the dough almost gathers into a ball. Carefully remove the dough from the work bowl, place on a piece of waxed paper, and shape it into a 6-inch disc. Wrap it securely, and chill for 30 minutes.

To make the dough by hand, place both flours and salt in a mixing bowl. Cut in the butter with a pastry blender until the mixture resembles coarse crumbs. Toss with a fork, while gradually adding the water. Continue mixing with a fork until the dough gathers into a ball. Wrap and chill as directed above.

Roll the dough into a 14-inch circle on a lightly floured surface (a canvas pastry cloth works best). Transfer the dough to an 11-inch-diameter, 1-inch-deep tart pan with a removable bottom. Gently work the pastry into the corners, but do not stretch it. Use scissors to trim the overhanging pastry to ½ inch beyond the edge of the pan. Fold the overhanging pastry back onto the pastry lining the sides of the tart, pressing the two together to make the sides double in thickness and extending about ¼ inch above the pan rim. Place the tart pan on a baking sheet and freeze for 20 to 30 minutes. Meanwhile, adjust the oven rack to center position and preheat the oven to 400°.

Line the chilled pastry shell with aluminum foil and fill it with dry beans or rice. Bake for about 20 minutes, or until the edge of the pastry is light golden. Remove the foil and beans or rice and return the pastry to the oven for about 5 more minutes, or until it appears set and is only very lightly browned. If the pastry puffs up during baking, gently prick it with a fork to deflate. Cool the pastry until ready to use.

To make the filling, bring 2 quarts of water to a boil in a 3- or 4-quart saucepan. Drop in the asparagus tips and blanch uncovered for 3 to 4 minutes, or until they are crisp-tender. Drain well. Place the asparagus in a large bowl of cold water. Allow the tips to stand until they are cool, then drain well and set aside on paper towels. Preheat the oven to 350°.

In a medium-sized bowl, whisk together the eggs and yolk to combine well. Whisk in the cream, milk, salt, pepper, and nutmeg. Scatter the cooked chanterelles over the bottom of the partially baked pastry shell. Arrange the asparagus tips on top. Carefully pour in the cream mixture and sprinkle the Parmesan evenly over the top. Place the tart on a baking sheet and bake for 30 to 40 minutes, until it is puffed, set, and light golden brown on top. Remove the tart from the oven and let cool in its pan for 5 minutes, then carefully remove the sides of the pan and slide the tart onto a serving platter. Cut into 12 wedges and serve on plates.

Note: To bake as individual tartlets or miniquiches, roll the pastry until it is quite thin, between $1/16$ and ⅛ inch thick. To prevent sticking, lightly coat each miniature muffin cup with nonstick cooking spray before lining with pastry. Cut the pastry into 3-inch circles and fit them into the cups. The dough should make 24 to 30 tartlet shells. Cut the cooked asparagus tips into 3 or 4 pieces each. Place about 2 teaspoons of mushrooms and 2 or 3 pieces of asparagus into each shell, fill almost to the top with the custard mixture, and sprinkle with the Parmesan cheese. Bake on the center rack at 400° for 10 to 15 minutes, or until pastry is nicely browned and the filling is puffed and set. Carefully remove the pastries and serve immediately.

Fava Bean Dip

• *Yield: 2½ cups* •

Fava beans, or broad beans, are commonly eaten in Asia, Europe, Africa, and South America. In China, favas have been part of the diet for about 5,000 years. Only recently, however, has the bean begun to catch on in the United States. Favas' bright green pods contain beans that look much like limas, but the similarity ends there. They have a unique taste that is slightly bitter, but otherwise indescribable. Favas grow very well in cool climates and reach their peak here in July, but you don't have to grow your own to enjoy this dip. Favas are becoming readily available in markets all over the United States. On the West Coast, they may be found from late March through early May. Because there is so much more pod than bean in each fava, and because each bean must be skinned before it is used, this exquisite dip takes a lot of pods and time to make, but is well worth it.

4 pounds fava beans in the pod

1 cup water

¾ teaspoon ground cumin

3 cloves garlic, peeled and sliced

½ teaspoon salt

½ teaspoon freshly ground black pepper

3 tablespoons extra virgin olive oil

1 tablespoon freshly squeezed lemon juice

½ teaspoon paprika

Sliced crusty French bread or split and toasted pita triangles (see Note)

Shell the favas and place the beans in a large pot of rapidly boiling water to blanch for 15 to 30 seconds. Remove the beans with a slotted spoon and transfer them to a large bowl of very cold water. After 5 to 10 minutes, drain them well. Pierce the skin of a bean with a fingernail, then slip off and discard the skin; repeat for each bean. You should have 2½ cups of bright green beans. Combine the favas, water, cumin, and garlic in a 2- to 3-quart saucepan. Bring the mixture to a boil over high heat. Reduce the heat to medium and cook, partially covered, about 20 minutes, or until the favas are tender. Most of the liquid should be gone. Transfer the favas to a wire strainer to drain excess liquid. Set aside for a few minutes to cool.

Place the favas in the work bowl of a food processor fitted with the metal blade. Add the salt, pepper, 2 tablespoons of the olive oil, and the lemon juice. Purée about 2 minutes, or until smooth, stopping to scrape the work bowl as necessary. If the purée is too thick, thin it with a little water. It should be thick enough to spread or use as a dip, not soupy. Transfer the dip to a serving dish and smooth the top. Drizzle the remaining 1 tablespoon of oil over the dip and sprinkle it with the paprika. Cover the dish tightly with plastic wrap and let it stand at room temperature for 1 hour or so before serving.

Note: To toast pitas, split them into individual rounds with a sharp knife and coat the inside surfaces lightly with olive oil cooking spray. Cut each round into 8 wedges and arrange them close together, oiled side up, on a baking sheet. Bake at 350° for about 10 minutes, or until lightly browned. They will crisp as they cool. Store them in an airtight plastic bag for up to 3 days.

Friday, June 4 [1852]. This is a day long to be remembered for hard work. Paid $1.00 per wagon and 25 cents per yoke of oxen for the privilege of ferrying ourselves over the Missouri in a flat boat which took us all day and till after dark. Made 1 mile. Our company now consists of 6 wagons, one of which is bound for California. A great many Mormons are starting for the Salt Lake.

Home
what so sweet!
So beautiful on Earth! So Rare
as kindred love and family repose:
The busy world
With all the tumult and stir of life
Pursues its wonted course; on pleasure some
And some on commerce and ambition bent
And all on happiness, while each one loves
With nature's holiest feelings. One sweet spot
And calls it home. If sorrow is felt
There it seems through many bosoms and a smile
And if disease intrudes
The sufferer finds
Rest on the breast beloved.

—Cecelia Adams and Parthenia Blank
in their *Oregon Trail Diary of Twin Sisters*

Green Tomato Pizza

• Yield: 6 to 8 servings •

"Do you think the tomatoes will ripen before the frost comes?" We ask that question every year toward the end of August, when the tomatoes reach their peak in the Rocky Mountain West. Even when Mother Nature grants us an abundant tomato harvest, there are always some laggards on the vine. This is what we do with them. Incidentally, I like to dissolve the yeast in a glass measuring cup because the pouring spout makes it easy to add the mixture to the dry ingredients without spills. Instead of using a pizza pan, I prefer to bake free-form pizzas on unglazed quarry tiles or on a pizza stone, both of which are available at gourmet specialty stores or through the mail (see page 249), because they create a crispier crust.

Dough

1 teaspoon active dry yeast

¼ cup warm water

1½ cups (7½ ounces) unbleached all-purpose flour

¾ teaspoon salt

⅓ cup cold water

Topping

1½ ounces cream cheese

¼ cup (1 ounce) goat cheese

1 small clove garlic, minced

1½ tablespoons olive oil

3 firm green tomatoes

2 ounces fontina cheese, thinly sliced

To make the dough, stir the yeast into the warm water in a glass measuring cup and let stand about 10 minutes, or until the yeast has dissolved and the mixture is creamy. Meanwhile, measure the flour by scooping a measuring cup into the flour container, filling it to overflowing, and sweeping off the excess with a metal spatula. Place the flour and salt in the work bowl of a food processor fitted with the metal blade. Stir the cold water into the yeast mixture. Start the food processor and gradually add the yeast mixture through the feed tube in a steady stream. The dough will gather into a ball. Process for 1 minute. The dough should be moist and slightly sticky. When you work it between your hands, it will lose some of its stickiness.

Place the dough in an ungreased 2- to 3-quart bowl, cover it tightly with plastic wrap, and set it aside to rise at room temperature until it is almost triple its original size, about 2 hours. If you're not ready to work with the dough after it has risen, deflate it, reshape it into a ball, and return it to the rising bowl. Cover tightly, refrigerate, and use within 24 hours.

Place the tiles or a pizza stone on an oven rack close to the bottom of the oven. Preheat the oven to 500° about 45 minutes before baking. If you use a pizza pan, brush it lightly with olive oil and preheat the oven just 20 minutes in advance.

To make the topping, place the cream cheese, goat cheese, garlic, and olive oil in a small bowl and mash thoroughly with a fork to make a smooth, creamy mixture. Slice the tomatoes ⅛ inch thick and set them on paper towels.

Shape the risen dough into a ball, dust it lightly with flour, and set it aside, covered, about 20 minutes to allow the gluten to relax before shaping. If the dough was refrigerated, bring it to room temperature before shaping. Roll the dough into a 12-inch circle on a lightly floured surface. Lightly dust a board or baker's peel with cornmeal and place the dough on it or in the prepared pizza pan. Spread the cheese mixture on the dough, arrange the tomato slices on top, and place the fontina over the tomatoes. Quickly slide the pizza onto the hot tiles or place the pizza pan in the oven. Bake for about 10 minutes, or until the edges of crust are lightly browned and the cheese and tomatoes appear bubbly. Remove from the oven and let stand for 2 to 3 minutes before cutting into wedges.

DEAR JANEY...

When Calamity Jane was near death at the age of fifty, she wrote the following to her imaginary daughter:

Dear Janey

I guess my diary is just about finished. I am going blind—can still see to write this yet but I cant keep on to live an avaricious old age...

I hate poverty & dirt & here I shall have to live in such in my last days. Dont pity me Janey.

Forgive all my faults & the wrong I have done you.

Rock Creek Trout
in Tomato and Onion Sauce

• Yield: 4 to 6 servings •

Rock Creek is a blue-ribbon trout stream located 45 minutes from my home in Missoula. Anglers from all over the United States come to Rock Creek for the plentiful trout its waters hold. It is the first and only stream I've ever fished. The first time out, I landed a 14-inch brown trout—beginner's luck for sure. I learned quickly that I am not a fisherman by nature, and so now I buy fresh trout at the market. This is a quick, easy, and delicious way to enjoy it. I like to serve it with French or Italian bread to sop up the excess sauce. The recipe may be doubled.

1 pound boneless and skinless trout fillets, cut into 1½-inch pieces

¾ teaspoon salt

½ teaspoon freshly ground black pepper

¼ cup unbleached all-purpose flour

¼ cup extra virgin olive oil

3 carrots, peeled and shredded

1 large sweet onion, peeled and finely chopped

1 (16-ounce) can tomato purée (2 cups)

¼ cup dry white wine or dry white French vermouth

1 tablespoon freshly squeezed lemon juice

Sprinkle the trout lightly with salt and pepper. Place the flour in a plastic bag, add the fish, and toss gently until all the pieces are well coated. Remove the fish, shaking off excess flour.

In a large skillet, heat 2 tablespoons of the oil over medium-high heat until very hot, but not smoking. Add the fish in batches and fry until golden and just done, about 1 minute on each side. (Don't crowd the pieces.) Use a slotted spoon to transfer the fish to paper towels to drain. Repeat until all of the pieces are cooked.

Discard the oil from the skillet and add the remaining 2 tablespoons of oil. Return the pan to medium-high heat and stir in the carrots and onion. Reduce heat to medium-low, cover, and cook 5 minutes. Stir in the tomato purée, wine, lemon juice, and salt and pepper to taste. Cover and cook another 5 minutes, or until the onion is barely tender. Add the cooked fish, very gently stirring it into the sauce. To serve hot, cover and cook 1 to 2 minutes, to heat fish through. To serve at room temperature, remove the pan from the heat after adding fish and let it stand, uncovered, until ready to serve. Adjust seasoning, adding salt, pepper, and lemon juice as desired.

Fishing on Rattlesnake Creek in Missoula, MT, in 1903.

Vietnamese Seafood Imperial Rolls

• *Yield: 6 dozen* •

In Vietnamese, these are called *Cha Gio* (pronounced j-eye YAW). My good friend Chu Chu Pham, who moved to Montana from Southeast Asia twenty years ago, taught me how to make them for a television program we did together on the cuisine of Vietnam. In the broadest sense, these are a Vietnamese version of Chinese egg rolls. Rice paper, brushed with beer or water to moisten and make it flexible, is wrapped around a filling of ground pork, crab, jicama, and other ingredients. The rice paper is rolled around the filling to make a small, compact cylinder, fried in oil until very brown and crisp, and then wrapped in a lettuce leaf along with cucumber, bean sprouts, cilantro, and mint. The *Cha Gio* is then dipped into Vietnamese fish sauce and eaten. Although there is a fair amount of work to the preparation, it's worth it. The bean thread, tree ear mushrooms, fish sauce, and rice paper are all available in well-stocked supermarkets or in Asian food stores. Vietnamese fish sauce has a strange taste and a stranger smell to some people, but don't be put off by it. It lends a delicious and special taste to these seafood rolls. The rolls are particularly excellent when accompanied by a fresh vegetable platter (recipe follows).

½ to 1 (3.85-ounce) package bean thread noodles

⅓ cup (½ ounce) dried tree ear mushrooms

2 pounds lean ground pork

½ pound crabmeat

1 cup peeled, shredded jicama

1 large yellow onion, finely chopped

½ to 1 teaspoon freshly ground black pepper

1 teaspoon salt

1 large egg

3½ tablespoons Vietnamese fish sauce (nuoc mam)
    plus additional for dipping

Beer or water, for brushing rice paper

18 (12-inch-diameter) sheets rice paper

Vegetable oil, for frying

Place the bean thread noodles in a medium-sized bowl and cover completely with warm tap water. Place the tree ear mushrooms in another bowl and cover them with warm water. Let both stand 20 to 30 minutes. The noodles will soften and lose their brittle consistency and the mushrooms will soften and swell a great deal.

Drain the noodles and set aside on paper towels. Drain the mushrooms and rinse in fresh water to remove any sand or grit; drain on paper towels. Cut the noodles into 1-inch lengths, chop the mushrooms coarsely, and set aside. Mix the pork and crab together in a large bowl. Add the noodles, mushrooms, jicama, onion, pepper, salt, egg, and fish sauce, and combine thoroughly.

Place the beer in a bowl and, using a pastry brush, lightly brush both sides of each sheet of rice paper at a time. Don't use too much beer; the rice paper will fall apart. After brushing, cut the rice paper with scissors evenly into quarters. Set aside 3 pieces on your work surface and place the fourth piece in front of you with its rounded edge nearest you. Put about 2 tablespoons of the Cha Gio mixture in a 3- to 4-inch-long horizontal strip about 1 inch from the rounded side of the rice paper. Fold both sides of the rice paper over the filling, pressing firmly. Then fold the rounded edge over that and roll up the Cha Gio to form a tight, compact cylinder measuring about 4 inches long. (The moistened rice paper will stick to itself.) Place the Cha Gio on a baking sheet. Continue making the Cha Gio until all the filling is used. If the rice paper tears, you can either patch it with a piece of beer-brushed rice paper, patted down firmly so that it sticks to the torn sheet, or you can overlap two quarter-sheets of rice paper to cover the damage. Packages of rice paper usually have a defective sheet or two; I break these up and moisten them for emergency repairs. Completed Cha Gio may be refrigerated for an hour or so, they can be cooked immediately, or they may be frozen (see Note, page 38).

To cook the Cha Gio, pour vegetable oil to a depth of ¼ to ½ inch into a large electric frying pan set on 375° or into a large skillet over medium heat. To test the heat of the oil in a regular skillet, stick the tips of a pair of wooden chopsticks into the pan; if bubbles form around the chopsticks, the oil is hot enough.

Place several Cha Gio about ½ inch apart in the oil. Do not move them once they are in place for at least a few minutes or the rice paper may tear. When the Cha Gio have browned lightly, turn them over carefully (chopsticks work best). Continue cooking, turning the Cha Gio 2 or 3 times for about 10 minutes, or until they are dark brown all over and the rice paper is crisp. Drain by propping cooked rolls on top of the cooking Cha Gio and lean them against the side of the pan briefly for a minute, then transfer them to paper towels to drain further. Add uncooked Cha Gio to the pan as the cooked ones are removed. Add oil to the pan, if necessary, to maintain a depth of about ¼ inch. As long as a temperature of 375° is maintained, the Cha Gio will not become greasy or absorb oil. Do not overcrowd the pan at any point.

When all of the Cha Gio are done, leave them at room temperature until ready to serve. They should be served within an hour or two, with the vegetable platter and additional fish sauce.

(continued)

Fresh Vegetable Platter

The amount of fresh vegetables you prepare will depend upon how many *Cha Gio* are served. Here I've given the amount that goes with the above recipe. How you serve the vegetables is up to you. The instructions below explain how I present them.

6 dozen Boston or butter lettuce leaves

2 English cucumbers

2 cups fresh bean sprouts, rinsed and drained

2 cups fresh cilantro leaves, rinsed and patted dry

2 cups fresh mint leaves, rinsed and patted dry

Wash and dry the lettuce leaves and arrange them attractively in the center of a large round platter. Peel the cucumbers and cut them in half lengthwise. Cut each half crosswise into thin slices and arrange at the outer edge of the platter. Place the bean sprouts between the lettuce and the cucumbers. Arrange clumps of cilantro and mint leaves on top of the cucumbers and bean sprouts.

If the Cha Gio are being served at the dinner table, provide each diner with a personal small bowl of fish sauce. Hold a lettuce leaf in your hand and place a Cha Gio on it. With chopsticks or a fork, pick up some cucumber, bean sprouts and cilantro and mint from the vegetable platter and put them on the lettuce leaf. Enclose everything in the leaf, dunk into the fish sauce, and eat.

Note: Cha Gio are best when freshly made and freshly cooked, but I've kept them frozen—either raw or cooked—and served them later with good results. The best way to keep Cha Gio is to freeze them right after they are shaped. Freeze them in single layers on baking sheets lined with waxed paper or plastic wrap. When solidly frozen, transfer them to airtight heavy-duty plastic bags and store them in the freezer for up to 2 weeks. To cook them, place the frozen rolls into cold oil. Then turn on the heat to medium (or set thermostat to 375° if using an electric frying pan) and fry for 10 to 15 minutes until they're crisp and well browned. Drain and cool before eating. Cha Gio can be frozen after cooking, but they're not as good reheated. To reheat cooked frozen Cha Gio, place them on a baking sheet in the center of a preheated 375° oven and bake for about 10 minutes, or until thoroughly heated and crisp. Cool, then serve.

Cha Gio may also be served in smaller pieces as a bite-sized appetizer. Snip each cooked Cha Gio into thirds with scissors, and arrange on platters. Serve with the vegetables and Vietnamese fish sauce.

NEW FLAVORS FOR THE NEW WEST

When I was growing up in Shanghai, I loved eating all kinds of Chinese food, most of it prepared by our *amah* (female cook). In San Francisco, I could always find what I needed in Chinatown. By the time my family and I moved to Missoula, Montana, my cooking interests included the cuisines of Southeast Asia. But the only way I was able to get those ingredients was either by mail order or by having friends send me care packages. A few years after we moved here, new Asian products began appearing in our supermarkets. I was thrilled. I brought them home, but didn't know much about how to use them. Soon, a mutual friend introduced my family and me to Chu Chu Pham. That's when I discovered why and how Missoula supermarkets began stocking "exotic" Asian ingredients. Chu Chu tells the story:

When we first came here [in 1975], there weren't many Asian people. We were the second Vietnamese family. I went to the market and looked to see what I could find. There was carrot, and potato, and cabbage. I had no clue what celery was. For seasoning all they had was soy sauce, and my husband doesn't like it. So I decided that since I could speak the language, I'd be brave and stubborn. I went to the supermarket and said, "This is what I want. I want to see more Oriental food." But they didn't know what to do, where to buy it. So I said, "Okay, I see you have soy sauce. Where do you get it?" The man said it came from a supplier in Seattle. So I asked if he could get them to send a list of what they sold. And they did. I can still see the long list on that old computer paper with the thick green bars. I studied it. All I wanted was to get *nuoc mam* for my husband. But then I thought while I'm here I might as well ask them to get some other stuff if they're willing to. I'll take the risk and promise to buy everything if they can't sell it. So they ordered rice paper and tree ear mushrooms, bean thread, and *nuoc mam*. Then more people came in and asked for other Oriental stuff and they got more and more. Other stores got it too as more and more Asians moved to the area.

Flathead Lake Whitefish Cakes

• Yield: 6 servings •

This makes an excellent appetizer for a formal dinner party because the fish cake mixture needs to be refrigerated for several hours after shaping and takes only minutes to cook. Whitefish are plentiful in lakes and streams of the Northwest. Because of an abundant food supply in Montana's Flathead Lake (see sidebar, page 190), the average size of whitefish has increased in the past few years from just under ½ pound to more than 2 pounds. The flesh is firm and sweet, and holds its shape beautifully in these fish cakes. Since whitefish is usually sold frozen (for ordering information, see page 249), I don't bother thawing them for this recipe. If you can't get whitefish, don't be concerned. Trout is an excellent substitute. Coating the fish cakes with untoasted wheat germ gives them a thin, crunchy crust, which contrasts nicely with the tender flesh.

1½ pounds boneless and skinless frozen or fresh whitefish fillets

1 cup water

½ cup dry white French vermouth

3 bay leaves

¼ cup finely chopped flat-leaf parsley

2 large shallots, finely chopped

1 clove garlic, minced

1 teaspoon Old Bay seasoning

½ teaspoon salt

¼ teaspoon freshly ground black pepper

¼ cup fine dry unseasoned bread crumbs

¼ cup lowfat mayonnaise

1 egg

2 teaspoons Dijon-style mustard

¾ cup untoasted wheat germ

¼ cup vegetable oil

½ cup sour cream

¼ cup buttermilk

1 tablespoon minced fresh chives

Place the frozen whitefish in a 12-inch heavy skillet. Add the water, vermouth, and bay leaves. Cover the pan and cook for several minutes over medium-low heat until the liquid comes to a simmer. Do not let it boil. Carefully turn the fish with a wide metal spatula, cover the pan, and cook 2 minutes longer. Remove the pan from the heat and let it stand, covered, for 15 minutes, or until the fish is cooked through. Test by separating the flesh with the tip of a sharp knife. It should be opaque. If using fresh fish, remove the pan from the heat immediately after turning the fish. Cover and let stand about 10 minutes before testing for doneness.

Transfer the fish to a dish lined with paper towels to drain and cool completely. Break the fish into large flakes and remove any small bones. Place the fish into a large mixing bowl. Add the parsley, shallots, garlic, Old Bay seasoning, salt, pepper, and bread crumbs. Fold gently with a rubber spatula to combine well and avoid breaking the fish into small pieces.

In a small bowl, combine the mayonnaise, egg, and mustard with a fork. Add to the fish mixture and fold in with the rubber spatula. Divide the fish into 6 equal portions and shape each between the palms of your hands into a cake measuring about 3 inches in diameter and 1 inch thick. Press gently but firmly so that the cakes hold their shape. Place the cakes on a plate lined with plastic wrap. Cover loosely with more plastic wrap and refrigerate for several hours. (The fish cakes may be prepared up to 12 hours ahead up to this point.)

When ready to cook, spread the wheat germ on a large sheet of waxed paper, and coat each fish cake lightly on all surfaces. Heat the oil in a 12-inch heavy skillet over medium to medium-high heat. When hot, add the fish cakes, leaving a bit of space between them, and cook on each side about 5 minutes, until nicely browned. Meanwhile, whisk together the sour cream and buttermilk. When the fish cakes are done, drain them briefly on paper towels and transfer to a serving platter. Spoon some of the sour cream sauce over them, sprinkle with the chives, and serve hot.

SOUPS

Soup is comfort food any time and in any season, but hot soups are especially welcome in cool mountain climates or in foggy and breezy coastal areas. The San Juan Islands, where my wife and I lived for two years, wasn't foggy, but the brisk Puget Sound winds made us crave soups often. One summer, when we were students in a marine biology class, the group got so hungry on the return leg of a long collecting trip that our instructors cooked up a soup of fresh-caught scallops and shrimp right on the boat. It was one of the best things we have ever eaten.

At home in Montana I make soups often. Hearty soups like the Oyster Mushroom and Oyster Chowder bring to mind those days in Puget Sound. Lighter soups such as Summer Vegetable Soup and Tomato-Tarragon Soup satisfy during the hot weather. The wild mushroom harvest during spring, summer, and fall provide abundant inspiration. Chanterelle Mushroom Soup is one creation inspired by a basket of plump mushrooms.

The best soups begin with the best stocks. When I was a teenager, I worked as an usher at a movie theater in San Francisco and Edna Allen, the telephone operator there, always said, "You have to put in good to take out good." That phrase has become a sort of mantra for me, and influences the way I cook, especially when it comes to soup making. Try the stock recipes in the Basics chapter (pages 11 to 16) and put some good in your soups.

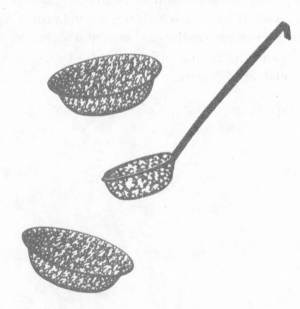

Chanterelle Mushroom Soup

• Yield: 4 to 6 servings •

I t's hard to beat the combination of chanterelles and cream. This soup is easy to make and is a wonderful way to savor that special chanterelle taste. Make it once, and you'll have something to remember for an entire year.

3 tablespoons butter

2½ tablespoons unbleached all-purpose flour

3½ cups unsalted chicken stock (page 11), boiling

¼ cup sherry (see Note)

1 cup whipping cream

1 teaspoon salt

⅛ teaspoon freshly ground black pepper

1 cup cooked chanterelles (see page 18)

1 teaspoon finely chopped fresh thyme leaves, for garnish

Melt the butter in a 3-quart saucepan over medium heat. When hot and bubbly, stir in the flour with a wooden spoon. Stir continuously for 2 minutes to cook the flour without browning. Remove pan from heat and pour in the boiling chicken stock all at once. Stir well with a wire whisk and return pan to heat. Bring the mixture to a boil and cook, stirring with the whisk, until it is only slightly thickened, just a minute or so. Stir in the sherry and simmer over low heat, partially covered, for 10 minutes. Add the cream, salt, pepper, and the chanterelles. Stir briefly just to heat through without boiling. Ladle into small bowls, sprinkle with a pinch of the thyme, and serve at once.

Note: I like to use equal parts dry sherry and cream sherry.

Borscht

• Yield: 12 to 16 servings (5 quarts) •

I loved borscht as a child growing up in Shanghai. My Russian grandmother prepared it often and after we moved to San Francisco, my mother frequently made the soup. I have carried on the tradition and make this soup in Montana, especially during the first fall harvest, when beets, leeks, carrots, and onions are ready to be picked at about the same time. This recipe makes a large batch because I've found that people usually want seconds. Leftovers can be refrigerated for several days or frozen for longer storage. The slight browning of the beets emphasizes their sweetness.

6 small to medium beets

2 leeks

¼ cup butter

1 large yellow onion, coarsely chopped

1 large carrot, peeled and cut into thin half-circles

3 cloves garlic, minced

1½ pounds Yukon gold potatoes, peeled and cut into ¾-inch cubes

1 large green bell pepper, cored, seeded, and cut into ½-inch pieces

3 quarts rich beef stock (page 12)

1 (14½-ounce) can peeled, diced tomatoes with juices, or 2 cups fresh

4 teaspoons salt

½ teaspoon freshly ground black pepper

6 cups shredded green cabbage (about 1 pound)

¼ cup freshly squeezed lemon juice plus additional to taste

Sour cream, for garnish

Chopped fresh dill, for garnish

Wash the beets and wrap them securely in heavy-duty aluminum foil. Bake in the center of a preheated 350° oven about 1¼ hours, or until tender when pierced with a small sharp knife. When the beets are cool, peel and cut them into ⅓-inch cubes. Set aside.

Thinly slice the white part of the leek and about 1 inch of the green portion. Melt the butter in a heavy-bottomed 8- to 9-quart stockpot over medium heat. Add the onion and leeks. Stir and cook for 2 to 3 minutes. Add the beets and cook for about 10 minutes, stirring occasionally, until they begin to brown slightly. Stir in the carrot and garlic and cook for 5 minutes. Add the potatoes and bell pepper and cook for 2 minutes.

Add the beef stock, tomatoes and juices, salt, and pepper, and bring mixture to a boil, uncovered, over medium-high heat. Stir in the cabbage and bring the mixture back to a boil. Reduce the heat and simmer, uncovered, about 15 minutes, or until the cabbage and potatoes are tender. Stir in the lemon juice. Adjust the seasoning to taste with salt, pepper, and lemon juice.

To serve, ladle the soup into bowls and place a dollop of sour cream in the center. Sprinkle with chopped dill.

Supper time in a cowboy camp on the banks
of the Yellowstone River (circa 1900).

Portobello and Bacon Soup
with Oyster Sauce

• Yield: 6 servings •

This is a multinational soup that showcases classic flavors from several countries. The true western foods here are the bacon and mushrooms. The bacon adds a smokiness to the mushrooms, emphasizing their meaty taste, while the oyster sauce contributes a slight saltiness. The garlic toasts and cilantro bring all the flavors together.

6 slices French or Italian bread, about ½ inch thick

Extra virgin olive oil, for brushing

3 cloves garlic, peeled and cut in half, for rubbing

¼ pound thick-sliced bacon, cut crosswise into ¼-inch strips

6 cups unsalted chicken stock (page 11)

1 pound portobello mushrooms

½ cup dry white French vermouth

2 cloves garlic, minced

1 tablespoon extra virgin olive oil

1 teaspoon salt

¼ teaspoon freshly ground black pepper

1 tablespoon minced fresh oregano

4 teaspoons oyster sauce

3 tablespoons chopped fresh cilantro leaves, for garnish

Brush the bread slices lightly with olive oil and brown them under the broiler on both sides. While the slices are still hot, rub both sides with the 3 cut garlic cloves.

Cook the bacon slowly in a large skillet until most of the fat is rendered and the bacon is lightly browned and almost crisp. Drain on paper towels. Pour off the fat, leaving the browned bits in the skillet. Set the skillet aside.

Place the chicken stock in a 3-quart saucepan. Remove the stems from the portobellos and trim off their sandy ends. Slice the stems and add them to the chicken stock. Simmer for about 10 minutes, then remove and discard the stems. Cut the caps into cubes measuring about $^3/_8$ inch. Add them to the skillet along with 1 cup of the chicken stock, the vermouth, and the minced garlic. Cook, covered, over medium heat for 5 minutes. Then uncover and cook over high heat, stirring often, until the liquid has almost evaporated, about 5 minutes. Add the tablespoon of olive oil and continue to cook, stirring and tossing for 1 to 2 minutes, to brown the mushroom pieces slightly. Remove from the heat and set aside.

Combine the cooked mushrooms with the remaining 5 cups of chicken stock in the saucepan. Add the salt, pepper, oregano, and oyster sauce. Stir well, then add the bacon pieces. Bring the soup to a simmer. Place a slice of prepared bread in each soup bowl. Ladle in the soup, sprinkle with cilantro, and serve.

Note: If you use salted chicken stock, decrease the amount of salt and oyster sauce as desired.

"Bacon should be packed in strong sacks of a hundred pounds to each; or, in very hot climates, put in boxes and surrounded with bran, which in a great measure prevents the fat from melting away. If pork be used, in order to avoid transporting about forty per cent of useless weight, it should be taken out of the barrels and packed like the bacon; then so placed in the bottom of the wagons as to keep it cool. The pork, if well cured, will keep several months in this way, but bacon is preferable."

—Randolph Marcy, *The Prairie Traveler*, 1859

Curried Butternut Squash Soup

• Yield: 8 servings •

At my house, we compost all vegetable trimmings in the backyard garden. Sometimes volunteer plants spring up, and we wonder what in the world they are. During the last growing season, which was long and hot, several intriguing-looking vines bearing blossoms that clearly belonged to the squash family spread all over the place. We didn't have the heart to uproot them, so we let them flourish and were rewarded with huge butternut squashes. This soup is one of the results of that bounty.

2 tablespoons butter

1 large or 2 medium yellow onions, coarsely chopped

1 large fresh jalapeño chile, seeded and finely chopped (about 2 tablespoons)

1 teaspoon curry powder

3 pounds butternut squash, peeled, seeded, and cut into 1-inch chunks (about 6 cups)

4 cups water

2 teaspoons salt

1 cup half-and-half

2 tablespoons dry sherry

Salt to taste

Melt the butter in a heavy 5-quart stockpot over medium heat. Add the onion and stir to coat it well with the butter. Cover and cook until tender but not browned, about 5 minutes. Add the jalapeño and curry powder, and cook, stirring, 1 to 2 minutes more. Add the squash, water, and salt. Stir well and bring to a boil over high heat. Cover the pan, reduce heat to medium-low, and simmer slowly until the squash is very tender, 30 to 40 minutes. Purée in batches in a blender until very smooth. Return to the pot and stir in the half-and-half and sherry. Add the salt to taste, if desired. Heat slowly, stirring occasionally, until very hot, but not boiling. Ladle into bowls and serve.

SQUASHES

Winter squash have wonderfully distinct flavors. Butternut squash is my favorite—it grows well in our garden, keeps for months in a cool place, and tastes terrific. That's why it is the squash of choice in the recipes here. Squashes and pumpkins are native to the Americas, where they have been cultivated for more than nine thousand years. Because squashes grow best during warm weather, they probably originated in Mexico and South America. And they are extremely promiscuous—we are always finding new scouts in our garden as a result of crossbreeding. The longer the summer, the more likely a different volunteer will reach maturity. We never know exactly what we are eating when we cook these garden volunteers, but for the most part they are very tasty.

Oyster Mushroom and Oyster Chowder

• *Yield: 6 servings* •

This is a perfect soup for late spring, when wild oyster mushrooms are abundant. Although oyster mushrooms don't taste like oysters, their cooked texture matches that of barely poached oysters. The corn highlights the sweetness of the mushrooms and oysters. If you can get lemon thyme, by all means use it. The thyme provides a slight citrus background that acts as a welcome counterpoint to the sweet ingredients.

1 pound yellow Finn potatoes, peeled and cut into ½-inch cubes (2 cups)

2 tablespoons butter

1 large sweet yellow onion, finely chopped

1 carrot, peeled and finely chopped

½ pound oyster mushrooms

2 (10-ounce) jars oysters

1 cup fresh sweet corn kernels

1 teaspoon Worcestershire sauce

½ teaspoon salt

¼ teaspoon Tabasco sauce

2 cups milk

2 cups half-and-half

2 tablespoons dry sherry

¼ cup minced parsley

1 tablespoon minced fresh lemon thyme (optional)

Place the potatoes in a 3-quart pot of rapidly boiling, lightly salted water. Cover and cook over high heat for 5 minutes. Drain and set potatoes aside. In a heavy 5-quart saucepan, melt the butter over medium heat. Stir in the onion and carrot. Cover the pan and cook slowly until the vegetables are tender but not browned, about 5 minutes. Wipe away any dirt from the mushrooms and slice them about ½ inch thick. Stir them into the onion and carrot mixture, cover the pan, and continue cooking slowly for another 5 minutes.

Drain the oysters in a large wire strainer set over a bowl. Reserve the oyster liquor; quarter the oysters and set them aside. Add the oyster liquor, corn, Worcestershire, salt,

Tabasco, milk, half-and-half, and sherry to the saucepan. Stir well and bring the mixture almost to a boil; do not allow it to boil because the milk and half-and-half may curdle. Add the oysters and cook, stirring continuously, over medium-high heat for a few minutes, or until oysters are just cooked. They should remain soft and tender.

To serve, ladle about 2 cups into each of 6 large soup bowls. Combine the parsley with the lemon thyme and sprinkle the herbs over the soup. Serve immediately.

———————

August 4, 1866

"We do have the most remarkable weather here [Fort Dalles, Columbia River Gorge], one day you roast with the thermometer at 115 degrees, next day a wind arises that takes you off your feet if you dare to go outside the door, the third day the heat is almost stifling during the few hours near midday, while in the morning and evening you can wear an overcoat comfortably. I never saw such a climate in my life."

—Julia Gilliss, in a letter dated August 4, 1866, to her parents

Summer Vegetable Soup

• Yield: 6 servings •

I make this sweet soup in the heart of summer when turnips are small and tender, the sweet white corn and vine-ripened tomatoes are bursting with flavor, and the fava beans and zucchini are ready to pick. The lemongrass adds a wonderful accent to the vegetable stock. You can prepare the broth a day or two ahead and refrigerate it. There will be enough stock for two batches of this soup. I suggest freezing the extra or using it to make the Cauliflower Soup with Roasted Red Pepper Purée (page 56).

Vegetable Stock

1 ear sweet white corn, husked

¼ pound fresh shiitake mushrooms

1 head garlic, separated into cloves, unpeeled

2 large carrots, cut into 1-inch pieces

3 stalks celery with leaves, washed and cut into 1-inch pieces

2 stalks lemongrass, cut into ½-inch pieces

½ pound small white mushrooms, cut in half

2 large leeks, split, washed well, and cut into 1-inch pieces

12 sprigs parsley

2 bay leaves

1 teaspoon black peppercorns

12 cups water

Vegetables

2 pounds fresh fava beans in the pod

2 tablespoons butter

1 large sweet yellow onion, peeled and coarsely chopped

1 large carrot, peeled and cut into ¼-inch cubes

5 small white turnips, peeled and cut into ½-inch pieces

Reserved shiitake mushrooms caps, sliced ¼ inch thick

1½ teaspoons salt

1 large ripe tomato, peeled, seeded, and diced

1 small zucchini, cut into ½-inch cubes

Reserved corn kernels

4 cups strained vegetable stock

2 tablespoons minced fresh thyme leaves, for garnish

Cut the kernels off the corn with a sharp knife and reserve them for the soup. Place the corn cob in a heavy 6-quart pot. Cut off the stems from the shiitake mushrooms and add them to the pot, reserving the caps. Add the garlic, carrots, celery, lemongrass, white mushrooms, leeks, parsley, bay leaves, peppercorns, and water. Bring to a boil over medium-high heat, uncovered. Reduce heat and allow the stock to simmer slowly for 1 hour. Strain through a fine-mesh strainer and discard the solids. You will have about 8 cups vegetable stock. Cool, cover, and refrigerate. The stock keeps refrigerated for 2 days or up to 3 months frozen in an airtight container.

Shell the favas and place the beans in a large pot of rapidly boiling water to blanch for 15 to 30 seconds. Remove the beans with a slotted spoon and transfer them to a large bowl of very cold water. After 5 to 10 minutes, drain them well. Pierce the skin of a bean with a fingernail, then slip off and discard the skin; repeat for each bean. You should have 1½ scant cups of bright green beans. Set them aside.

Melt the butter in a heavy 5-quart saucepan over medium-low heat. Stir in the onion, carrot, turnips, mushroom caps, and salt. Cover and cook, stirring 2 or 3 times, until the vegetables are almost tender, about 15 minutes. Raise the heat to high and add the tomato. Cook, stirring, for 1 to 2 minutes. Add the zucchini, corn kernels, fava beans, and vegetable stock. Lower the heat and simmer a few minutes, or until the vegetables are slightly al dente. Ladle into soup bowls, sprinkle with the thyme, and serve.

Tomato-Tarragon Soup

· *Yield: 6 to 8 servings* ·

Because of a typically short growing season, vine-ripened tomatoes are a precious commodity in the Mountain West. When we're fortunate enough to get them, there are usually three things we make: a fresh tomato salad drizzled with extra virgin olive oil and sprinkled with chopped basil and shallots; Tomatoes Stuffed with Fresh Herbs and Bread Crumbs (page 201); and this incredible soup. The color is a bright orange-red, and the taste is sensational.

8 large cloves garlic, peeled

2 tablespoons extra virgin olive oil

2 sweet yellow onions, coarsely chopped

1 large carrot, peeled and coarsely chopped

4 pounds ripe tomatoes

1½ teaspoons salt

¼ teaspoon freshly ground black pepper

¼ cup chopped fresh tarragon leaves

½ cup whipping cream

1 tablespoon minced fresh tarragon leaves, for garnish

Adjust an oven rack to the center position and preheat the oven to 300°. If the garlic cloves vary in size, cut them into equal fragments. Place the garlic in a small (6-ounce) heatproof custard cup and add the olive oil. Cover tightly with foil and bake for 1 hour, or until the garlic is very tender. Turn into a small wire strainer set over a 5-quart saucepan and allow the oil to drain. Reserve the garlic.

Set the saucepan over medium-low heat and add the onions and carrot. Stir well, cover the pan, and cook for about 15 minutes, or until the vegetables are tender but not browned. Stir occasionally.

Place half of the tomatoes in a large pot of rapidly boiling water and blanch for 30 seconds. Remove the tomatoes with a slotted spoon and transfer them to a large bowl of very cold water. Repeat with the remaining tomatoes. When the tomatoes are cool enough to handle, drain, stem, and peel them. Cut the tomatoes in half crosswise and squeeze gently to remove the juices and seeds. (Freeze the juices and seeds to use in stock.) Cut the tomatoes into large chunks.

Add the tomatoes to the onions and carrot along with the salt and pepper. Stir well, cover the pan, and continue cooking over medium-low heat for another 15 minutes.

Add the ¼ cup chopped tarragon and cook, covered, another 10 minutes. Stir in the roasted garlic.

Purée in batches in a blender until smooth. Return to the pan and add the cream. The soup may be made ahead and refrigerated to this point. When ready to serve, heat gently, stirring often, until piping hot. Do not allow the soup to boil. Ladle into bowls and sprinkle with the minced tarragon.

HERBS IN THE WEST

Emigrants on the Oregon Trail used little else to season their food besides salt and pepper. The added flavor boost that herbs gave to foods was virtually unknown at the time and only became common in the decades following the settlement of the West. Home gardeners in the late 1800s usually grew parsley and sage, but little else in the way of herbs. Although *The Web-Foot Cook Book*, published in Portland, Oregon, in 1885, contains many recipes that use spices such as cinnamon, cloves, allspice, nutmeg, mustard, curry powder, and cayenne, just a handful of recipes call for fresh parsley or dried sage, marjoram, thyme, or bay leaves. It's only been in the last decade and a half that the popularity of fresh herbs has nearly surpassed that of the dry form.

Supermarkets carry the most commonly used fresh herbs, such as tarragon, thyme, oregano, sage, and rosemary. Fresh herbs add a flavor to food unmatched by the dried versions. For example, fresh French tarragon has an aniselike taste that is completely lost after drying. If you grow tarragon, it is important to start with the French variety and not the Russian kind. The latter has no taste or aroma and adds nothing to food. Similarly, you'll want to grow Greek oregano, which has white flowers, and not a milder version with pinkish to lavender-colored blossoms. There are so many different varieties of thyme and basil, each with its unique taste, that to simply call for "basil" or "thyme" in a recipe may not be adequate in the future. Mint, which is also a member of the basil, oregano, and marjoram family, also has a number of varieties. Do you want a chocolate mint taste, a spearmint taste, or a peppermint overtone? In tabbouleh, for example, I wouldn't dream of using chocolate-mint; my preference is spearmint.

It's easy to grow herbs indoors if you don't have a garden. And it is always gratifying to rub a leaf of oregano or basil between your fingers and inhale the promise of a warm summer day during the heart of winter.

Cauliflower Soup with Roasted Red Pepper Purée

• *Yield: 6 to 8 servings* •

Cauliflower, like its relative broccoli, grows very well in the cool mountain air of the Rocky Mountains. Both make excellent soups, but cauliflower results in a rather sweet soup when used alone. Red bell peppers reveal an intriguing background acidity. When the pepper purée is swirled into the cauliflower soup, the look and the taste are tantalizing.

1 head cauliflower

2 large red bell peppers

2 tablespoons extra virgin olive oil

1¾ teaspoons salt

4 tablespoons butter

1 large or 2 medium sweet yellow onions, chopped

4 tablespoons unbleached all-purpose flour

4 cups vegetable stock or chicken stock (page 11), boiling

¼ teaspoon freshly ground black pepper

1 cup half-and-half

2 tablespoons snipped fresh chives (optional)

Break the florets off the cauliflower stem and cut them into 1-inch pieces. Discard the stem. Steam the florets for about 5 minutes, or until they are tender when pierced with the tip of a sharp knife. Set aside to cool. The cauliflower may be wrapped when cool and refrigerated for 1 day before using.

Roast the red peppers over a charcoal grill or under the broiler, turning them as necessary, until the skins are black and blistered all over. Place the peppers in a paper bag, seal the top, and set aside until cool. Using your fingers, remove the skins and stems and discard. Cut the peppers into sections and wipe away the seeds with paper towels. Do not rinse the peppers under water or you will wash away most of their flavor. Purée the peppers in a food processor until smooth, stopping to scrape the work bowl as necessary. With the machine running, gradually drizzle in the olive oil. Add ¼ teaspoon of the salt and process 1 minute longer. Transfer to a small bowl, cover, and set aside.

Melt the butter in a 5-quart saucepan over medium heat. Stir in the onion, cover the pan, and cook for 5 to 8 minutes, or until the onion is tender but not browned. Add the flour and cook, stirring with a wooden spatula, for 2 to 3 minutes, but do not let it brown. Remove the pan from the heat and add the hot stock. Stir well with the wooden spatula and set the pan over high heat. Bring the mixture to a boil and cook, stirring continuously, for 1 minute, or until the soup is slightly thickened. Add the cauliflower and cook, stirring for another 2 minutes. Purée the soup in a blender in batches until smooth. Return the soup to the saucepan and stir in the remaining 1½ teaspoons salt, the black pepper, and the half-and-half. Heat slowly over medium heat until piping hot, stirring occasionally; do not allow the soup to boil. Taste the soup and adjust seasoning. Ladle the soup into bowls and place a generous spoonful of red pepper purée in the center. Swirl the purée into the soup with the tip of a dinner knife, using two or three broad strokes. Sprinkle with the chives and serve.

Chicken and Corn Soup with Tequila, Jalapeño Chile, and Tomatoes

• *Yield: 6 to 8 servings* •

The Latin flavors brought by early settlers to the southern Rocky Mountain region of Colorado and New Mexico have spread north and west and now influence all aspects of cooking in the new West. This is sort of a Mexican-style chicken minestrone in the making. I say this because you could easily turn it into a full-blown minestrone by adding more vegetables such as shelled peas, diced cooked green beans, and potatoes. The soup is only mildly hot, but feel free to increase the heat with more jalapeños. This is a perfect soup for a hot summer day. Note that there are choices of garnishes. Each gives a different taste to the soup, but the combinations are harmonious.

1 pound boneless and skinless chicken breasts, cut into ½-inch pieces

1 jalapeño chile, seeded and finely chopped

2 cloves garlic, finely chopped

2 tablespoons tequila

1 tablespoon freshly squeezed lime juice

¾ teaspoon ground cumin

1 teaspoon salt

¼ teaspoon freshly ground black pepper

1 teaspoon sugar

2 tablespoons extra virgin olive oil

1 pound plum tomatoes

6 cups unsalted chicken or turkey stock (page 11)

3 ears corn, husked, kernels cut off the cob

Salt

Freshly ground black pepper

Freshly squeezed lime juice

⅓ cup snipped fresh chives, chopped green onion, chopped cilantro, or chopped flat-leaf parsley, for garnish

Combine the chicken, jalapeño, garlic, tequila, 1 tablespoon of lime juice, cumin, salt, pepper, sugar, and 1 tablespoon of the olive oil in a medium-sized bowl. Refrigerate for 30 minutes. This step may be completed several hours ahead.

Place the tomatoes in a large pot of rapidly boiling water and blanch for 30 seconds. Remove the tomatoes with a slotted spoon and transfer to a bowl of very cold water. When the tomatoes are cool enough to handle, drain, stem, and peel them. Cut the tomatoes in half crosswise and squeeze gently to remove juice and seeds. (Freeze the juices and seeds to use in a stock.) Dice the tomatoes and set them aside.

Heat the remaining 1 tablespoon olive oil in a 12-inch skillet over medium-high heat and add the chicken mixture. Cook and stir for 3 to 4 minutes, or until the chicken is cooked through. Set aside.

Bring the stock to a boil in a 5-quart saucepan over medium-high heat. Add the corn and cook for 2 minutes. Stir in the tomatoes and the chicken mixture and heat briefly just until piping hot. Taste and add more salt (about 1 teaspoon), pepper, and a few drops of lime juice. Ladle the soup into serving bowls and garnish each with about 2 teaspoons of chopped chives, green onions, cilantro, or parsley.

Fava Bean Soup with Basil and Tomato Pesto

• Yield: 6 generous servings •

A friend who grows favas every year once went on vacation just as the plants were reaching their maximum production. She asked my wife and me if we'd like to harvest her garden while she was away. I picked so many pounds I lost track. If you are unfamiliar with fava beans, this soup will help you get acquainted nicely.

Soup

3 pounds fava beans in the pod

6 cups medium-strength unsalted chicken stock (see page 12)

1 carrot, peeled and sliced into half-circles

¾ to 1 teaspoon salt

¼ teaspoon freshly ground black pepper

Pesto

3 cloves garlic, peeled

1 cup loosely packed fresh basil leaves

2 tablespoons chopped walnuts

¼ cup extra virgin olive oil

½ cup grated Parmesan cheese

½ teaspoon salt

¼ cup tomato paste

2 tablespoons chopped flat-leaf parsley, for garnish

To make the soup, shell the favas and place the beans in a large pot of rapidly boiling water to blanch for 15 to 30 seconds. Remove the beans with a slotted spoon and transfer them to a large bowl of very cold water. After 5 to 10 minutes, drain them well. Pierce the skin of a bean with a fingernail, then slip off and discard the skin; repeat for each bean. You should have 2 cups of bright green beans. Set them aside. The favas may be prepared up to this point a day ahead; cover and refrigerate.

Bring the chicken stock to the simmer in a 4-quart saucepan. Add the carrot and cook, partially covered, 5 minutes. Add the favas and simmer, uncovered, another 5 minutes. Season with the salt and pepper. Set aside until serving time.

To make the pesto, place the garlic in the work bowl of a food processor fitted with the metal blade. Process 15 seconds. Add the basil and walnuts and process 20 seconds. Add the olive oil, cheese, salt, and tomato paste and process another 10 seconds. The mixture will be a thick paste. Transfer to a small bowl.

To serve, reheat the soup over medium heat. Ladle into serving bowls, making sure each gets a generous amount of fava beans. Place a rounded teaspoonful of pesto in the center of each bowl (see the Note for ways to use the leftover pesto), and sprinkle the parsley around the pesto. Serve immediately. Before eating, stir the pesto into the soup.

Note: This pesto recipe makes enough for 12 servings, but it has many uses. For example, you can spread it on grilled bread, serve it as a topping for pasta, mix it into mashed potatoes, or add it to a potato salad.

~ BREADS ~

Yeast breads, especially those made with a sourdough starter, were a staple for the western pioneers. The term "sourdough" even became eponymous, referring not only to the substance but to the person who made bread with it. This was long before the days of active dry yeast, and there was no way to transport highly perishable fresh yeast during the long journeys by covered wagon. Sourdough starters—firm or liquidy doughs containing living yeast cells—were the answer. All that was needed to transform them into bread-making yeast factories was more flour and water.

This chapter features many sourdough breads, not only because of their historical importance to the West, but because they have a taste unrivaled by any other leavening agent and stay fresh longer than breads made with commercial yeast. I began experimenting with sourdough starters about twenty-five years ago. I was fascinated by the notion that a mixture of flour and water or flour and milk would actually trap wild yeast cells when set out in the warm air. If properly nurtured, these cultures can be used to leaven all sorts of breads indefinitely, provided the starter survives. In addition to sourdough breads, English muffins, and waffles, this chapter includes recipes for breads made with commercial yeast and for quick breads.

As you will see, starters can be finicky. Sourdough bakers tend to have different experiences depending on where they live and what season they collect the wild yeast cells, but all find that it's worth the effort to nurture a successful culture. More than any other kind of baking, bread making is a living, interactive process, uniting the baker with the dynamics of another living organism: yeast.

Most of the pioneer breads were made with white flour because of its long shelf life. I have kept the recipes in this chapter simple by using only two kinds of flour: white and whole wheat. Basic additions—carrots, beers, or grains—turn traditional fare into flavorful, nutritious, moist loaves and rolls. Once you've made some of these recipes, feel free to create your own variations.

I am a fan of heavy-duty electric mixers when making bread. For years I made bread by hand, and while I find the process satisfying, a mixer's power can knead more dough than my arms in a fraction of the time.

Sourdough Starters

In *The Bread Book*, Betsy Oppenneer writes, "More important than pigs, cattle, or sheep, starters were part of brides' dowries and were jealously guarded by pioneer wives as their caravans trundled across the country. These women kneaded the starter into a firm ball, nestled it in the flour barrel, and softened it with water when they needed to bake bread. The starter meant life, and as prospectors rushed to California and then to the Yukon and Alaska, they, too, carried a supply of starter for biscuits and other sustaining breads."

In America before the mid-1870s, the only way to make a yeast bread was with a sourdough starter, a batter containing live yeast cells. Although no one knows for sure how and when making sourdough breads with starters began, we do know that it is a very ancient technique that existed for at least five thousand years.

Yeast breads need yeast to rise, and there are many sources for that yeast. Packaged yeast wasn't known in America until the late nineteenth century, when the Fleischmann brothers, a pair of immigrants, perfected a method for a compressed yeast cake that reliably produced yeast breads. This yeast was perishable and required refrigeration, but by then ice boxes were common in American homes. The Fleischmann brothers, along with their business partner James Gaff, introduced their revolutionary product to the world at the Centennial Exposition of 1876, in Philadelphia. A boom in home yeast baking began, and the use of homemade sourdough starters fell by the wayside. During World War II, the Fleischmann Laboratories in Peekskill, New York, developed active dry yeast for the armed forces. The yeast required no refrigeration and could be transported all over the world, thus furthering the popularity of commercial yeast. Most often, commercial yeast, usually in a dry form, is dissolved in warm water and mixed into doughs. When a small amount of sugar is added to the yeast and water, the mixture foams and bubbles, indicating the yeast is alive and active. This step is called "proofing."

In the following recipes, whenever dry yeast is called for, I simply measure 1 tablespoon from the large bag of yeast I keep in the refrigerator. If you bake a lot of bread, it's far cheaper to buy yeast in bulk and store it this way. If you use individual packets of active dry yeast, keep in mind that each one contains 2¼ teaspoons. It's easier to measure 1 tablespoon, and doesn't alter the results of the recipes, so I opt for that. Incidentally, be sure to use regular active dry yeast in these recipes and not the quick-rising type, which is a completely different strain and is handled in a different way.

"However improbable it may seem, the health of many a professional man is undermined, and his usefulness curtailed, if not sacrificed, because he habitually eats *bad bread*."

—Mrs. Cornelius, *The Young Housekeeper's Friend*, 1850

Basic Sourdough Starter

1 tablespoon, or 1 package active dry yeast

¼ teaspoon sugar

1¼ cups warm water

1 cup (5 ounces) unbleached all-purpose flour

Combine the yeast and sugar with ¼ cup of the warm water in a small bowl or glass measuring cup. In a few minutes, the mixture will foam and bubble, indicating the yeast is alive and active. If it doesn't bubble, buy fresh yeast and start over. Transfer the yeast mixture to a 2-quart glass measuring cup. Measure the flour by scooping a measuring cup into the flour container, filling the cup to overflowing, and sweeping off the excess with a metal spatula. Add the flour to the yeast mixture along with the remaining 1 cup water and whisk to make a smooth batter about the consistency of pancake batter. Adjust the thickness with flour or water, if necessary. Scrape the side of the bowl and let the starter stand for a few hours at room temperature, loosely covered, until the mixture has almost tripled in volume. Stir the batter, cover with plastic wrap, and let rest overnight at room temperature. The next day, it will be ready to use.

Threshing oats with the aid of "modern" machinery (circa 1920).

Maintaining a Healthy Starter

Starters gain character if you feed them with more flour and water over time and store them in the refrigerator. When starter is stored in the refrigerator, a liquid layer ("hooch") will eventually separate from the flour mixture below it. Before using, always stir the two together. As long as the hooch is not pink or tinged with orange, it is all right to use. Sometimes the liquid layers of my various starters will be yellowish, gray, or even black, but they are usable. If your starter goes bad, simply begin again.

Before using a starter for the first time, whisk in 1 cup each of flour and water and transfer the mixture to a larger glass or plastic container. Let the mixture stand at room temperature, uncovered, until it has again almost tripled in volume. Then stir the mixture, cover tightly with plastic wrap, and refrigerate. Bring to room temperature before using. Each time you use some of the starter, replenish it with equal amounts of flour and warm water. For example, if you use 1 cup starter, replenish the remaining starter by whisking in ½ cup each of flour and water. Let the replenished starter rest, uncovered, at room temperature until it is bubbly and active; then stir, cover, and store in the refrigerator.

It is a good idea to refresh your starter every week or so. If you haven't used the starter in a few weeks or a couple of months, discard all but 2 cups of it and whisk in 1 cup each of flour and water. Let it stand at room temperature for a few hours until bubbly, then store as directed above. Sometimes you will need to feed it over a period of days before the starter comes back to life. The discouraging part is that after days of waiting, watching, and hoping, the starter may be dead (it will have very few or no bubbles in it), or the population of yeasts and bacteria in it may have changed so much that it is no longer capable of making bread. If you have the heart for it, begin all over again and keep your fingers crossed. I assure you that once you have made bread with your own starter you will be hooked on the whole experience.

Wild Yeast

Yeast cells live all around us, blown about by the wind. It is possible to rig various traps to capture wild yeast and create your own starter from them. Mix equal amounts of flour and water or flour and milk together in a container. After covering the container with cheesecloth to prevent insects, twigs, and leaves from taking up residence in the mixture, set it outdoors on a warm day—80° to 90° is ideal. After a few hours, bring the container back into the kitchen and leave it for 3 to 5 days in a warm place. During this time, if your trap was successful, the mixture will bubble and smell sour. If the mixture loses too much water due to evaporation or becomes too thick at any time, stir in tepid water to bring it back to its original thickness.

I spent two entire summers in different locations experimenting with various methods of trapping yeast cells. What I found was not always encouraging; the types of yeast cells and bacteria conducive to making great bread may not be available from one locale to another. When I worked as a chef at a guest ranch about 90 miles south of Missoula, I didn't have to add any commercial yeast to my wild sourdough starter doughs to produce fabulous breads. The starters were always potent. A starter made by boiling potatoes until tender, mashing them in their liquid, and whisking in flour while the potato mixture was warm seemed to work best there. After covering the container with cheesecloth, I set it outside. Potatoes are great yeast magnets, but sometimes they will attract the "wrong" kind, as they did at my home in Missoula during another summer. The starter I made there looked bubbly and very alive. It made my bread doughs rise spectacularly. But when I went to shape the bread, the dough became hopelessy gluey, wet, sticky, and impossible to use. I tried many times over a period of months using various starter mixtures: water and flour alone; potatoes, water, and flour; and milk and flour. Except for the milk-based starter, all my other starters failed at producing a decent loaf of bread—despite their appearance of bubbliness! Even when I added commercial yeast to my sourdough batters, the results were a disaster.

The reason for the mixed results is that milk and flour starters are consistently better than water and flour starters because milk is a better medium for growing many strains of yeast and bacteria that affect the bread's texture and flavor. The right balance of both organisms is needed to make a good starter. My water-based starters were apparently excellent at trapping wild yeasts or other microorganisms that altered gluten from its normally strong and elastic form to one that was wet, dense, and sticky.

Wild Yeast Starter

2 cups whole milk

2 cups (10 ounces) unbleached all-purpose flour

Place the milk in a 2-quart glass measuring cup and let it stand at room temperature for 24 hours. Measure the flour by scooping a measuring cup into the flour container, filling the cup to overflowing, and sweeping off the excess with a metal spatula. Whisk the flour into the milk. Cover the mixture with cheesecloth and leave outside for several hours on a warm day out of direct sunlight. Bring the container back into the kitchen and let it rest uncovered at around 80° (near a pilot light or in a "cold" electric oven with the light on) for 3 to 5 days, or until the starter becomes bubbly and smells and tastes sour. If some of the liquid evaporates and the starter becomes too thick, whisk in a bit of warm water to return it to its original consistency. Every time you use some of the starter, replace it with equal amounts of milk and flour, whisking them in until smooth. Let the replenished starter rest at room temperature for several hours or until the starter becomes full of bubbles. Stir, cover, and refrigerate.

Grape Starters

A few years ago, I read about starters that were made from yeasts growing on grape skins. I was intrigued. Here was a source of wild yeasts that didn't have to be lured into a liquid trap. The grapes were mixed with the flour and liquid and the yeast cells fed on the abundant supply of carbohydrates bathing them. I have done countless trials using grapes for sourdough starters. The results have been far from consistent, but good enough to keep me trying. My last starter seems to be working just fine; it produces chewy, deliciously tangy bread.

Making an active grape starter takes 10 days, but if you're a die-hard bread fan, I urge you to try it. Expert Steve Sullivan, founder of Acme Bakery (in Berkeley, California), uses wine grapes and master baker Nancy Silverton, owner of La Brea Bakery (in Los Angeles) calls for red or black grapes. The grapes that produced my best starter were called "black grapes." They were organically grown and had a chalky bloom on their skins, which I took to mean that yeasts were living there happily. Be that as it may, the grape culture and resulting starter worked.

Grape Starter

5 cups (1 pound 9 ounces) bread flour

5 cups warm water

½ pound organic black grapes, stems removed

1 large square washed cheesecloth

Measure the flour by scooping a measuring cup into the flour container, filling the cup to overflowing, and sweeping off the excess with a metal spatula. Whisk together 2 cups of the flour and 2 cups of the warm water in a 2-quart glass or plastic container. It's not necessary to break up any small lumps of flour. The remaining flour and water will be used several days later. Place the grapes on the cheesecloth and tie the ends securely to enclose grapes completely. Gently pound the grapes with a rolling pin to crush them a bit, then stir the bag of grapes into the flour-water mixture. Cover tightly with plastic wrap and leave at room temperature (75° to 80° is ideal) for 6 days. Every day, stir the mixture briefly and re-cover it. Over time, the mixture will bubble and then the bubbles may subside. A liquid layer will rise to the top and may have an odd purplish color. At the end of 6 days, the process of fermentation is complete, and the carbohydrate supply in the batter will have been exhausted by the multiplying yeast cells. You will have to feed the batter over a period of days to strengthen it. Remove the bag of grapes, squeezing the liquid back into the container; discard the grapes. Stir the starter with a rubber spatula and transfer it to a 3-quart glass bowl. Whisk in 1 cup flour and 1 cup warm water. Let the starter stand at room temperature, uncovered, for several hours, or until bubbly, then cover tightly with plastic wrap and refrigerate overnight. Repeat this procedure twice, adding 1 cup each of the remaining flour and water at each feeding. At the end of the third feeding, and after the starter has stood at room temperature until bubbly, it is ready to use. It may have an odd grayish color, which is fine. Stir, cover, and store in the refrigerator.

CHOOSING A STARTER

Some of the following sourdough recipes call for one of the three starters I've given. For best results, use the starter recommended. In some cases, though, any of the above starters will work, so use whichever one you happen to have on hand.

ABOUT SPONGES

Some of these bread recipes start off with a sponge, which is simply a mixture of sourdough starter, water, and flour that is allowed to ferment for a few hours or overnight in order to kick the starter into high gear. During this time, the sponge doubles or even triples in volume. The term "sponge" probably originated because the mixture is full of large holes and has the appearance of a sponge.

Sourdough English Muffins

• *Yield: 18 muffins* •

Once you make your own English muffins, you won't want to buy them again. These call for a milk-based starter and are light and tender. This recipe is based on one in *The Sunset Cookbook of Breads*. As with most sourdough breads, the batter is started the night before. I made these every week for Sunday brunch to serve with Eggs Benedict when I was a chef at a Montana guest ranch. The muffins are also delicious hot off the griddle, split, buttered, and eaten with slices of creamy Havarti cheese or preserves.

1½ cups whole or lowfat warm milk

¾ cup milk-based sourdough starter (page 67)

4 cups (1 pound 2 ounces) unbleached all-purpose flour

2 tablespoons sugar

1 teaspoon salt

¾ teaspoon baking soda

Cornmeal

Combine the milk and starter in a large bowl. Measure the flour by spooning it into a measuring cup, filling the cup to overflowing, and sweeping off the excess with a metal spatula. Stir 3 cups of the flour into the milk-starter mixture to make a stiff batter (the batter does not have to be smooth). Cover tightly with plastic wrap and let rest overnight at room temperature.

The next day, combine ¾ cup of the flour with the sugar, salt, and baking soda, and stir it into the dough with a wooden spoon. Sprinkle a work surface with the remaining ¼ cup of flour. Turn the dough out onto the floured surface and knead it until smooth and no longer sticky, adding more flour if needed. Cover loosely with a towel and let it rest 15 minutes. Sprinkle two baking sheets with cornmeal. Roll or pat out the dough until it is about ¾ inch thick. Using a sharp 3-inch-diameter cookie cutter, cut out the muffins. Place them 1 to 2 inches apart on the prepared baking sheets. Gather, reroll, and cut the dough scraps to make a total of about 18 muffins. Cover loosely with dry kitchen towels and let the muffins rise in a warm place until they are puffy and light, about 45 minutes.

Heat a griddle to 275°. (If your griddle has no thermostat, adjust the heat to medium.) Cook the muffins for about 10 minutes on each side, or until they are nicely browned and cooked through. Test by splitting one with a fork to be sure the inside is cooked. Serve warm, or let cool, then split and toast. Leftover muffins freeze well; just thaw, split, and toast before serving.

Ranch Hand Sourdough Loaves

• *Yield: 2 large loaves* •

These huge loaves are named in honor of the insatiable appetites of hard-working ranch hands. The loaves weigh 2 pounds each and make excellent ham, salami, and cheese sandwiches or toast. A heavy-duty electric mixer is highly recommended.

6 to 6½ cups (1 pound 14 ounces to 2 pounds ½ ounce) bread flour

2 cups Basic or Grape Starter (pages 64–68)

1½ cups warm water

1 tablespoon or 1 package active dry yeast

½ teaspoon plus ¼ cup sugar

1 tablespoon salt

¼ cup vegetable oil

Measure the bread flour by scooping a measuring cup into the flour container, filling it to overflowing, and sweeping off the excess with a metal spatula. The night before baking, make the sponge. Beat the starter, 1 cup of the warm water, and 2½ cups of the bread flour in the bowl of a heavy-duty mixer with a wooden or rubber spatula until smooth. Cover tightly with plastic wrap and let rise overnight at room temperature.

The next day, stir the yeast and ½ teaspoon of the sugar into the remaining ½ cup of the warm water and let stand 10 minutes, or until the yeast is dissolved and mixture is very foamy. Add the yeast, ¼ cup of the sugar, the salt, oil, and 1 cup of the bread flour to the sponge.

Using the flat beater of the mixer, beat on low speed to combine well. Increase the speed to medium and beat 3 minutes. Scrape down the bowl and beater. Replace the beater with the dough hook. Beating on low speed, gradually add the remaining 2½ to 3 cups bread flour to make a smooth, elastic, and slightly sticky dough. Knead 8 to 10 minutes on low to medium speed. Shape the dough into a ball. Lightly coat a 6-quart bowl with nonstick cooking spray. Transfer the dough to the bowl and turn to coat all surfaces. Cover tightly with plastic wrap and let rise at room temperature until almost tripled in volume, about 1½ hours. (It should rise nearly to the top of the container.)

Lightly flour a work surface. Turn the dough out onto the floured surface and gently pat it to a 15-inch square. Coat two 9 × 5 × 3-inch loaf pans with nonstick cooking spray or grease with vegetable shortening. Cut the dough in half with a sharp knife. Roll each piece tightly, jelly-roll style, to form a cylinder. Pinch the edges to seal. Turn seam side down and seal the ends, tucking them under the loaf. Place the dough seam side down in the prepared pans. Cover loosely with lightly oiled plastic wrap and let rise at room temperature until the loaves are 1½ to 2 inches above the rim of the pans, about 1½ hours.

Meanwhile, adjust an oven rack to the lower-third position and preheat the oven to 400°. Remove the plastic wrap and place the loaf pans a few inches apart in the oven. Bake for 35 to 40 minutes, or until the bread is well-browned and the loaves sound hollow when removed from the pans and tapped lightly on the bottom. Cool completely on a wire rack before slicing. Use the bread within 2 days, or freeze in airtight plastic bags for up to 2 months.

Whole Wheat Variation: Substitute 2 cups of whole wheat flour for the 2½ cups of bread flour in the sponge. Complete the recipe as directed, using a total of 4 cups bread flour.

Milk-Based Sourdough Loaves

• Yield: 3 loaves •

This bread is light and tender but has real substance. It makes marvelous toast and is excellent for sandwiches. This recipe makes almost 5 pounds of dough, about the limit for a 5-quart heavy-duty electric mixer.

1 cup milk-based sourdough starter (page 67)

2 cups warm whole or lowfat milk

1 tablespoon, or 1 package active dry yeast

½ teaspoon plus ⅓ cup sugar

½ cup warm water

5 cups (1 pound 9 ounces) bread flour

3 cups (15 ounces) unbleached all-purpose flour

1 egg

1 tablespoon salt

½ teaspoon baking soda

Combine the sourdough starter and warm milk in the bowl of an electric mixer. Stir the yeast and ½ teaspoon of the sugar into the warm water and let it stand about 5 minutes, or until the mixture is very bubbly and the yeast is dissolved. Measure the flours by scooping a measuring cup into the flour containers, filling the cup to overflowing, and sweeping off the excess with a metal spatula. Add the yeast mixture along with the bread flour, ⅓ cup sugar, egg, salt, and baking soda to the bowl of the mixer. Using the flat beater, beat on medium speed for 5 minutes. The dough will be ropy, elastic, and very sticky. Scrape down the bowl and beater. Replace the beater with the dough hook and gradually knead in the all-purpose flour to make a smooth, elastic dough that is only slightly sticky. If necessary, finish the kneading by hand.

To make dough by hand, combine the starter and milk in a large bowl. Dissolve the yeast and ½ teaspoon of the sugar in the water as directed above and add it to the bowl along with 4 cups of the bread flour, ⅓ cup sugar, egg, salt, and baking soda. Beat with a sturdy wooden spoon or wooden spatula for about 3 minutes. Beat in the remaining cup of bread flour until the dough is ropy, elastic, and very sticky. Stir in 2 cups of the all-purpose flour to make a stiff dough. Sprinkle the work surface with the remaining 1 cup of all-purpose flour and turn the dough out onto the surface. Knead for about 10 minutes, adding more flour if necessary to make a dough that is smooth, elastic, and satiny.

Lightly coat a 6-quart bowl with nonstick cooking spray. Transfer the dough to the bowl and turn to coat all surfaces. Cover tightly with plastic wrap and let rise at room temperature until doubled in size, about 2 hours.

Coat three 8½ × 4½ × 2¾-inch loaf pans with nonstick cooking spray and set aside. Turn the dough out onto the work surface and divide it into 3 equal pieces. Pat each piece into an 8 × 12-inch rectangle. If the dough is sticky, dust it lightly with flour. Starting with a short end, roll each piece, tightly, jelly-roll style, to form a cylinder. Pinch the edges to seal. Turn seam side down and crimp the ends, tucking them under the loaf. Place the dough in the prepared pans and cover loosely with lightly oiled plastic wrap. Let rise at room temperature until the loaves have risen about 1½ inches above the rim of the pans, about 1½ hours.

Adjust an oven rack to the lower-third position and preheat the oven to 375°. Remove the plastic wrap and bake the loaves for 35 to 40 minutes, until they are dark brown on top and sound hollow when removed from pan and tapped on the bottom. Cool completely on wire racks before slicing. Use the bread within 2 days, or freeze in airtight plastic bags for up to 2 months.

French Sourdough Baguette

· *Yield: 1 large loaf* ·

Crusty French bread, which is normally full of large holes and has a tender yet chewy interior, is transformed into a sturdier loaf with more character when made with a sourdough starter. This bread is excellent for bruschetta or garlic bread. I prefer to use the grape starter because the taste is a bit sweeter and more subtle than the milk- or water-based starters, but use whatever starter you like. This dough needs to be made with a heavy-duty mixer; you will enjoy your results a lot more without an arm in a sling.

After the first rise, I shape this bread into a fairly fat baguette and let it rise again in a canvas-lined *banetton*—a basket specially made for rising bread. *Banettons* come in several sizes and shapes (see page 249 for mail-order sources).

I have always used tiles to produce breads with crusty exteriors and moist interiors. I've also found that frequently spritzing the oven with water during the first 15 minutes of baking ensures a crisp and substantial crust. (Be sure to spritz only the walls of the oven and not the bread; if the bread is spritzed, the top of the loaf will be splotchy when removed from the oven.) I urge you to line an oven rack with a pizza stone or with square unglazed tiles. I leave my tiles on the lower-third rack all the time, so that I have a ready hearthlike surface for breads and pizzas.

1 cup grape starter (page 68)

⅔ cup warm water

3½ cups (1 pound 1½ ounces) bread flour, plus more if needed

1 tablespoon or 1 package active dry yeast

½ teaspoon sugar

2 teaspoons salt

Cornmeal

The night before baking, combine the starter and ⅓ cup of the warm water in a 1-quart bowl. Measure the flour by scooping a measuring cup into the flour container, filling the cup to overflowing, and sweeping off the excess with a metal spatula. Add 1 cup of the flour to the starter mixture, beating it in with a rubber spatula to make a smooth batter. Cover tightly with plastic wrap, and let rest overnight in a warm place.

The next day, stir the yeast and sugar into the remaining ⅓ cup warm water. Let the mixture stand until the yeast is dissolved and the mixture is very foamy, about 10 minutes. Transfer the starter mixture to the large bowl of an electric mixer. Stir in the dissolved yeast and 1½ cups of the remaining bread flour. Using the flat beater, beat on low speed until the dough is well mixed, then increase the speed to medium and beat for 3 minutes to form a smooth, creamy, thick batter. Scrape down the bowl and beater. Replace the beater with the dough hook and add the remaining 1 cup of bread flour and the salt. Knead first on low, then increase the speed to medium for 8 to 10 minutes to make a firm, elastic, nonsticky dough. Add a little more flour, if necessary. Shape the dough into a ball. Lightly coat a 3-quart bowl with nonstick cooking spray. Transfer the dough to the bowl and turn to coat all surfaces. Cover tightly with plastic wrap and let rise at room temperature until nearly tripled in volume, about 2 hours (it will nearly fill the bowl).

Sprinkle a work surface with flour. Turn the dough out onto the floured surface and shape it into a tapered loaf measuring about 16 inches long. Pat the dough into a 12-inch rectangle. Roll it tightly, jelly-roll style, to form a cylinder. Pinch the edges to seal. Turn seam side down and lengthen the cylinder by gently rolling it back and forth with your palms until it is the right length. If you have a baguette-shaped, canvas-lined banneton, coat it with flour and place the loaf in it seam side up. Enclose the loaf in a large plastic bag, leaving plenty of room to rise, and seal with a twist tie. Let it rise at room temperature until the loaf is slightly more than double in volume, about 2 hours. If you don't have a banneton, place the loaf seam side down diagonally on a large, lightly oiled baking sheet. Cover loosely with plastic wrap and let rise as directed.

About 45 minutes before you expect the loaf to be ready for baking, line the lower-third of the oven with a large pizza stone or unglazed quarry tiles. Preheat the oven to 450°. When the loaf is ready to bake, remove it from its plastic bag and carefully invert it onto a baker's peel or board lightly sprinkled with cornmeal. (If the loaf is on a baking sheet, simply remove the plastic wrap). With a sharp razor, make four diagonal slashes about 4 inches long and ½ inch deep along the top of the loaf, keeping the blade almost parallel to the loaf as you cut. Spray the oven generously with water and slide the bread off the peel onto the tiles (or place the baking sheet in the oven on the lower-third shelf.) Close the oven door immediately. Spray the oven every 3 minutes for the first 15 minutes of baking, then lower the oven temperature to 400° and continue baking for another 20 minutes, or until the bread is well-browned and sounds hollow when tapped on the bottom.

Turn off the oven, and prop the door open a few inches. Leave the bread in the cooling oven for 45 minutes to 1 hour, then transfer it to a wire rack to finish cooling before slicing. Use the bread within 2 days, or freeze in an airtight plastic bag for up to 2 months.

Sourdough Whole Wheat Waffles

• Yield: 6 to 8 waffles •

These waffles are ideal for a late and lazy Sunday brunch. The batter is started the night before and takes only a few minutes to complete the next morning. Once mixed, the batter can stand at room temperature for a few hours. It may not look as bubbly after an hour or so, but the results will be the same. The waffles are crunchy on the outside and light and tender on the inside. They are similar to Belgian waffles and can be enjoyed with sliced strawberries and whipped cream or with butter and maple syrup.

1 cup (4½ ounces) whole wheat flour

1 cup sourdough starter (pages 64–68)

½ cup warm water

1 cup plain nonfat yogurt

½ cup nonfat or lowfat milk

2 egg yolks

2 tablespoons melted butter

1 tablespoon pure vanilla extract

1 cup (4½ ounces) unbleached all-purpose flour

½ teaspoon salt

1 teaspoon baking powder

½ teaspoon baking soda

3 egg whites

3 tablespoons sugar

Measure the whole wheat flour by spooning it into a measuring cup, filling the cup to overflowing, and sweeping off the excess with a metal spatula. To make the sponge, combine the starter, water, and whole wheat flour in a large mixing bowl, beating with a wooden or rubber spatula until smooth. Cover tightly with plastic wrap and let rise overnight at room temperature.

The next morning, combine the yogurt, milk, egg yolks, melted butter, and vanilla in a small bowl and whisk the mixture into the sponge. Measure the all-purpose flour as described for the whole wheat flour, then sift the all-purpose flour, salt, baking powder, and baking soda together. Stir gently into the batter with a rubber spatula just until smooth. The batter will rise and bubble almost immediately.

In a small bowl, beat the egg whites with a handheld electric mixer until soft peaks form. Gradually beat in the sugar on medium speed; increase the speed to high and continue beating until the whites form stiff, shiny peaks. Carefully fold the whites into the batter.

Preheat a waffle iron and brush it lightly with vegetable oil or coat it lightly with nonstick cooking spray. Spoon in just enough batter to cover the bottom of the iron (about 1¼ cups). Close the iron and cook for about 6 minutes, or until the waffle is a deep golden brown. Serve immediately, repeating until all of the batter is used.

MOUNTAIN WEST WHOLE WHEAT FLOUR

Hard winter wheat from the plains of eastern Montana and the rolling Palouse Hills of Idaho make excellent yeast breads because of their high gluten content. One problem with 100 percent whole wheat flour bread recipes has been that they tend to be on the heavy side and don't rise as high as their white flour counterparts. Flourgirls flour from Pullman, Washington, has overcome that problem. The Unifine Milling Company has patented a process that literally explodes the wheat berry as the mill rotates at more than 5,600 revolutions per minute, causing the bran, endosperm, and wheat germ to become very fine and evenly mixed. It is the coarse bran in ordinary whole wheat flour that normally interferes with gluten development during kneading, typically resulting in a poor gluten network incapable of supporting the carbon dioxide bubbles that form as the dough rises. In addition, the uniform distribution of the endosperm's natural antioxidants gives the flour a long shelf life.

Whenever I use 100 percent whole wheat flour in a recipe, I always use Flourgirls. It is sold in stores in Idaho, Oregon, Washington, and Montana. If you cannot find it in your area, ask your grocer to order it for you, or order it yourself directly from the mill by calling or writing the company (see page 249 for ordering information). The flour is sold in 5-, 10-, 25-, and 50-pound bags. It also may be ordered in bales of five 10-pound bags or eight 5-pound bags. Since the flour stays fresh for many months (some people have kept it successfully in a cool, dry place for well over a year), order more rather than less and save on shipping costs.

Sourdough Sage Biscuits

• *Yield: 15 biscuits* •

Sage grows very well in the West. One summer, I decided to add some to sourdough biscuit dough to serve with a stewed chicken. We liked the biscuits so much, they have become a staple during fresh sage season in late summer and early fall. Dry sage will not give you the same results.

2½ cups (11¼ ounces) unbleached all-purpose flour

1 cup milk-based sourdough starter (page 67)

½ cup buttermilk

¾ teaspoon salt

1 tablespoon sugar

1 tablespoon baking powder

¼ teaspoon baking soda

¼ cup cold butter, cut into 4 pieces

1½ tablespoons chopped fresh sage leaves

Measure the flour by spooning it into a measuring cup, filling the cup to overflowing, and sweeping off the excess with a metal spatula. The night before, make the sponge. Combine the starter, buttermilk, and 1 cup of the flour in a medium-sized bowl. Cover tightly with plastic wrap and let rest overnight at room temperature.

The next day, combine 1 cup of the flour, the salt, sugar, baking powder, and baking soda in a separate bowl. Cut in the butter with a pastry blender until the mixture resembles coarse meal. Stir in the sage. Add the sponge and stir to make a soft dough. Sprinkle a work surface with the remaining ½ cup flour. Turn the dough out onto the floured surface and knead for 2 to 3 minutes, adding more flour if necessary. The dough should be slightly sticky when properly kneaded. Cover loosely with a dry kitchen towel and let rest 15 minutes.

Preheat the oven to 450°. Pat or roll out the dough to a ¾ inch thickness. Using a 2½-inch-diameter cookie cutter, cut out the biscuits, dipping the cutter into flour as necessary to prevent sticking. Place the biscuits about 1 inch apart on a 15½ × 10½ × 1-inch jelly-roll pan. Gather, reroll, and cut the scraps. Place on the pan. Bake in the center of the oven until the tops are golden brown, 10 to 12 minutes. Serve hot with butter.

Variation: For a delicious breakfast biscuit, omit the sage and serve with honey butter (blend equal parts honey and softened butter with a fork until smooth).

A group of cowhands enjoy a meal south of Twin Falls, Nevada, in the fall of 1919. Tony Grace was the chuck wagon cook and some of his treasured cooking pots are seen in the foreground.

"Most often I'd make baking powder biscuits, but sometimes I'd use my sourdough starter. I put the flour, baking powder, and salt in a large pan and add just enough water to make a nice dough. This I'd turn out onto a floured canvas on my work table, knead it a little, and pat it out 'till it was the right thickness. Then I cut the biscuits with an empty can of evaporated milk. Those cans made real good cutters, and I always had cases of evaporated milk in the chuck wagon. First, I heated the edge of the can over the coals to soften the thick lip, then I just popped it off with a knife, leaving a nice sharp edge. After I cut my biscuits I put them in a Dutch oven with some beef suet in the bottom and then set the pan on the coals to bake. I served them with butter, but I never made the dough with butter or any other fat.

"When it rained, I had to prepare all the food under the chuck wagon. I even mixed my biscuit dough down there right in the sack of flour. I made a well in the flour and added the baking powder, salt, and water right into the well. I mixed in flour from the sides with my hands until I had a nice clump of dough, which I put on my canvas on the ground. Since the ground was uneven, I just shaped the biscuits by hand. I got coals going under the wagon, too, so that's how everything kept dry."

—Tony Grace, on his days as a chuck wagon cook, beginning in 1913

Sourdough Buttermilk Pancakes

• Yield: sixteen 5-inch pancakes •

My wife and I became sourdough pancake addicts while we were graduate students living in Friday Harbor on San Juan Island. A friend gave us some starter and a recipe, and we faithfully made the pancakes almost every weekend. Then we became parents, which quickly altered our routine. As a result, the starter fell into disuse and ultimately died. We still kept the recipe, though, and I was able to resurrect it many years later, using either the sourdough grape starter or milk-based starter. The pancakes are hearty but tender with the slightly chewy texture that is characteristic of sourdough starters. I use buttermilk for a rich, tangy taste. During blueberry or huckleberry season, I sprinkle the tops of each pancake with a few of the berries as the first side cooks. Serve with butter and maple syrup.

1½ cups grape- or milk-based sourdough starter (pages 67–68)

1¾ cups (8¾ ounces) unbleached all-purpose flour

½ teaspoon salt

1 teaspoon baking powder

½ teaspoon baking soda

2 tablespoons sugar

1½ cups buttermilk

1 egg

2 tablespoons melted butter

1 teaspoon pure vanilla extract

2 cups fresh blueberries or huckleberries (optional)

Remove the starter from the refrigerator and let it stand overnight, covered, at room temperature. Measure the flour by scooping a measuring cup into the flour container, filling the cup to overflowing, and sweeping off the excess with a metal spatula. Sift the flour, salt, baking powder, baking soda, and sugar into a 2-quart bowl. In a separate bowl, whisk the starter with the buttermilk, egg, melted butter, and vanilla. Gently fold the wet ingredients into the dry ones with a rubber spatula, mixing just until the dry ingredients are thoroughly moistened. The batter will be bubbly and may have some lumps.

Heat the griddle to 375°. (If your griddle doesn't have a thermostat, adjust the heat to medium-high.) Lightly coat the griddle with nonstick cooking spray. For each pancake, spoon about ⅓ cup batter onto the griddle lightly. Sprinkle the berries over the pancakes. When the top sides are full of broken bubbles and start to lose their glossy look, flip the pancakes and cook until the undersides are golden brown, about 1 minute. Serve immediately.

Buttermilk-Yogurt Pancakes

• Yield: twelve 5-inch pancakes •

This recipe is for those who love light and tender pancakes that practically fly off the plate. The combination of buttermilk and yogurt gives the pancakes a taste that suggests a sourdough starter, but the texture tells you no starter was used. You can prepare the dry and liquid ingredients separately the night before and combine the two the next morning for breakfast or brunch. As usual, serve these cakes hot of the griddle with butter and syrup.

1⅔ cups (7½ ounces) unbleached all-purpose flour

¼ cup sugar

1¾ teaspoons baking powder

¾ teaspoon baking soda

½ teaspoon salt

1 cup buttermilk

⅔ cup plain lowfat yogurt

1 egg

1 tablespoon pure vanilla extract

2 tablespoons vegetable oil

1½ cups fresh huckleberries or blueberries (optional)

Measure the flour by spooning it into a measuring cup, filling the cup to overflowing, and sweeping off the excess with a metal spatula. Sift the flour together with the sugar, baking powder, baking soda, and salt into a medium-sized bowl and set aside. In a separate bowl, whisk together the buttermilk, yogurt, egg, vanilla, and oil. Add the liquid mixture to the dry ingredients and fold both together gently with a rubber spatula just until the dry ingredients are thoroughly moistened. It is not necessary to break up any small lumps of flour.

Heat the griddle to 375°. (If your griddle doesn't have a thermostat, adjust the heat to medium-high.) Lightly coat the griddle with nonstick cooking spray. For each pancake, spoon about ¼ cup batter onto the griddle. Sprinkle the berries over the pancakes. When the top sides are full of broken bubbles and start to lose their glossy look, flip the pancakes and cook until the undersides are golden brown, about 1 minute. Serve immediately.

Black Quinoa Whole Wheat Bread

• Yield: 2 large loaves •

Almost any bread can profit nutritionally from the addition of a whole grain. In this case, 100 percent whole wheat flour is combined with protein-rich cooked quinoa to make loaves that pack a nutritional wallop. I like to use the black quinoa because of its varied texture and color, but you can use regular quinoa if black is unavailable. This bread makes great sandwiches and is especially good toasted. I recommend using Flourgirls whole wheat flour (see page 249) and a heavy-duty electric mixer.

½ cup black quinoa

1 cup hot water

4 tablespoons butter, softened

⅓ cup firmly packed light brown sugar

1 egg

2 teaspoons salt

2 tablespoons or 2 packages active dry yeast

½ teaspoon granulated sugar

½ cup warm water

6 to 7 cups (1 pound 14 ounces to 2 pounds 3 ounces) whole wheat flour

1½ cups buttermilk

Rinse the quinoa in a wire strainer under cold running water for about 1 minute. Shake off excess water and place the quinoa in a 2-quart saucepan with the hot water. Bring the mixture to the boil over medium-high heat. Cover the pan, reduce the heat to medium-low, and cook for 15 minutes, or until the quinoa is tender and the water is absorbed. Remove from the heat and stir in the butter. When the butter is incorporated, add the brown sugar, egg, and salt and stir to mix well. Set aside.

In a small bowl, combine the yeast and granulated sugar with the warm water. Set aside for a few minutes until the mixture is very foamy and bubbly. Meanwhile, measure the flour by scooping a measuring cup into the flour container, filling the cup to overflowing, and sweeping off the excess with a metal spatula. Place 4 cups of the flour in the mixing bowl of an electric mixer and stir in the yeast mixture and buttermilk. With the flat beater, beat on low to mix well, then increase the speed to medium and continue beating for 5 minutes. The mixture will be heavy, sticky, and elastic. Add the quinoa mixture (which may be warm), and beat it in on low to medium speed until thoroughly incorporated. Scrape down the bowl and beater. Replace the beater with the dough hook and gradually knead in 2 to 3 cups of the flour, waiting until each addition is incorporated before adding the next. Knead on low to medium speed for several minutes, or until the dough is firm, moist, and only slightly sticky. Do not add too much flour or the resulting bread will be dry and crumbly instead of moist and tender. (You have quite a bit of leeway in this regard, but be careful nevertheless.)

To mix the dough by hand, cook the quinoa and add the butter and other ingredients to it as described above. Dissolve the yeast as described above. Place 4 cups of the flour in a large bowl and add the quinoa mixture, dissolved yeast, and buttermilk. Stir well with a heavy wooden spoon or spatula and beat for several minutes until the batter is thick and elastic. (This takes a lot of arm power.) Cover the bowl loosely with a kitchen towel and let the dough stand at room temperature for 30 minutes. Beat again for about 1 minute. Gradually stir in about 1½ cups of the flour to make a firm dough. Sprinkle a work surface with the remaining ½ cup of flour. Turn the dough out onto the floured surface and knead for 10 to 15 minutes, adding up to 1 more cup of flour as needed. If the weather is very humid, you may have to add more flour, but go easy. When properly kneaded, the dough should be smooth, moist, elastic, and slightly sticky.

Lightly coat a 6-quart bowl or casserole with nonstick cooking spray. Transfer the dough to the bowl and turn to coat all surfaces. Cover tightly with plastic wrap and let rise at room temperature until the dough triples in size and fills the container, about 2 hours. Sprinkle the work surface with flour. Turn dough out onto the surface and pat it into a 15-inch rectangle, flouring your hands as needed. Divide the dough in half and roll each piece tightly, jelly-roll style, to form a cylinder. Pinch the edges to seal. Turn seam side down and seal the ends, tucking the edges under the loaves. Coat two 9 × 5 × 3-inch loaf pans with nonstick cooking spray. Place the loaves in the prepared pans. Cover loosely with lightly oiled plastic wrap and let rise at room temperature until the loaves have risen about 2 inches above the rim of the pans, 1½ to 2 hours. They should look plump. The bread will not rise much more when baked.

About 30 minutes before the loaves are ready to be baked, adjust an oven rack to the lower-third position and preheat the oven to 400°. Remove the plastic wrap and bake the loaves for 40 to 45 minutes, or until they are well browned and sound hollow when removed from the pans and thumped on the bottom. Cool completely on wire racks before slicing. Use within 1 day, or freeze in airtight plastic bags for up to 2 months.

Whole Wheat Carrot Bread

• Yield: 2 large loaves •

Montana and Idaho are known for their hard wheats, which make great-tasting breads with light but hearty textures. The high gluten content of these flours assures an expandable elastic fabric strong enough to contain the carbon dioxide bubbles that cause the bread to rise. This bread is a gorgeous orange color from the carrot juice. You can buy carrot juice in a can, or you can make it yourself in a blender or vegetable juicer. The bread is excellent for making sandwiches or for toasting and spreading with butter and honey.

2 tablespoons or 2 packages active dry yeast

½ teaspoon sugar

⅓ cup warm water

1 large carrot, peeled and shredded

⅔ cup water

1 cup buttermilk

1 egg

⅓ cup unsulphured molasses

⅓ cup melted butter

1 tablespoon salt

4 cups (20 ounces) whole wheat flour

2 to 3 cups (10 to 15 ounces) bread flour

Stir the yeast and sugar into the warm water and let stand about 10 minutes, or until the yeast is dissolved and mixture is very foamy. Meanwhile, place the shredded carrot and the ⅔ cup water in a blender. Cover and blend on high speed until the mixture is a thick purée. Remove 1 cup for the recipe and combine it with the buttermilk in a small saucepan. (Reserve any leftover purée for another use, such as soup.) Heat the mixture just until it is warm to the touch.

In the large bowl of an electric mixer, combine the dissolved yeast and buttermilk-carrot mixture. Stir in the egg, molasses, melted butter, and salt. Measure the flours by scooping a measuring cup into the flour containers, filling the cup to overflowing, and sweeping off the excess with a metal spatula. Add the whole wheat flour. With the flat beater, beat on low until flour is moistened, then increase the speed to medium and beat for 3 minutes. Scrape down the bowl and beater. Replace the beater with the dough hook and gradually knead in 2½ cups of the bread flour on low to medium speed until the dough is soft, smooth, and elastic, about 8 minutes. If the dough is very sticky, knead in more flour as necessary.

Lightly coat a 6-quart bowl with nonstick cooking spray. Place the dough in the bowl and turn to coat all surfaces. Cover tightly with plastic wrap and let rise at room temperature until doubled in size, about 2 hours. Sprinkle a work surface with flour. Turn the dough out onto the surface and flatten it with your palms into a 15-inch square. Cut the dough in half and roll each piece tightly, jelly-roll style, to form a cylinder. Pinch the edges to seal. Turn seam side down and seal the ends, tucking them under the loaves. Coat two 9 × 5 × 3-inch loaf pans with nonstick cooking spray and place the loaves in the pans seam side down. Cover loosely with lightly oiled plastic wrap. Let rise at room temperature until the loaves have risen almost 2 inches above the rim of the pans.

About 30 minutes before the loaves are ready to bake, adjust an oven rack to the lower-third position and preheat the oven to 375°. Remove the plastic wrap and bake the loaves for about 35 minutes, or until they are well browned and sound hollow when removed from the pans and tapped on the bottom. Cool completely on wire racks before slicing. Use within 2 days, or freeze in airtight plastic bags for up to 2 months.

DUTCH OVEN BAKING

Detailed descriptions of bread baking during the cross-country trek by covered wagon are rare, but here's one that tells how the Dutch oven—the heavy cast iron pot that was the universal appliance of every emigrant family—made it possible to create tasty loaves in the middle of nowhere.

This is a pleasant place to camp for Sunday. A nice spring nearby, and plenty of good grass for the horses....Today we washed some and it is Sunday too...and I have also baked some light bread which is quite a luxury after so much hot bread called Flapjacks...the way I bake light bread is this. I have a large camp kettle, flat bottomed with a tight cover [Dutch oven]. I put my dough in the kettle and set it by the fire to rise. in the meanwhile I have a hole dug in the ground, and build a fire in it. When my dough is light, and the hole in the ground is hot, I take the coals out, and put them in a pile at one side. Then leaving a few small coals at the bottom of the pit, set the kettle of bread on them, put the pan [lid] snugly in the top of the kettle, fill it with coals & hot ashes, then pile the rest of the hot ashes around the kettle in the pit and in an hour I can bake a large loaf. I have baked 7 or 8 such loaves in a day, besides doing considerable else. I begin to enjoy this kind of life very much.

—Lucy Clark Allen, August 7, 1881

Great Big Hamburger Buns

• *Yield: 12 buns* •

I first tasted these buns at a cookout for the board of directors of Missoula's farmers market, and practically demanded the recipe on the spot. The buns are great with hamburgers, buffalo burgers, barbecued beef brisket, sloppy joes, or whatever else you want to put inside them.

2 tablespoons or 2 packages active dry yeast

⅓ cup plus ½ teaspoon sugar

⅓ cup warm water

2¼ teaspoons salt

⅓ cup vegetable oil

⅔ cup milk

3 eggs

4½ cups (1 pound 6½ ounces) unbleached all-purpose flour,
   plus more if needed

Sesame seeds

Stir the yeast and ½ teaspoon of the sugar into the warm water and let stand until the yeast is dissolved and the mixture is very foamy, about 10 minutes. Combine the ⅓ cup sugar, 2 teaspoons salt, oil, milk, and 2 of the eggs in the bowl of an electric mixer. Measure the flour by scooping a measuring cup into the flour container, filling the cup to overflowing, and sweeping off the excess with a metal spatula. Add the dissolved yeast and 3 cups of the flour to the bowl of the mixer and mix on low speed with the flat beater. Increase the speed to medium and beat for 5 minutes. Scrape down the bowl and beater. Replace the beater with the dough hook. Gradually knead in the remaining 1½ cups of flour on low to medium speed until the dough is soft, moist, elastic, and slightly sticky. The dough must be moist or the baked buns will be dry.

To make dough by hand, follow the directions above for dissolving yeast through adding the 3 cups of flour. Beat well with a sturdy wooden spoon or spatula for several minutes, or until the dough is smooth and elastic. Gradually add and stir in the remaining 1½ cups flour to make a soft dough. Sprinkle a work suface with flour. Turn the dough out onto the floured surface and knead until smooth and elastic, about 8 minutes. Add only enough flour to keep the dough soft and barely sticky. Lightly coat a 3-quart bowl with nonstick cooking spray. Place the dough in the bowl and turn to coat all surfaces. Cover tightly with plastic wrap and let rise at room temperature until the dough almost reaches the top of bowl, about 1 hour.

Remove the dough from the bowl and knead it briefly on a lightly floured surface to redistribute the yeast cells. Divide the dough into 12 equal (3½-ounce) pieces. Lightly grease 2 large baking sheets with vegetable shortening so that the buns will adhere to the pans later when you flatten them. Shape each piece into a smooth ball and place the balls several inches apart on the prepared baking sheets, 6 per sheet. Cover loosely with dry kitchen towels and let rest for 10 minutes. With your fingers, flatten the balls of dough into 4-inch rounds. Cover them loosely with plastic wrap and let rise at room temperature until doubled in size, about 45 minutes.

Adjust two oven racks to divide the oven into thirds and preheat the oven to 350°. Lightly beat the remaining egg and remaining ¼ teaspoon of salt with a fork. Brush the egg wash on the buns and sprinkle with the sesame seeds. Bake for 20 minutes, switching the top and bottom pans and rotating them front to back after about 10 minutes to ensure even baking. The buns should be well browned. Using a wide metal spatula, transfer the buns to wire racks and cool completely before splitting. Unused buns may be frozen in airtight plastic bags for up to 2 months.

TRAIL BREAD

Making bread on the Oregon Trail was a daily chore and the variety was usually limited to quick bread. The routine went something like this: Generous amounts of soda and water were stirred together in a large tin pan. Salt and enough flour were mixed in to make a firm dough. Then the mixture was kneaded right in the pan. After the dough was patted into a 1-inch disc, it was placed in a Dutch oven or large skillet and covered with an iron lid. The pan was set over the fire and the bread baked, usually by the time the meat had been fried and the coffee brewed. Sometimes, if the fire was too hot, the outside of the bread might be burned and the center raw. To avoid this, some women prepared the dough the night before, and then shaped it into small cakes and fried it in the morning.

Indian Fry Bread

• *Yield: 6 servings* •

Fry bread migrated up to the Rocky Mountain West from the Southwest. It has become such a favorite here that vendors always sell out at fairs and expositions. Makers of fry bread are very secretive about their recipes. I once asked a vendor whether she used sugar in the dough and my question was met with stony silence. Two basic types are commonly made, one with baking powder and the other with yeast. I prefer the yeast version because of its chewy texture. After conversations with several Native Americans who were willing to share their hints for success with me, I came up with this recipe. Fry bread is delicious drizzled with honey or sprinkled with cinnamon sugar. Or you may use it like a taco shell and stuff it with any savory filling.

1½ teaspoons active dry yeast

1 tablespoon plus ½ teaspoon sugar

¼ cup warm water

1 tablespoon vegetable oil

½ cup evaporated milk

2 cups (9 ounces) unbleached all-purpose flour, plus additional for kneading

½ teaspoon salt

Vegetable oil for deep frying

Stir the yeast and ½ teaspoon of the sugar into the warm water and set it aside until the yeast is dissolved and the mixture is very bubbly, about 10 minutes. Add the 1 tablespoon of oil and the evaporated milk to the yeast mixture and stir to combine. Measure the flour by spooning it into a measuring cup, filling the cup to overflowing, and sweeping off the excess with a metal spatula. Place the flour, salt, and the 1 tablespoon of sugar in a medium-sized bowl and stir well. Add the yeast-milk mixture and stir to make a soft dough.

Sprinkle a work surface with flour. Turn the dough out onto the surface and knead for several minutes, or until the dough is smooth and elastic. Lightly coat a bowl with nonstick cooking spray. Place the dough in the bowl and turn to coat all surfaces. Cover tightly with plastic wrap, and let rise at room temperature until it has more than doubled in volume, about 1 hour.

Divide the dough into 6 equal pieces and shape each into a ball. Cover with a kitchen towel and let the dough rest 10 minutes. Meanwhile, pour oil into an electric frying pan to a depth of ¾ inch. Set the thermostat to 375°. Roll out each piece of dough to form a circle or rectangle about ⅛ inch thick. Cover with a towel and let the dough rest for 10 minutes. Just before frying, make a 3-inch-long cut in the center of the dough with the tip of a small sharp knife. Fry one piece at a time until nicely browned on both sides, 1 to 2 minutes per side. Remove with a slotted spoon and set aside on paper towels to drain. Serve hot or warm.

Note: If you don't have an electric frying pan, heat the oil in a large skillet over medium to medium-high heat. Insert the tip of a wooden spoon into the oil, if bubbles form around it, the oil is hot enough to fry the bread.

FRIED CAKES

Take a little flour & water & make

some dough, roll it thin, cut it into

square blocks, then take some beef fat

and fry them. You need not put either salt

or pearl ash in your dough.

—Missionary Narcissa Whitman, 1836

Beer Bread

• *Makes 2 loaves* •

This recipe is a tribute to the wonderful microbreweries that have sprung up all over the Northwest. Beer gives bread a tenderness in texture usually associated with milk. It also contributes a unique taste, depending on the type of beer you use. Light beers give the bread a milder taste than dark beers. Consider what you are serving with the bread when selecting which beer to use. You will have two nice fat loaves with a beautiful rich brown, soft crust—ideal for slicing and eating with butter.

1 tablespoon or 1 package active dry yeast

2 tablespoons plus ½ teaspoon sugar

¼ cup warm water

2½ cups (12½ ounces) whole wheat flour

2 cups (10 ounces) bread flour

1½ teaspoons salt

12 ounces beer

2 tablespoons vegetable oil

1 egg white, lightly beaten

Stir the yeast and ½ teaspoon of the sugar into the warm water and let stand until the yeast is dissolved and the mixture is very foamy, about 10 minutes. Measure the flours by scooping a measuring cup into the flour containers, filling the cup to overflowing, and sweeping off the excess with a metal spatula. Combine the whole wheat flour with the salt and remaining 2 tablespoons sugar in the large bowl of an electric mixer. Add the beer, oil, and dissolved yeast and mix with the flat beater on the lowest speed just until the flour is moistened. Increase the speed to medium and beat for 5 minutes. With a rubber spatula, stir in 1 cup of the bread flour. Scrape down the bowl and beater. Replace the beater with the dough hook and gradually add the remaining 1 cup of bread flour while kneading first on low, then increasing the speed to medium until the dough is smooth, moist, elastic, and only slightly sticky, 6 to 8 minutes.

To make dough by hand, dissolve the yeast as directed and stir together with the salt, remaining 2 tablespoons sugar, beer, and oil in a large bowl. Add the whole wheat flour and beat with a sturdy wooden spoon or spatula for several minutes, or until the dough is thick and elastic. Stir in 1 cup of the bread flour. Sprinkle the remaining 1 cup of bread flour on a work surface. Turn out the dough onto the surface and knead until the dough is smooth, satiny, and only slightly sticky, 10 to 15 minutes.

Lightly coat a 3-quart bowl with nonstick cooking spray. Place the dough in the bowl and turn to coat all surfaces. Cover tightly with plastic wrap and let stand at room temperature until dough reaches the top of the bowl, 1 to 1½ hours. Punch down the dough and divide it in half. Cover loosely with a towel and let the dough rest for 10 to 15 minutes. Flatten each piece into an 12 × 8-inch rectangle and roll up tightly, jelly-roll style, beginning with a long side. Pinch the edges to seal. Turn seam side down and taper both ends. The loaves will be about 13 inches long. Grease a 17 × 14-inch baking sheet with vegetable shortening and place the loaves seam side down on the sheet, leaving about 5 inches between them. Cover loosely with lightly oiled plastic wrap and let the dough rise at room temperature until puffy, light, and doubled in size, about 45 minutes to 1 hour. Meanwhile, adjust an oven rack to the center position and preheat the oven to 375°. Before baking, make 3 or 4 slashes about 3 inches long and ¼ inch deep down the length of each loaf at a slight angle with a sharp knife. Brush the loaves with some of the beaten egg white and bake for about 35 minutes, or until the bread is well browned and the loaves sound hollow when removed from the pan and tapped on the bottom. Brush the tops again with egg white and transfer the loaves to wire racks to cool completely before slicing.

Variation: To make Beer and Cheese Bread, divide the dough in half after it has risen the first time. Work ½ pound of sharp Cheddar cheese cubes (½ inch) into each piece of dough, enclosing the cheese completely. Shape into loaves as directed above and continue with the recipe.

Day-Ahead Apple and Hazelnut Coffee Cake

• Yield: 12 servings •

This coffee cake is unusual in that it defies one of the cardinal rules of baking: best when fresh. This recipe is best if made a day ahead. The apples need time to flavor and moisten the cake. Pioneer women would have loved the convenience of this recipe.

A few years ago, I fell in love with an Apple Baba recipe I baked from a superb Russian cookbook, *Please To The Table*, by Anya von Bremzen and John Welchman. It was a huge tube cake with a special texture filled with apple slices. The memory of the cake has been with me ever since. In creating the batter for this coffee cake, I adapted the authors' method. Both hazelnut oil (to order, see page 249) and toasted hazelnuts contribute to the cake's taste and texture. Be sure to use a firm-textured tart cooking apple, such as Granny Smith. We use one of our locally grown varieties—Sweet Sixteen, Lyman's Large, or Kidd Orange. If you like your cake warm, simply reheat it for a few minutes in a 300° oven while your coffee brews.

Streusel Hazelnut Topping

¼ cup (1¼ ounces) unbleached all-purpose flour

½ cup granulated sugar

½ teaspoon pumpkin pie spice

¼ cup cold butter

Coffee Cake

2 cups (9 ounces) unbleached all-purpose flour

¾ teaspoon baking powder

¼ teaspoon salt

2 cups peeled, thinly sliced tart baking apples (about ¾ pound)

2 tablespoons granulated sugar

1 teaspoon ground cinnamon

2 eggs

1 cup firmly packed brown sugar

1 teaspoon pure vanilla extract

¼ cup hazelnut oil

¼ cup corn oil

Finely grated zest of 1 large orange

3 tablespoons freshly squeezed orange juice

1 tablespoon freshly sqeezed lemon juice

½ cup blanched, toasted hazelnuts (page 10), chopped

To prepare the topping, measure the ¼ cup flour by scooping a measuring cup into the flour container, filling the cup to overflowing, and sweeping off the excess with a metal spatula. Combine the flour, sugar, and pumpkin pie spice in a small bowl. With a pastry blender, cut in the butter until the mixture resembles coarse meal. Set aside.

For the cake, adjust an oven rack to the center position and preheat oven to 350°. Grease a 13 × 9 × 2-inch baking pan and set aside. Measure the 2 cups flour by spooning it into a dry measuring cup, filling the cup to overflowing, and sweeping off the excess with a metal spatula. Sift the flour with the baking powder and salt and set aside. Combine the apples, granulated sugar, and cinnamon in a medium-sized bowl, tossing to coat the apples well.

In the bowl of an electric mixer, beat the eggs, brown sugar, and vanilla together on high speed for 5 to 10 minutes, or until the mixture has tripled in volume and is thick and light colored. Combine the oils in a glass measuring cup. While beating on high speed, gradually add the oils in a thin stream. Continue beating for about 1 minute after all the oil has been incorporated. Beat in the orange zest. Combine the orange and lemon juices in a glass measuring cup, then slowly drizzle it into the batter while beating on high speed. Scrape down the bowl. While beating on the lowest speed, add the sifted dry ingredients, mixing only until thoroughly incorporated, 1 to 2 minutes. Fold in the apple mixture into the batter. Spread the batter evenly in the prepared pan. Sprinkle with the hazelnuts and scatter the streusel topping evenly over the top. Bake 40 to 45 minutes, or until the cake is golden brown and a toothpick comes out clean when inserted in the center of the cake. Cool on a wire rack and serve warm or at room temperature.

A breakfast break near Missoula, MT (circa 1900).

Huckleberry Muffins

· *Yield: 12 muffins* ·

These are light-textured, easy-to-make muffins that almost demand to be eaten with sweet butter. For many years, I made them nearly every weekend during huckleberry season and there were never any leftovers. Much of the preparation can be done the night before, leaving only the mixing and baking for the morning. Nonstick muffin pans work best. When huckleberries are in short supply, blueberries will work just fine.

1 cup sugar

1 teaspoon ground cinnamon

2 cups (9 ounces) unbleached all-purpose flour

2 teaspoons baking powder

¼ teaspoon baking soda

½ teaspoon salt

6 tablespoons cold butter, cut into 6 pieces

1 cup buttermilk

1 egg

1 teaspoon pure vanilla extract

1½ cups fresh or frozen huckleberries

Adjust an oven rack to the center position and preheat the oven to 350°. Lightly coat 12 standard nonstick muffin cups with cooking spray; set aside. Combine 2 tablespoons of the sugar with the cinnamon and set aside.

Measure the flour by spooning it into a measuring cup, filling the cup to overflowing, and sweeping off the excess with a metal spatula. Sift the flour with the remaining ¾ cup and 2 tablespoons of sugar, the baking powder, baking soda, and salt into a large bowl. Cut in the butter with a pastry blender until the mixture resembles coarse meal. (The recipe may be prepared up to this point the night before; just cover tightly and refrigerate.)

In a small bowl, combine the buttermilk, egg, and vanilla and pour it evenly over the dry ingredients. Add the huckleberries (unthawed, if frozen), and fold everything together gently with a rubber spatula just until the dry ingredients are well moistened. The batter will be fairly stiff. Spoon into the prepared muffin cups, filling them almost completely. Sprinkle each muffin with about ½ teaspoon of the sugar-cinnamon mixture. Bake for 20 to 25 minutes, or until the tops are golden brown and spring back when gently pressed with a fingertip. Remove the pan from the oven and cool for 5 minutes. The best way to remove these delicate muffins is to invert the pan onto a baking sheet, wait a few seconds, then carefully lift the pan away. The muffins should fall out easily. If necessary, coax them out of the pan with the tip of a small sharp knife. Place the muffins in a large napkin-lined basket and serve immediately.

BAKING SODA

Travelers on the Oregon Trail were advised to pack several pounds of saleratus, or baking soda, for each adult. In many cases, this was not enough for the months-long trip, so more was often gathered at the edges of natural soda springs, where it dried into crusty white beds. One emigrant, Amelia Hadley, described the saleratus "as white as snow" and "3 or 4 inches deep," adding, "you can get chunks…as large as a pint cup just as pure as that you buy." As is true of modern day baking soda, saleratus worked best when mixed into a batter and baked immediately in a moderately hot to very hot oven.

FAREWELL TO A ROLLING PIN

Sometimes even a rolling pin was too heavy to transport in the westward trek over the mountains and had to be left along the wayside. Here's one such account of that:

"A man named Smith had a wooden rolling pin that it was decided useless and must be abandoned. I shall never forget how that big man stood there with tears streaming down his face as he said, "Do I have to throw this away? It was my mothers. I remember she always used to roll out her biscuits and they were awful good biscuits."

—Mrs. Matthew Dready, emigrant on the Oregon Trail, 1846

BAKING ON THE TRAIL

The quick breads that were baked along the Oregon Trail used saleratus or baking soda. Baking powder became commercially available in the 1850s and was called yeast powder. Sold in airtight cans, it was popular with emigrants because of its stability and dependability. Yeast baking, which requires more time for doughs to rise, also took place on the trail. Sourdough starters were used by some women, but others carried along a homemade portable yeast called patent yeast. Early cookbook author Eliza Leslie described how to make it in *Directions for Cookery,* published in 1857:

> Boil half a pound of fresh hops in four quarts of water, till the liquid is reduced to two quarts. Strain it, and mix in sufficient wheat flour to make a thin batter, adding half a pint of strong fresh yeast (brewer's yeast, if it can be procured). When it is done fermenting, pour it into a pan, and stir in sufficient Indian meal (cornmeal) to make a moderately stiff dough. Cover it, and set it in a warm place to rise. When it has become very light, roll it out into a thick sheet, and cut it into little cakes. Spread them out on a dish and let them dry gradually in a cool place where there is no sun. Turn them five or six times a day while drying; and when they are quite dry, put them into paper bags, and keep them in a jar or box closely covered, in a place that is not in the least damp.

> When you want the yeast for use, dissolve in a little warm water one or more of the cakes (in proportion to the quantity of bread you intend making), and when it is quite dissolved, stir it hard, thicken it with a little flour, cover it, and place it near the fire to rise before you use it. Then mix it with the flour in the usual manner of preparing bread. [This] is a very convenient way of preserving yeast through the summer, or of conveying it to a distance.

MEATS

Because beef has become such an integral part of our diet since the West was settled, I've included many recipes featuring it. The difference between pioneer days and now is that instead of eating beef three times a day, which was typical at least for ranch hands, beef consumption has significantly declined. Beef is still the most popular commercially available meat in the Rocky Mountain West, it's just that people eat less of it because of health concerns and because pork has gained in popularity. The beef recipes included here are lighter versions of such classic main dishes as beef stew or new combinations, as in Stir-Fried Beef with Asian Noodles and Mizuna.

Smoking and barbecuing meats has long been a favorite way of flavoring and tenderizing, so you will also find recipes for smoked beef brisket and smoked pork loin. If you've never smoked foods, I encourage you to try; it's not difficult and you will feel a real sense of accomplishment when you serve what you've made.

I have also included several lamb recipes, partly inspired by the significant amount of quality lamb that is raised on the rugged landscape of the Mountain West. Strangely enough, lamb is not widely popular in my region, perhaps because the beef industry is so dominant. If our lamb is shipped to your part of the country, I hope you'll take advantage of your good fortune and give the recipes a try.

"Just remember these three things. Meat, biscuits, and gravy. That's what the cowhands wanted, and that's what they got—three times a day."

—Tony Grace, on his days as a chuck wagon cook, beginning in 1913

New West Beef Stew

This recipe clearly shows the difference between the new and old cooking of the West. In the old days, all the ingredients for a stew were cooked together for hours until everything was overcooked. Hungry ranch hands wanted nourishing food as soon as their work was done, so stews were put on the stove and cooked for a variable number of hours. Today, we cook each ingredient in a stew so that its integrity is maintained, making the dish all the more enjoyable.

3½ pounds trimmed beef chuck, cut into 2-inch chunks

Unbleached all-purpose flour, for coating

⅓ cup vegetable oil

1 cup water

4 cups beef stock (page 12)

2 bay leaves

½ teaspoon dried whole leaf thyme or 1 tablespoon chopped fresh thyme

1 tablespoon salt

2 pounds boiling potatoes, such as yellow Finn, peeled and cut into 1-inch chunks

16 small turnips (1 to 1½ inches in diameter), peeled and cut in half

4 large carrots, peeled and sliced ½ inch thick

Salt and freshly ground black pepper

1 cup shelled fresh peas

1 cup fresh corn kernels

¼ cup mixed chopped fresh parsley, thyme, and oregano

Coat the beef in flour. Place the oil in a 5-quart Dutch oven or a wide, deep ovenproof skillet and set the pan over medium heat. When the oil is hot, add the meat in batches and brown on all sides. Remove meat and set aside. Repeat until all meat is browned.

Remove the pan from the heat and discard fat and any burned pieces of meat stuck to the bottom of the pan. Add the water, and scrape the bottom of the pan with a wooden spoon to dislodge any browned bits. Strain and reserve the liquid. Return beef to pan, add the beef stock, the strained liquid, bay leaves, and thyme. The liquid should just reach the top of the meat without actually covering it. Simmer slowly, covered, until meat is very tender, 2 to 3 hours.

Meanwhile, bring 3 to 4 quarts water to a rolling boil over high heat in an 8-quart pot. Add the salt and potatoes. Cover and cook until potatoes are just tender, 8 to 10 minutes. Test with the tip of a sharp knife. Remove the potatoes with a large skimmer and set aside. Add the turnips to the pot of water and boil until tender, about 5 minutes. Remove the turnips and set aside with the potatoes. Finally, add the carrots to the water and cook until tender, 5 to 8 minutes. Drain and add them to the potatoes and turnips. Set aside until ready to use. The recipe may be completed hours in advance up to this point.

When the beef is tender, taste the cooking liquid and season with salt and pepper. Add the potatoes, turnips, carrots, peas, and corn to the beef and stir together carefully without breaking up the meat or the vegetables. Cover the pan and place it in a pre-heated 350° oven until piping hot and the peas and corn are cooked, about 30 minutes.

To serve, transfer beef and vegetables to large soup bowls with a slotted spoon and ladle some of the broth into the bowls. Sprinkle with the chopped fresh herbs and serve immediately. If you are not going to serve the stew right away, cool, cover, and refrigerate.

SAVORING THE PAST

After reading almost two thousand original sources over many years, cookbook author and restaurateur Sam Arnold has gathered a wonderful collection of Old West recipes. In his book *Fryingpans West*, you'll find recipes for Rocky Mountain Oysters, Fort Laramie Chicken Salad, Indian Pemmican, Broiled Buffalo Marrow Bones, Buffalo Tongue with Caper Sauce, and a stew-like soup called Bowl of the Wife of Kit Carson. Sam serves many of these delicious creations at his restaurant, The Fort, outside of Denver, Colorado. The restaurant was patterned after the original Bent's Fort in eastern Colorado.

One stew on his menu, Washtunkala, was originally made by Sioux Indians, using beef, deer, or buffalo jerky and dried corn. The dried corn kernels were removed from the cob and soaked in water overnight. Sam Arnold says the rehydrated corn "tasted almost as good as fresh corn." The corn was put into a large kettle over a fire and the cut up jerky added, along with wild onions and prairie potatoes. The prairie potatoes "taste somewhat like turnips and are often strung like garlic by the old Sioux people," according to Sam. (Small new potatoes may be substituted for the prairie potatoes.) Native Americans added no salt or pepper to the stew.

Herding cattle on the Western prairie (circa 1900).

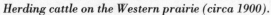

"After breakfast the cowhands did their work and I got ready for lunch. I'd start a pot of beans, stew some dried fruit for dessert, make more biscuits, and fry steak or make a roast. If I made a roast, I'd add potatoes near the end of the cooking so they wouldn't turn to mush. I seldom made stews. Cowboys just didn't like boiled beef! We also had canned peas, beans, and corn. Occasionally we had canned hominy. But what everybody really wanted was meat, potatoes, biscuits, and gravy."

—Tony Grace, on his days as a chuck wagon cook, beginning in 1913

Roasted Armagnac-Marinated Fillet of Beef

• Yield: 4 to 6 servings •

Some of the best-tasting beef in America is raised in the West, in California, Nevada, Wyoming, Montana, and Colorado, which continue to be prominent cattle-ranching states. I make this roast when we have something to celebrate with a few close friends. You'll probably need to special-order the beef from your butcher, and it should be of even thickness. The Armagnac does something wonderful for the meat, but cognac will also work. Roasted potatoes and freshly shelled peas are an excellent accompaniment. The roast is also great served cold as part of a buffet.

⅓ cup finely chopped shallots

2 cloves garlic, finely chopped

1 teaspoon salt

½ teaspoon freshly ground black pepper

2 tablespoons finely chopped fresh tarragon

2 teaspoons finely chopped fresh thyme

½ cup extra virgin olive oil

⅓ cup Armagnac or cognac

2½ pounds fully trimmed center-cut beef fillet

Additional olive oil, for roasting

Combine the shallots, garlic, salt, pepper, tarragon, thyme, olive oil, and Armagnac in a 1-gallon resealable plastic bag. Add the beef, seal the bag, and let it marinate in the refrigerator for 4 to 6 hours.

Remove the meat from the marinade and pat dry. Adjust an oven rack to the center position and preheat the oven to 450°. Tie the roast with kitchen twine crosswise in 4 or 5 places along its length, then tie it once circling the length of the meat. This will keep the meat cylindrical in shape during roasting. Rub the meat lightly with additional olive oil and place it in a shallow roasting pan. Cook for a total of 30 minutes for medium-rare, turning the roast carefully every 5 to 7 minutes. The meat will feel slightly springy to the touch, and the internal temperature should be between 125° and 130° when an instant-read thermometer is inserted into an end of the roast. Let the roast sit at room temperature or in a warm oven for 10 minutes before removing the strings and carving. Cut the meat into ½-inch-thick slices and serve as soon as possible with any pan juices.

Stir-Fried Beef with Asian Noodles and Mizuna

• Yield: 4 to 6 servings •

F lank steak is the best meat to use in stir-fries because it is tender and cooks very quickly. Slice it fairly thin crosswise against the grain or it will be tough when you cook it. Placing the meat in the freezer for 15 to 20 minutes will firm it sufficiently to make slicing very easy. Fresh Chinese lo mein noodles are readily available in well-stocked supermarkets, as are the other Asian ingredients.

1 pound fully trimmed flank steak, cut crosswise into ¼-inch strips

4 tablespoons vegetable oil

2 tablespoons dry sherry

1 tablespoon Vietnamese fish sauce (nuoc mam)

2 cloves garlic, chopped

12 ounces fresh lo mein noodles

1 tablespoon dark sesame oil

2 tablespoons light soy sauce

2 tablespoons dark soy sauce

⅓ cup rich beef stock (page 12)

⅓ cup water

1 tablespoon cornstarch

1 ounce dried shiitake mushrooms

2 bunches mizuna (about 1 pound total), washed and cut into 3-inch lengths

2 broccoli stems, peeled and sliced thin

1 large red bell pepper, cored, seeded, and cut into thin strips

4 scallions, trimmed and thinly sliced

Combine flank steak, 2 tablespoons of the oil, the sherry, fish sauce, and garlic in a bowl; cover and refrigerate. These steps may be completed hours ahead or shortly before cooking.

Cook the noodles according to directions on the package. Drain well and cool briefly in a large bowl of cold water. Drain well again and return noodles to the cooking pot. Mix in the sesame oil, cover, and set aside.

Stir together both soy sauces, the beef stock, water, and cornstarch; set aside. Soak the mushrooms in hot water to cover until soft. Squeeze out excess moisture, cut away and discard stems, and cut mushroom caps into 1-inch pieces.

Place a large wok over medium-high heat. When hot, add the beef mixture. Stir and toss 3 to 4 minutes, or until the meat is just cooked. Remove and set aside. Add the remaining 2 tablespoons oil to the wok and heat. Add the mizuna, stir and toss for about 2 minutes, or until the leaves are wilted. Add the mushrooms, broccoli stems, and red bell pepper. Stir and cook for another 2 minutes. Add the noodles and scallions and toss well to heat thoroughly. Stir the sauce mixture to distribute the cornstarch evenly and add it to the wok. Add the beef mixture and stir well for about 1 minute, or until the sauce is slightly thickened and the stir-fry is heated through. Transfer to a large serving dish and serve immediately.

THE SPICY GREEN

Mizuna is an all-purpose tender leafy green with a delightful spiciness that is not overwhelmingly hot. It loves the climate in the West and grows well in any weather, hot or cold. Mizuna has attractive lacy leaves that look pretty in salads or in stir-fries. Buy mizuna that is young and tender, preferably at farmers markets, or grow it yourself. The entire plant can be eaten as long as the stems are very thin, about ⅛ inch.

Leg of Lamb Stuffed with Garlic and Herbs

• Yield: 6 to 8 servings •

For this dish, I like to buy a boneless leg of lamb. Even so, you will need to trim the meat well to remove the outer membrane and inner pockets of fat. The garlicky herb purée is an ideal foil for this robust meat. The lemongrass powder, which is available in Asian markets, is a nice addition but it's not essential to the success of the recipe. Try to serve the lamb pink. Stuffed Tomatoes with Fresh Herbs and Bread Crumbs (page 201) and roasted potatoes are perfect accompaniments.

1 boneless leg of lamb (about 6 pounds)

¼ cup chopped garlic

1 teaspoon salt

6 tablespoons extra virgin olive oil, plus extra to rub on the lamb

⅓ cup finely chopped fresh oregano

¼ teaspoon ground cayenne pepper

1 teaspoon freshly ground black pepper

3 tablespoons freshly squeezed lemon juice

1 teaspoon lemongrass powder (optional)

1 tablespoon sweet paprika

1½ cups rich chicken stock (page 11)

½ cup dry white French vermouth

2 tablespoons butter

Carefully remove the outer membrane from the lamb with a sharp boning knife. Open the inside of the lamb leg (using the incision already made to remove the bones as a starting point) so that the whole leg lies flat on your work surface in a rough triangular shape. Cut away as much of the fat as you can, but don't be obsessive about it. Make shallow slashes in the thicker portions of meat so that the marinade can penetrate. You will wind up with about 4 pounds of meat from a trimmed 6-pound boneless leg.

Pound the garlic and salt to a purée in a mortar with a pestle or mash with a fork in a small bowl. Gradually stir in the olive oil. Add the oregano, cayenne, black pepper, lemon juice, lemongrass powder, and paprika and mix in well. Rub the mixture all over the meat. Roll the lamb into a cylinder and tie it securely in 4 or 5 places crosswise with kitchen twine. Tie one string lengthwise around the lamb. The meat should be an even cylinder shape. Rub the outside surface lightly with olive oil. Place the lamb in a shallow dish, cover loosely with plastic wrap, and refrigerate 4 to 6 hours.

To cook lamb, adjust an oven rack to the center position and preheat the oven to 450°. Place the lamb in a shallow roasting pan and cook, uncovered, for 15 minutes. Reduce the oven temperature to 350° and continue cooking until the internal temperature of the lamb is between 125° (rare) and 130° (medium-rare). After 1 hour of total cooking time, test for doneness by inserting an instant-read thermometer about halfway into the lamb while it is in the oven. Immediately remove the meat from oven and wait about 15 seconds to read the temperature. If lamb is not ready, remove the thermometer, return the meat to the oven, and keep retesting every few minutes until the lamb is cooked to your liking.

When the lamb is ready, transfer it to a cutting board and cut away the twine. Create a loose tent with foil, place it over the lamb, and let it stand 15 minutes before carving so the juices can be reabsorbed into the meat. While the lamb rests, pour off any juice from the roasting pan and reserve it. Add the chicken stock and vermouth to the pan and set it over high heat. Scrape the bottom of the pan with a wooden spoon to dislodge any browned bits and boil briefly to reduce the sauce by about one-third. Swirl in the butter and add the reserved juices. Adjust the seasonings, as desired. Carve the lamb into thin slices and serve with the sauce.

Three thousand sheep being herded through "downtown" Belt, MT (circa 1900).

Vietnamese Be-Boon

• *Yield: 6 servings* •

My Missoula friend Chu Chu Pham is to thank for this recipe. It is a Vietnamese version of barbecued pork served with rice stick noodles, fresh vegetables, and fish sauce. The secret ingredient is ground browned rice, which is easy to make. This is a spicy and exciting eating experience.

½ cup long-grain white rice

1 pound pork tenderloin

7 tablespoons Vietnamese fish sauce (nuoc mam)

2 teaspoons dry white French vermouth

¼ teaspoon freshly ground black pepper

1 tablespoon vegetable oil

¼ cup sugar

3 tablespoons water

2 tablespoons rice vinegar or apple cider vinegar

1 large lime

¾ cup finely shredded carrot

¾ cup peeled, finely shredded jicama

1 fresh hot chile pepper (such as serrano, jalapeño, or habanero)

4 cloves garlic, peeled and coarsely chopped

1 English cucumber, peeled and sliced

2 cups fresh bean sprouts

1 cup fresh cilantro leaves

1 cup fresh mint leaves, torn into small pieces

5 to 10 ounces rice stick noodles

Wash rice thoroughly in several changes of cool tap water, then drain and dry it well on a kitchen towel. Place the rice in a small, heavy skillet (cast iron is best) over medium heat. Do not add any oil to the pan. Stir occasionally with a wooden spoon until the rice grains begin to brown. Then stir almost continuously until all the rice is a deep caramel color. Do not allow the rice to burn. This whole process takes about 20 minutes. Transfer the rice to a bowl and allow it to cool. Grind to a fine powder in a blender, mini-grinder, or spice mill. Transfer it to an airtight container. It will keep in a cool cupboard for up to several weeks.

Slice the pork about ½ inch thick. In a medium-sized bowl, combine the pork with 2 teaspoons of the fish sauce, the vermouth, pepper, and oil. Cover and refrigerate 1 hour or longer. Mix the remaining 6 tablespoons and 1 teaspoon of the fish sauce, the sugar, water, and vinegar together in a medium-sized bowl. Stir until the sugar is dissolved.

Remove the rind from the lime. The easiest way is to slice both ends off and stand the lime upright. Cut the peel and white pith away from lime in strips with a small sharp knife. Hold the lime over a mortar or a small bowl and remove the sections by cutting them out between the membranes. Collect the sections and juice in the mortar or bowl. Squeeze the remains of the pulp to extract all of the juice. Crush the lime sections in the juice with a pestle or mash with a fork. Add the juice and pulp to the fish sauce mixture and stir in the carrot and jicama. Cover and refrigerate.

Wearing protective gloves, stem and chop the chile coarsely. Leave in the seeds and ribs if you like ultraspicy foods. Combine the garlic and chile on the chopping board and finely chop both together, or crush them to a paste with a mortar and pestle. Place in a small dish and set aside, covered. Arrange the cucumber, bean sprouts, cilantro, and mint on a platter. Cover and refrigerate until serving time. The recipe may be made hours ahead up to this point.

Rice stick noodles come dried in packages of 3 to 4 stacks. Each stack weighs about 5 ounces. Fill a large stockpot with 12 cups of water and bring it to a boil. Place 1 or 2 stacks of the noodles in the stockpot. Cook, stirring occasionally, for about 3 minutes, or until just tender. Drain in a large colander and rinse under warm tap water. Drain well. To prevent the noodles from sticking together, divide them into small piles on a serving dish. Let them stand loosely covered until serving time. The noodles may be prepared 1 hour or so ahead.

When ready to serve, heat a large nonstick skillet over medium-high heat and sauté the pork on both sides just until done, about 3 minutes total. Remove from the pan and set aside to cool briefly. Cut the pork into thin strips and combine them in a serving bowl with 1 to 2 tablespoons of the ground browned rice.

To serve, set the pork, the vegetable platter, bowls of the fish sauce mixture, the garlic and hot pepper purée, and the rice stick noodles on the table. Provide each person with a bowl and a pair of chopsticks. Each diner places some rice stick noodles in the bowl, adding some of the vegetables, pork, fish sauce mixture, and a dab of the garlic-pepper purée, if desired. Mix well with the chopsticks (or a fork!) and enjoy.

Note: You can substitute hot boiled rice for the rice stick noodles, if you prefer. Plan on about 1 cup cooked rice per person.

Smoked Beef Brisket with Tamarind Barbecue Sauce

· *Yield: 10 to 12 servings* ·

This is what barbecue is all about—long, slow cooking at a low temperature until the meat is so tender it practically falls apart. Allow 8 to 10 hours, or longer, to smoke and cook the brisket. Start early in the day when you've got someone to share cooking duties and chat with.

Beef brisket comes from a well-exercised part of the chest muscle of a steer. It is an ideal cut to barbecue because it starts out tough; slow cooking breaks down the fibers and tenderizes the meat. It is also fairly high in fat. But this is desirable, because during cooking the fat melts out of the beef, basting it with flavor. This results in meat that is tender, moist, and ultimately low in fat. You will probably have to special-order the brisket at your market. Ask for a whole brisket with about ½ inch of fat covering most of one side. It should weigh 7 to 8 pounds. Brisket known as a "packer cut" is larger, weighs about 12 pounds, and has a thicker layer of fat and a tougher end. If you have a choice, opt for the former cut. You'll waste a lot less, and the results will be moist, juicy, and tender. According to Charlie and Ruthie Knote in *Barbecuing and Sausage Making Secrets*, brisket and other tough cuts of meat require prolonged cooking at an internal temperature of 160° to become tender. Since that temperature is an internal one, I start cooking the brisket wrapped in foil for 3 hours, then unwrap the beef and continue cooking it for 5 to 7 hours, or until it is very tender. I use an electric smoker because it easily maintains a steady temperature better than a charcoal smoker.

The spice rub gives the meat a mildly hot taste. If you like yours more fiery, increase the amount of cayenne and use a hot paprika instead of a sweet one. The tamarind barbecue sauce is served with the brisket on the side. It is terrific with all sorts of barbecued meats. Tamarind is a tropical legume and is one of the ingredients that gives Worcestershire sauce its distinctive taste. I buy it in moist pulp form loaded with seeds in 8-ounce or 1-pound packages in Asian or Latin American markets. It is easy to prepare your own tamarind purée, and it is best to do so before you start with the brisket. Be sure to allow time for the brisket to marinate overnight.

1 (8-ounce) package moist tamarind pulp with seeds

2 cups boiling water

⅓ cup sweet paprika

¼ cup firmly packed light brown sugar

2 tablespoons ground cumin

2 tablespoons plus 2 teaspoons salt

1 tablespoon plus 2 teaspoons freshly ground black pepper

2 teaspoons ground cinnamon

2 teaspoons ground cayenne pepper

7 to 8 pound beef brisket

36 to 40 hickory chunks

2 tablespoons vegetable oil

3 large yellow onions, coarsely chopped

10 cloves garlic, coarsely chopped

3 jalapeño chiles, seeded and coarsely chopped

1 teaspoon ground cloves

½ cup distilled white vinegar

1 cup unsulphured molasses

¼ cup granulated sugar

3 (14.5-ounce) cans peeled whole tomatoes in juice

1 tablespoon dried whole thyme leaves

Break the tamarind pulp into walnut-sized pieces and place them in a bowl. Pour the boiling water over and let the mixture stand undisturbed for 1 hour. Break up the tamarind with your fingers to separate the pulp from the seeds and let it soak for 3 hours more. Press the mixture through a coarse sieve, reserving the purée. You will have about 1½ cups of purée. Cover and refrigerate until needed. (It keeps well for several days.)

Combine the paprika, brown sugar, cumin, 2 tablespoons salt, 1 tablespoon black pepper, the cinnamon, and cayenne in a small bowl. Pat the brisket dry with paper towels and rub all of the spice mixture over it. Cover the brisket with plastic wrap and refrigerate overnight. Wrap the brisket in heavy-duty aluminum foil and let it stand at room temperature while you soak the hickory chunks and prepare the smoker.

Soak the hickory chunks in cold water for at least 2 hours.

Prepare the smoker, preheating the chamber to 200° to 220°. Add 3 or 4 hickory chunks and some water to the smoker, according to the manufacturer's instructions, and place the brisket on the top rack. Smoke for 3 hours, adding 3 or 4 chunks and additional water as needed while maintaining the smoker temperature between 200° and 220°. Unwrap the brisket and return it to the smoker fat side up. Continue cooking until the meat is very tender and pulls apart easily with a fork, about 5 to 7 hours. Test the temperature of the brisket occasionally with an instant-read thermometer. It should be about 165°. The brisket will look black but will be fine.

While the brisket cooks, prepare the barbecue sauce. Heat the oil in a heavy 4-quart saucepan over medium heat. Add the onions, cover the pan, and cook for 10 minutes without browning, stirring once. Add the garlic and jalapeños. Cover and cook for 5 minutes. Stir in the cloves, the remaining 2 teaspoons of black pepper, and 2 teaspoons salt. Cover and cook 5 minutes more over medium heat. Add the reserved tamarind purée, vinegar, molasses, granulated sugar, tomatoes, and thyme. Stir well. Break the tomatoes up with a spoon, pressing them against the side of the pan. (If you

(continued)

taste the sauce now it will seem very sour and you will be tempted to add more sugar. Don't. Long, slow cooking will mellow the acidity.) Cover the saucepan and simmer the sauce over medium heat for 10 to 15 minutes. Set the lid askew on the pan and regulate the heat so that the sauce simmers very slowly for about 3 hours. Stir occasionally. At the end of cooking, the sauce will be slightly thickened. Cool it slightly and purée until smooth with a food processor. The sauce will have a deep brown color and be the consistency of a thick tomato purée. You'll have about 6 cups of sauce. Cover and refrigerate leftovers.

To serve the brisket, slice it thinly with a sharp knife at a 45° angle across the grain. Pass the sauce separately.

Note: The sauce keeps in the refrigerator for 4 to 6 weeks and improves with time. It can also be frozen in an airtight container.

"During roundups we were often off a long time and a long distance from town, so we had to have everything we needed and plenty of it. In the spring, when we branded and castrated the males, we'd throw the testicles right on the coals where they'd roast and cook. Everybody loved those mountain oysters!"

—Tony Grace, on his days as a chuck wagon cook, beginning in 1913

Working up an appetite (circa 1920).

THE MAKING OF A CHUCK WAGON COOK

Tony Grace made his way west from Milwaukee at the age of 17, in 1907. He saw a poster of a cowboy and that got his imagination going. At first he earned his living working on the railroad and then he landed a job as a ranch hand in Roundup, Montana. The only horse riding he'd done up to that point had been on a merry-go-round. He tells the rest of the story:

I decided to try my hand at cooking instead of riding while I was in Arizona. One reason was there weren't so many men in the outfits, maybe 8 or 10. So I could always put a meal together in a hurry. Another reason was the horses weren't so good there. They were small, more like ponies, and riding them didn't look good to me.

Well, since they needed a cook, and since I was used to "baching" it in the winter, when we were laid off, I decided to give it a try. Besides, the pay was $25 a month more!

The chuck wagon itself had everything I needed. We kept the big cast iron Dutch ovens inside—couldn't do without those pots, and the back of the wagon had all kinds of drawers for storing salt, sugar, pepper, and even butter. The back of the wagon was a lid that folded down to use as a prep table. It had a leg that stood on the ground for support. The chuck wagon was the heart of the camp. During roundups, the cowboys would ride out each morning after breakfast and return for meals.

I'd get up around three in the morning during spring roundups and start fixing breakfast. First I'd make a good fire with wood that was in the area. When the coals were right, I'd get a pot of coffee going. Had to have coffee hot and ready all the time. Then I'd get my biscuits ready and start them cooking. For the meat, I'd cut steaks about a half inch thick from the side of beef, coat them lightly in flour, and fry them in a Dutch oven with beef suet or lard. I made a gravy with flour and evaporated milk. This is what I made for breakfast every day. We all ate our meat well done. Everyone just filled his plate with food, found a spot on the ground, and sat down and ate.

Roasted Rack of Lamb with Rosemary and Thyme

• *Yield: 4 servings* •

Completely trimmed racks of lamb, marinated in wine, olive oil, and herbs, make a festive entrée for a special party. You can ask your butcher to trim the lamb for you, making sure all of the fat is removed, even between the ribs, or you can perform the operation yourself with a sharp boning knife. Lamb racks prepared this way are sometimes referred to as "Frenched." This dish goes very well with Sautéed Green Bean, Sweet Onion, and Yellow Beet Sauté (page 199) and roasted potatoes.

2 racks of lamb, 8 chops each, completely trimmed

1½ cups sauvignon blanc

⅓ cup extra virgin olive oil

½ cup sliced shallots

3 cloves garlic, coarsely chopped

1 tablespoon chopped fresh rosemary

1 teaspoon chopped fresh lemon thyme

1 teaspoon chopped fresh thyme

½ teaspoon freshly ground black pepper

Salt to taste

⅔ cup rich beef stock (page 12)

⅓ cup pinot noir

2 tablespoons butter

Place the lamb racks in a 9 × 5 × 3-inch glass loaf pan. Combine the sauvignon blanc, olive oil, shallots, garlic, herbs, and pepper and pour over the lamb. The liquid should just cover the lamb. Cover and marinate 4 to 6 hours, refrigerated. Turn the lamb 2 or 3 times while it marinates.

When ready to cook, adjust an oven rack to the center position and preheat the oven to 450°. Remove the lamb from the marinade and place it in a shallow roasting pan with the meat facing up. Sprinkle lightly with salt. Roast until medium-rare, about 25 minutes. An instant-read thermometer should register 130° when inserted in the roast. Transfer the lamb to a dish, cover it loosely with foil, and keep warm while you make the sauce.

Pour off and discard any fat from the roasting pan. Add the stock and pinot noir and cook over high heat, scraping the bottom of the pan with a wooden spoon to dislodge any browned bits. Reduce sauce by about half, or until slightly thickened. Add the butter and swirl it in. Strain the sauce through a fine-mesh sieve; there will be about ½ cup. Adjust the seasoning to taste and keep the sauce warm. To serve, slice the lamb into chops and divide it among 4 heated dinner plates. Spoon the sauce over the lamb and serve immediately.

SIX AND A QUARTER CENTS A POUND

In a letter started September 30, 1866, and finished on October 1 of that year pioneer Julia Gilliss describes the meat supply in Fort Stevens, on the Oregon Coast, where she and her husband James settled:

> We get our meat, the few times that there is any, from the Commissary at six and a quarter cents a pound. We are mighty glad to get it, and it adds to the interest that we have to guess what it is. We are told that it is always beef, but such shapes and such bones, I never saw before. Nothing like a steak or a roast exists, but the animal appears to be all cut into even chunks. Now of course, this is very impartial and therefore has its good side.

Beef, Turkey, and Pork Meat Loaf with Tomato-Mustard Glaze

• Yield: 8 to 10 servings •

If you're going to make meat loaf, you might as well fix a big one because leftovers make terrific sandwiches. This loaf is exceptionally moist, despite the use of lean ground meats, because of the liquid in the tomato purée, milk, and cooked onion and green pepper. But the baking has something to do with it, too. I followed Sylvia Woods' and Christopher Styler's recommendation in *Sylvia's Soul Food* and placed a pan of hot water on the rack below the baking loaf. The constant humid atmosphere in the oven guarantees a moist meat loaf. The loaf is so moist, in fact, it needs no sauce. Serve with Roasted Garlic Mashed Potatoes (page 205).

2 cups coarse fresh bread crumbs, made from day-old
    crustless French or Italian bread

½ cup milk

1 tablespoon butter

1 large or 2 medium sweet yellow onions, chopped

1 large green bell pepper, cored, seeded, and chopped

4 eggs

1 cup tomato purée

½ teaspoon Tabasco sauce

1 pound extra-lean ground beef

1 pound extra-lean ground turkey

1 pound ground pork

2 cloves garlic, minced (1 tablespoon)

1½ teaspoons rubbed sage

1 teaspoon dried oregano leaves, crumbled

½ teaspoon dried whole thyme leaves

2 teaspoons salt

1 teaspoon freshly ground black pepper

2 tablespoons Dijon-style mustard

1 teaspoon prepared horseradish

Combine the bread crumbs and milk in a large bowl and set aside. Melt the butter in a large skillet over medium heat and stir in the onion and bell pepper. Sauté, stirring occasionally, until the vegetables are tender but not browned, 6 to 8 minutes. Set aside to cool briefly.

Whisk the eggs, ¾ cup of the tomato purée, and Tabasco into the bread-milk mixture. Add the beef, turkey, pork, garlic, sage, oregano, thyme, salt, and black pepper and mix thoroughly with your hands. Transfer the mixture to a roasting pan and pat it into a loaf about 12 inches long and 5 inches wide. (The meat loaf may be made hours ahead up to this point; just cover and refrigerate. Bring to room temperature before baking.) When ready to bake the meat loaf, combine the remaining ¼ cup tomato purée with the mustard and horseradish and spread it evenly over the top of the loaf.

Adjust an oven rack to the lowest position and another to the center position, and preheat the oven to 350°. Fill a 13 × 9 × 2-inch baking pan halfway with boiling water and place it on the lower shelf. Place the meat loaf on the upper shelf. Bake for 1 to 1¼ hours, or until the juices run clear yellow when the loaf is pricked with a fork. Let it stand 10 minutes, then cut it into 1-inch slices.

"Whenever we needed meat we'd kill a cow, a yearling at least, and always a female. I'd dress it out and hang it up in the wagon so that the outside would dry out and form a hard shell. Then I'd wrap it in canvas and it would keep a good ten days. It aged nicely and didn't spoil."

—Tony Grace, on his days as a chuck wagon cook, beginning in 1913

FOR THE LOVE OF PIGS

I grew to love pigs when I worked as the chef at a guest ranch in southwestern Montana. We had a sow who suckled and reared almost a dozen piglets. She reveled in her motherhood, lolling contentedly on her side as her babies nursed. We fed the mother and piglets well with leftover vegetables and bread. As the piglets grew, they showed decidedly different personalities and their intelligence really impressed me. I grew to appreciate them so much that I couldn't eat them for a quite a while. But pigs figured so prominently as a food source during the settlement of the West, and are still one of our mainstays. So, I decided that no matter how I felt about the animals, I needed to include some pork recipes in this book.

Hickory-Smoked Barbecued Pork Loin

• Yield: 12 to 16 servings •

This recipe makes spicy, moist, succulent pork loin. After massaging in the dry rub, the meat is refrigerated for two to three days to allow the flavors to permeate it. During smoking, the meat is left uncovered for most of the time. Then it is wrapped in foil with a wet marinade for its final cooking. This two-step smoke cooking is what makes the meat so juicy. I like to make a lot of this at a time and either throw a big party or freeze half the pork for later use. Leftover barbecued pork is excellent in sandwiches. Or use it in Smoked Pork Lasagna with Salsa Verde and Red Pepper Purée (page 118). If you don't want to make this much, reduce all ingredients by half. The cooking time will be the same.

Dry Rub

1 tablespoon ground cinnamon

1 tablespoon rubbed sage

1 tablespoon whole dried thyme leaves

1 tablespoon dried oregano leaves

1 tablespoon ground cumin

1 tablespoon ground cayenne pepper

1 teaspoon ground cloves

1 tablespoon salt

1 tablespoon freshly ground black pepper

2 tablespoons granulated sugar

2 tablespoons firmly packed brown sugar

6 to 7 pounds pork loin roast

16 to 20 hickory chunks

Wet Cooking Marinade

6 cloves garlic, minced

4 tablespoons freshly squeezed lemon juice

4 tablespoons freshly squeezed orange juice

2 tablespoons extra virgin olive oil

Combine all of the dry rub ingredients thoroughly. Rinse the pork and pat it dry. Sometimes a thin layer of fat is on one side of the pork. Don't remove it completely, but cut away about a 1-inch-wide strip of the fat and the attached tough membrane that runs the length of the loin, to prevent the meat from curling during cooking. Cut the whole pork loin crosswise into two even pieces. Sprinkle dry rub over all surfaces and rub it in gently with your fingers, covering the pork completely. Place in an airtight plastic bag, seal, and refrigerate for 2 to 3 days. Let it stand at room temperature while you soak the hickory chunks and prepare the smoker.

Soak the hickory chunks in cold water for at least 2 hours.

Prepare the smoker, preheating the chamber to between 200° and 220°. Add 4 hickory chunks and some water to the smoker, according to the manufacturer's instructions, and place the pork on the upper rack. Smoke for 2½ hours, adding 2 to 3 hickory chunks and additional water as needed while maintaining the smoker temperature between 200° and 220°.

Meanwhile, combine the wet marinade ingredients in a small bowl. Remove the pork and test its internal temperature with an instant-read thermometer. It should register about 140°. Place each pork roast on a piece of heavy-duty aluminum foil, fold up the edges of the foil slightly to make a shell, and divide the marinade between the two pieces. Seal tightly and return the pork to the smoker. Continue smoking for another 1 to 1½ hours, or until the internal temperature of the pork is 160°. (If you are not ready to serve, the pork can be held at this temperature for an hour or so.) Let the pork stand for 10 minutes after removing it from the smoker. Place in a rimmed dish and carefully remove the foil. Slice the pork about ¼ inch thick, arrange on dinner plates or on a large serving dish, and spoon the marinade over it. Serve immediately.

"We bought our first hog late that spring, and how do you suppose hogs were brought into the valley? An enterprising resident of the valley went over into southern Oregon and bought a number of sows and stock hogs. He brought them by boat to Umatilla Landing and kept them there until the mountain roads were passable, then drove them afoot all that three hundred miles to the Boise Valley! We paid seventy-five dollars for a six-week-old sow. She soon brought us four little pigs, and from this one sow we got our start of hogs."

—Arabella Clemons Fulton, Boise, Idaho, settler in the late 1860s

Smoked Pork Lasagne with
Salsa Verde and Red Pepper Purée

• *Yield: 8 generous servings* •

This dish is my Western tribute to Italy, the land that gave the world lasagne. The three colors of the Italian flag—red, white, and green—are represented by the red pepper purée, lasagne noodles, and salsa verde, respectively. The smoked pork tastes particularly good with salsa verde, cheese, and red bell pepper. The tangy tomatillos in the salsa and the sweet taste of the pork and red pepper are a wonderful combination. All you need with this is a salad of tomatoes in an herb and garlic vinaigrette.

Salsa Verde

2 pounds tomatillos, with husks

8 cups water

3 teaspoons salt

2 cloves garlic, minced

4 jalapeño chiles, cut in half, seeded, and minced

½ cup loosely packed cilantro leaves, chopped

1 large yellow onion, finely chopped

1 tablespoon finely chopped fresh oregano

¼ teaspoon ground cumin

Roasted Red Pepper Purée

3 large red bell peppers

¼ teaspoon salt

⅛ teaspoon freshly ground black pepper

Lasagne

12 dried lasagne noodles

1 pound Hickory-Smoked Barbecued Pork Loin (page 116)

4 ounces lowfat cream cheese or Neufchâtel

1 cup (4 ounces) freshly grated Parmesan cheese

½ cup finely chopped flat-leaf parsley

1 egg

1 tablespoon extra virgin olive oil

3 cups (12 ounces) pepper jack cheese, shredded

To make the salsa, remove the thin husks from the tomatillos and place the tomatillos, water, and 2 teaspoons of the salt in a 4- to 5-quart saucepan. Cover and bring to a boil over high heat, then uncover, lower the heat to medium, and simmer the tomatillos just until they become soft, 6 to 8 minutes. (Their color will fade from bright green to olive drab.) Drain well and purée the tomatillos in a food processor or a blender. Transfer the purée to the saucepan and stir in the remaining 1 teaspoon salt and the rest of the salsa ingredients. Set the pan over low to medium-low heat and simmer the sauce, stirring every few minutes with a wooden spoon to prevent it from sticking to the bottom of the pan, about 40 minutes. You should have about 4 cups of sauce. Cool, cover, and refrigerate until ready to use. (The sauce keeps well in the refrigerator for several days.)

For the pepper purée, roast the peppers over a gas flame, charcoal grill, or under the broiler, until all sides are charred black. As soon as they are ready, place them in a paper bag and close the top securely. Let them cool slightly, then remove the skins. Core and seed the peppers using a small sharp knife. Do not rinse the peppers to wash away the seeds or you will also wash away most of the pepper taste. Pat peppers dry on paper towels and purée them in a food processor until very smooth, about 2 minutes. Season with salt and pepper and set aside, covered, until needed. Makes about 1¼ cups. (The peppers may be made a day ahead and refrigerated.)

Cook the lasagne noodles in a large pot of boiling water until they are just tender. Drain, rinse in cold water, and set aside in a single layer on kitchen towels to drain further. Chop the pork into small pieces with a heavy chef's knife or cut it into 1-inch chunks and use a food processor to pulse-chop it into very small pieces. You will have about 4 cups of chopped pork. Place the pork into a large bowl and add 2 cups of the Salsa Verde, the cream cheese, ½ cup of the Parmesan, the parsley, and egg. Beat well with a wooden spoon until thoroughly mixed. Combine ½ cup of the Salsa Verde with the olive oil in the bottom of a 13 × 9 × 2-inch baking dish and spread the mixture into an uneven layer. Place 3 lasagne noodles lengthwise over the salsa in a single layer. The strips should just cover the bottom of the pan. Spread with one-third (about 1 ½ cups) of the pork mixture, and sprinkle with one-third (1 cup) of the pepper jack cheese. Layer another 3 lasagne noodle strips over the cheese and spread with half the remaining pork mixture. Cover with 3 more lasagne strips, the remaining pork mixture, and 1 cup of the remaining pepper jack cheese. Arrange the last 3 lasagne strips lengthwise on top, spread with all the remaining Salsa Verde, and sprinkle with the remaining ½ cup Parmesan and the pepper jack cheese. (The lasagna may be made in advance up to this point; just cover and refrigerate. Bring to room temperature before baking.)

Adjust an oven rack to the center position and preheat the oven to 375°. Bake the lasagne, uncovered, until it is piping hot throughout and top is lightly browned, about 50 to 60 minutes. When the lasagne is almost ready, warm the pepper purée over very low heat in a small saucepan, but do not let it boil. Remove the lasagna from the oven and let it stand 10 minutes, then cut it into portions. Spoon a stripe of the red pepper purée diagonally over each serving of lasagne.

Roasted Pork Tenderloins, Potatoes, and Apples with Calvados Ginger Sauce

• Yield: 4 servings •

The key to the success of this recipe is using the proper potatoes and apples. The Mountain West has some of the best potato-growing farms in the country. Potato plants love our warm summer days and cool nights. I like to use yellow Finn potatoes in this recipe, but any firm-textured, boiling potato will work, including Yukon gold or red-skinned varieties. Using the right kind of apple is also important because you want the apple chunks to hold their shape during cooking. I prefer the locally grown antique variety Lyman's Large, which is a big apple with a pale greenish yellow skin that resembles a cross between a Granny Smith and a Golden Delicious in taste and texture. If you can get mature Granny Smith apples, use them. If not, firm Golden Delicious will do just fine. Serve with steamed tender green beans tossed with a touch of butter.

2 pork tenderloins (about 1½ pounds total)

3 teaspoons salt

¼ teaspoon freshly ground black pepper

3 teaspoons extra virgin olive oil

5 yellow Finn potatoes (about 1 pound), washed but unpeeled,
    cut into 1 inch pieces

1 large, firm, cooking apple, washed but unpeeled, cored,
    and cut into ¾-inch pieces (about 2 cups)

3 tablespoons butter

¼ pound fresh shiitake mushrooms, stems removed, caps thinly sliced

Salt and freshly ground pepper to taste

⅔ cup rich beef stock (page 12)

⅓ cup calvados

1 tablespoon peeled, finely shredded fresh ginger

1 tablespoon minced flat-leaf parsley, for garnish

Adjust an oven rack to the center position and preheat the oven to 400°.

Remove any membranes and fat from the pork with a small sharp knife. Rinse the pork and pat dry. Season each tenderloin with 1 teaspoon of salt and a pinch of pepper. Heat 2 teaspoons of the olive oil in a 12-inch nonstick ovenproof skillet over medium-high to high heat. When hot, add the tenderloins and cook for 6 minutes, or until all sides are nicely browned. Remove the pork and set aside on a plate.

Add the potatoes, remaining 1 teaspoon salt, and ¼ teaspoon pepper to the skillet. Stir well and cook for 1 minute over medium-high heat. Place the pan in the oven and roast the potatoes for 15 minutes. Combine the apples with the remaining 1 teaspoon olive oil. Add to the potatoes and roast for 10 minutes. While the apples and potatoes are in the oven, melt 1 tablespoon of the butter in a 10-inch skillet over medium-high heat. Add the mushrooms and salt and pepper to taste and cook until the mushrooms are lightly browned, about 2 minutes. Remove the mushrooms from the heat and add them to the potatoes and apples, which should be tender. Transfer to a dish, cover, and keep warm. (The recipe may be prepared several hours ahead up to this point. Just cool, cover, and refrigerate the pork, potatoes, apples, and mushrooms, then bring to room temperature before continuing.)

Place the pork in the skillet used to cook the potatoes and apples. Reserve any pork juices to make the sauce. Return the pan to the preheated 400° oven and roast for 15 to 20 minutes, or until the pork is only slightly pink in the center. An instant-read thermometer should register between 150° and 160° when inserted in the pork. Add the pork to the potato mixture; cover and keep warm.

Set the skillet over medium-high or high heat and add the beef stock, calvados, pork juices, and ginger. Bring to a boil, scraping the bottom of the pan with a wooden spoon to dislodge any browned bits, and reduce the liquid by almost half. Immediately add the remaining 2 tablespoons butter, swirling until it has melted into the sauce. Strain the sauce into a small bowl and taste for seasoning, adding salt and pepper if desired.

Slice each tenderloin at an angle into 8 pieces. Arrange 4 pieces on each dinner plate with some of the potato, apple, and mushroom mixture. Spoon the sauce over the pork, sprinkle with a little parsley, and serve immediately.

SON-OF-A-BITCH STEW

"Sometimes when we slaughtered for meat I'd make something called son-of-a-bitch stew. The main thing that went in the stew was the marrow gut, the tube connecting the young cow's two stomachs. It's got to be free of grass or the taste isn't right. First I cut the marrow gut into small pieces, about 2 inches long, dredged them in some flour seasoned with salt and pepper, and then fried the pieces in beef suet or lard in a Dutch oven until crisp. Next I chopped up the heart, kidneys, sweetbreads, and brains. After dredging those pieces in flour I added them to fry with the marrow gut so that everything was cooked crisp. Then I added enough water to cover everything. All of this was cooked until tender. You can't believe how good this tastes. Some of the hands used to squabble over pieces of kidneys and brains! They'd never eat kidneys cooked any other way."

—Tony Grace, on his days as a chuck wagon cook, beginning in 1913

TWO PIGLETS FOR A SIDESADDLE

From Arrow Rock, which was a bustling village by the Missouri River on the Santa Fe Trail, comes this tale:

Henry Nave, one of Arrow Rock's first settlers, had grown tired of the constant diet of deer, bear, and wild turkeys, so he visited a man who had some pigs. The man's wife didn't want to sell him any, but Nave finally persuaded her, trading his own wife's sidesaddle for two shoats for starting a pig farm. From that time on, pork in Arrow Rock has been more popular than beef, and "steak" on the menu more often means pork than beef.

Butchering hogs at a winter camp in 1912.

GAME

Hunting is a way of life in the Mountain West. At least half of the adults who live in the region hunt, and it's often a family affair. Before children go on a hunting trip, they are trained in the proper use and care of firearms and how to survive in the wild.

The new interest in game as a food source has resulted in the growing industry of raising of a variety of game animals, both in the United States and abroad. The animals are reared under strict conditions to make them as healthy as possible for the consumer; because of this, the meat is expensive. But game meats are far different in taste from domestic animals, and they are well worth the price.

It is important to remember that game is not new. It was the first meat our ancestors ate. As development occurred throughout the plains and mountain states and towns sprang up, game fell by the wayside as a food source and the cattle and poultry industries rose in prominence. Now, chefs all over the country feature game on their menus.

I never ate game until my wife and I moved to Montana. Now, with the generosity of friends who hunt and the availability of game through mail-order sources that offer overnight delivery, we enthusiastically embrace it as a regular part of our diet. During the various hunting seasons, many of our friends host game parties, giving everyone a chance to sample a variety of tasty meats. Many farm-raised game species are available to the home cook, including some exotic ones such as squirrel and rattlesnake, and more familiar animals such as deer, buffalo, and pheasant (see the mail-order sources on page 249). The key to game cookery is to not overcook the meat. This is especially true when preparing steaks or roasts. Game and fruit are natural partners. That doesn't mean that every game recipe has to include a fruit, but a sweet element tends to highlight the game's natural flavor.

For more information on all kinds of game and how to cook it, read *American Game Cooking* by John Ash and Sid Goldstein.

Elk Tenderloin Steaks with Chanterelles and Cream

• *Yield: 4 servings* •

Our friends Peggy and Ted Christian are avid hunters who generously shared some elk with us. Hunters in Montana will tell you that elk, a close relative of deer, is their favorite game meat. It has a wonderfully meaty taste without being heavy and lacks the gaminess that can be so off-putting if you're unfamiliar with wild meat. This combination of chanterelles, cream, and elk is too seductive to pass up. If you don't hunt, beg some elk from a friend who does, or order it (see page 249). Keep the rest of the meal simple, and serve the steaks with roasted potatoes and steamed green beans.

4 elk tenderloin steaks (5 to 6 ounces each, about ¾ inch thick)

1 tablespoon vegetable oil

1 tablespoon butter

1 cup cooked chanterelles (page 18)

⅔ cup rich beef stock (page 12)

½ cup dry white French vermouth

⅔ cup whipping cream

¼ teaspoon salt

⅛ teaspoon freshly ground black pepper

1 teaspoon freshly squeezed lemon juice

2 tablespoons finely chopped fresh tarragon leaves

Pat the elk steaks with paper towels. Heat the oil in a large nonstick skillet over medium-high heat, add the steaks and cook 2 minutes on each side for medium-rare. Transfer to a plate; cover and keep warm. Pour off fat in the skillet and return the pan to medium-high heat. Add the butter, and after it has melted, stir in the chanterelles. When the mushrooms are hot, pour in the stock and vermouth. Cook at a brisk boil, stirring occasionally, until the liquid has reduced by half and is syrupy. Add the cream, salt, and pepper, and continue reducing for several minutes until the sauce has thickened and coats a metal spoon. Stir in the lemon juice and taste carefully. Adjust seasoning with more salt, pepper, and lemon juice, if desired. Stir in the tarragon and return the steaks back to the pan. Cook briefly just to heat through, while spooning the sauce and mushrooms over the meat. Serve immediately.

Bison Tenderloins Au Poivre
with Zinfandel Sauce

• *Yield: 4 servings* •

This is my version of the French classic Steak au Poivre. Lean buffalo meat is ideal in this dish since the quick cooking over high heat ensures it will remain moist and tender. I've added tart cherries to tame the sweetness of the meat, and I use butter instead of cream so the sweetness of the cream doesn't dominate the taste of the meat.

4 (6-ounce) bison tenderloins, trimmed

2 tablespoons whole black peppercorns

Salt

2 tablespoons corn oil

¼ cup minced shallots

¼ cup dried sour cherries (Montmorency), soaked in hot water to plump

⅔ cup red zinfandel

½ cup rich beef stock (page 12)

1 teaspoon minced fresh thyme leaves

4 tablespoons butter

Thyme sprigs, for garnish

Pat the meat dry with paper towels and set it aside. Place the peppercorns on the work surface and crush coarsely with the bottom of a saucepan. Press pepper onto both sides of the steaks and refrigerate, covered, until ready to cook. This may be done several hours ahead.

Just before cooking, lightly season the bison with salt. Heat the oil in a large, heavy skillet over medium-high heat. Cook the steaks 2 to 3 minutes on each side, depending on whether you want the meat rare or medium-rare. Remove the meat from the pan, pour off the fat, and keep the steaks warm.

To make the sauce, place the shallots in the pan and return it to medium-high heat. Scrape the bottom of the pan with a wooden spoon to dislodge any browned bits while stirring the shallots. Drain the plumped cherries. Add the cherries, zinfandel, stock, and thyme to the pan. Boil the mixture and cook until it is reduced by half, then add the butter and any meat juices. Swirl the contents of the pan and cook until the liquid is thickened enough to lightly coat the steaks. Lower heat to medium-low, return the steaks to the pan, and baste continuously with the juices for about 1 minute, or just until the meat is heated through. Serve on warmed plates and garnish with the thyme sprigs.

Grilled Buffalo Rib-Eye Steaks
with Onion Confit

• *Yield: 4 servings* •

In this confit, onions are cooked with wine, vinegar, and a bit of sugar to make a tangy relish that goes especially well with mild, sweet-tasting game meat like buffalo. I recommend using Walla Walla sweet onions or Vidalias. The confit is based on a recipe in *Chez Panisse Pasta, Pizza, and Calzone* by Alice Waters, Patricia Curtan, and Martine Labro and is wonderful with hamburgers and Buffalo Burgers (page 128). Serve with Roasted Garlic Mashed Potatoes (page 205).

½ cup butter

4 large sweet yellow onions, peeled and cut in half vertically

¾ teaspoon salt

¼ teaspoon freshly ground black pepper

1 tablespoon firmly packed light brown sugar

2 cups pinot noir

¼ cup sherry wine vinegar

2 tablespoons balsamic vinegar

2 tablespoons red wine vinegar

2 tablespoons cassis

2 (4-inch-long) sprigs fresh rosemary

4 buffalo rib-eye steaks (8 ounces each and 1 inch thick)

1 tablespoon olive oil

Melt the butter in a small saucepan over medium-low heat and cook, without stirring, allowing the butter to bubble gently until it is lightly browned. Remove the foam layer with a spoon and discard. Carefully pour off clear butter into a wide, shallow 5-quart sauté pan.

Meanwhile, cut the onions crosswise into thin slices. Add them to the butter in the sauté pan and set over medium heat. Add the salt and pepper and stir to coat the onions well. Cover the pan and cook 5 minutes, until the onions begin to release their liquid. Stir in the brown sugar, cover the pan, and cook another 5 minutes. Add the pinot noir, the three vinegars, cassis, and rosemary and stir well. Bring the mixture to a boil, then cover the pan partially. Decrease the heat to low and cook about 1½ hours, or until the liquid is almost completely absorbed and the mixture is thick and slightly syrupy. Watch carefully toward the end of cooking and adjust the heat accordingly. Set aside and serve warm.

While the confit is cooking, prepare a charcoal grill. Pat the steaks dry with paper towels and rub their surfaces lightly with olive oil. Grill over hot coals about 4 minutes per side for medium-rare. Serve immediately on warm plates. Leftover confit will keep, refrigerated, for about a week.

THE BUFFALO HUNT

By the early 1840s, buffalo were already disappearing along the Santa Fe Trail and became a less common food source for trailgoers thereafter. When they did happen upon buffalo, the hunt was not as simple as one might think, as relayed by Colorado restaurateur and western food historian Sam Arnold:

When buffalo were killed on the prairie, there was a science to the killing. The biggest, most powerful buffalo bulls led the herd, and the young cows followed in the middle-front of the herd, protected by the lead bulls and the lesser bulls around the sides, while the old cows straggled behind. So, for the buffalo hunter, the tough job was to get at the young cows (the best eating) right in the middle-front of the herd. The skills necessary to obtain this young cow meat distinguished the professional hunter from the amateur.

Bringing bison back from extinction: The "Buffalo King,"
M. Pablo, overseeing his herd of bison in western Montana, 1908.

Buffalo Burgers with Shiitake Mushrooms and Onion-Cilantro Relish

• Yield: 4 servings •

Because buffalo is so lean, care must be taken during cooking to keep it moist. In these burgers, hydrated shiitake mushrooms, vermouth, and oyster sauce all contribute moisture as well as flavor to the buffalo. The onion and cilantro relish adds acidity to complement the sweetness of the meat. If you cannot get buffalo, don't despair; ground beef chuck will do in a pinch.

½ ounce dried shiitake mushrooms

1 pound ground buffalo

4 tablespoons oyster sauce

½ cup dry white French vermouth

1 English cucumber, washed and unpeeled

2 large sweet yellow onions

1 tablespoon vegetable oil, plus more for grilling or sautéing

1 tablespoon sherry wine vinegar

Vegetable oil, for frying

½ cup chopped fresh cilantro leaves

4 sesame seed hamburger buns

4 tablespoons mayonnaise

In a small bowl, soak the mushrooms in 1 cup warm water until softened, about 30 minutes. Squeeze out the excess moisture, and trim away and discard stems. Chop the mushrooms finely and set aside.

If cooking on a grill, prepare a hot charcoal fire. In a large bowl, combine the buffalo, mushrooms, 3 tablespoons of the oyster sauce, and ¼ cup of the vermouth. Mix well, taking care not to compact the meat. Divide the meat mixture into 4 equal portions, form the portions into round patties to fit the buns, and refrigerate.

Cut the cucumber into thin slices and refrigerate. Slice the onions crosswise about ¼ inch thick. Heat the oil in a 10-inch skillet over medium-high heat, add the onions, and cook about 5 minutes, stirring frequently until the onions are browned and slightly tender. Add the remaining 1 tablespoon oyster sauce, ¼ cup vermouth, and the sherry wine vinegar. Stir and cook several minutes until the onions are tender and the liquid is almost completely absorbed. Add the cilantro and remove pan from the heat. Set aside.

If grilling the burgers, brush the grill rack lightly with vegetable oil and place the patties on the grill. Cook until browned on the bottom. With a wide spatula, turn the patties and cook to desired doneness, 4 to 5 minutes total cooking time for medium-rare to medium burgers. If sautéing the burgers, set a large skillet over medium-high heat and add 1 tablespoon oil. When the oil is hot, cook the burgers until they are browned on both sides, about 6 minutes for rare to medium-rare.

After turning the patties to cook on the second side, toast the buns, cut side down, on the grill or set them cut side up a few inches under the broiler until nicely browned. To assemble the burgers, spread ½ tablespoon mayonnaise on each bun half. Arrange about 8 cucumber slices on the bottoms of the buns. Place the patties over the cucumbers and spoon the onion and cilantro mixture on top. Cover with the bun tops and serve immediately.

BUFFALO CONNOISSEURS

When buffalo were freshly killed, the most valued cuts were the tongue, liver, rib racks, and kidneys. The "fleece," fatty strips of meat on either side of the hump, were so coveted that hunters sometimes fought over them. Once these prized parts of the buffalo were eaten, the rest was either transported to a nearby fort, if one existed, or cut into strips and "jerked" (impaled on sticks or draped over twine and allowed to dry completely in the open air). Jerked meat could be kept indefinitely without spoiling and was a ready source of protein for the hunters and their families.

Stir-Fried Pheasant with Ginger and Orange

• *Yield: 4 servings* •

The leanness of game meats makes them ideal for the high-heat quick-cooking in stir-fry dishes. I suggest you order two whole pheasants weighing about 2½ pounds each and bone the breast meat yourself. That way you'll also have 4 leg-thigh cuts, which you can use in the next recipe.

1 pound boneless and skinless pheasant breast, cut into ¾-inch pieces

6 tablespoons freshly squeezed orange juice

4 tablespoons dry sherry

4 tablespoons hoisin sauce

2 tablespoons soy sauce

2 teaspoons cornstarch

½ cup chicken stock (page 11)

¼ teaspoon salt

½ pound fresh shiitake mushrooms

¾ pound fresh snow peas

2 tablespoons peanut oil or corn oil

2 tablespoons grated ginger

4 scallions, trimmed and sliced into ¼-inch pieces

4 cups hot cooked rice

Mix the pheasant with 3 tablespoons of the orange juice and 2 tablespoons of the sherry. Set aside.

Combine the remaining 3 tablespoons orange juice, 2 tablespoons sherry, the hoisin sauce, soy sauce, cornstarch, ¼ cup of the chicken stock, and the salt in a small bowl. Set aside.

Remove the stems from the mushrooms and save them to flavor stocks or soups. Slice the caps about ¼ inch thick. Snap the stems of the snow peas and pull gently toward the other end of the peas to "string" them.

Heat 1 tablespoon of the oil in a wok or 12-inch nonstick skillet over high heat. Add the mushrooms, snow peas, ginger, and scallions. Stir and toss everything together for 1 minute. Add 2 tablespoons of the chicken stock and continue tossing and cooking until the liquid evaporates, about 1 minute. Add the remaining 2 tablespoons of stock and cook again until it evaporates. Transfer the mixture to a large bowl and set aside.

Add the remaining 1 tablespoon oil to the pan and place it over high heat. Add the pheasant mixture and stir-fry about 3 minutes, until the pheasant is done. When the pheasant feels springy to the touch, stir the cornstarch mixture well and add it to the pheasant along with the vegetable mixture. Stir and cook about 1 minute, until the sauce bubbles and thickens. Immediately transfer to a serving bowl and serve with the hot rice.

Less than 20 years after the last covered wagon
crossed the United States, a pair of hunting dogs
guard the day's haul of pheasants, 1915.

Pheasant Thighs with Torpedo Onions and Savoy Cabbage

· *Yield: 4 servings* ·

This is a dish for a nippy fall evening. The newly dug onions and just-picked savoy cabbage are at their best, and practically beg to be paired with pheasant. Torpedo onions are spindle-shaped purple onions; "red" onions may be used as a substitute. Savoy cabbage, however, has no substitute. Its flavor is milder than regular cabbage and it works perfectly with pheasant or other poultry.

1 clove garlic, peeled and sliced

1 ½ teaspoons salt

¾ teaspoon freshly ground black pepper

½ teaspoon dried juniper berries (6 to 8)

¼ teaspoon dried whole thyme leaves

1 tablespoon olive oil

4 pheasant leg-thigh combinations

1 pound torpedo onions, peeled and sliced ¼ inch thick

2 tablespoons cider vinegar

1 teaspoon sugar

1 pound savoy cabbage, cut into 1-inch pieces

1 apple, peeled, cored, and shredded

¼ cup dry white French vermouth

½ cup chicken stock (page 11)

Using a mortar and pestle, crush the garlic, 1 teaspoon of the salt, ½ teaspoon of the pepper, the juniper berries, and thyme together, pounding them to a purée. Add the olive oil and work it in to form a pasty mixture. Rub over the pheasant, then cover and refrigerate several hours or overnight.

Adjust an oven rack to the center position and preheat the oven to 350°.

Place the pheasant, skin side down, in a large, ungreased ovenproof heavy skillet (cast iron works best) and set over medium-low heat. Cook the pheasant slowly on one side about 20 minutes, or until the skin is nicely browned. Remove and set aside. There should be about 2 tablespoons of fat in the pan; if not, make up the difference with olive oil. Add the onions, vinegar, and sugar to the pan. Raise heat to medium. Stir well and cook, covered, for 10 minutes. Add the cabbage, apple, remaining ½ teaspoon salt, remaining ¼ teaspoon pepper, vermouth, and stock and stir several minutes until the cabbage is wilted. Return the pheasant to the pan, placing the pieces skin side up on top of the vegetable mixture. Cover tightly and bake 1½ hours. The pheasant should be completely tender. If the cabbage mixture is soupy at the end of baking, set the skillet over high heat and boil rapidly until the juices are reduced and slightly syrupy. Adjust the seasoning with salt and pepper, if desired.

To serve, spoon the cabbage mixture onto 4 heated dinner plates and set the pheasant, skin side up, on top. Spoon pan juices over the pheasant and serve.

Elk Sirloin with Portobello Mushrooms and Soy-Lemon Marinade

· *Yield: 4 servings* ·

My friend Mike Schwartz presented me with beautiful elk sirloins one fall and told me to make something wonderful with them. It was a challenge I couldn't refuse. If you can't get elk sirloin from a supplier, use tenderloin instead. The dark soy sauce called for is available in Asian markets. It is a thick, almost black soy with some sugar added. If you can't find it, use regular soy sauce and add 1 teaspoon sugar to the marinade. The elk is terrific with savoy cabbage (prepared as described on page 132) and Roasted Garlic Mashed Potatoes (page 205).

1½ pounds trimmed elk sirloins or tenderloin, cut into 2 × 1 × 1-inch strips

½ cup thinly sliced scallions

2 tablespoons dark soy sauce, or regular soy sauce plus 1 teaspoon sugar

5 tablespoons extra virgin olive oil

2 tablespoons freshly squeezed lemon juice

2 cloves garlic, minced

½ teaspoon freshly ground black pepper

½ teaspoon crumbled whole dried thyme leaves

1 pound portobello mushrooms

Salt and freshly ground black pepper

1 cup rich beef stock (page 12)

1 cup dry white French vermouth

In a bowl, combine the elk, scallions, soy sauce, 3 tablespoons of the olive oil, the lemon juice, garlic, pepper, and thyme. To marinate, cover and refrigerate 2 hours or longer.

Remove mushroom stems and save them for another use. Slice the caps about ½ inch thick. Heat the remaining 2 tablespoons olive oil in a large skillet over medium-high heat. Add the mushrooms and stir well. Sprinkle with salt and pepper and cook, stirring frequently, until the mushrooms are tender, about 5 minutes. Remove the mushrooms and any liquid from the pan and set aside.

Place the pan over medium-high heat and add about half the elk with any marinade that adheres to it. Separate the elk pieces, so they don't steam as they cook. For rare or medium-rare, brown on all sides for about 2 minutes total. Remove from the pan and keep warm. Repeat with the remaining elk.

Pour off any fat remaining in the skillet, leaving any browned bits of meat. Add the beef stock and vermouth to the pan and return it to medium-high heat. Stir well, scraping the bottom of pan with a wooden spoon to dislodge the browned bits, and boil until the liquid is reduced and slightly thickened. Decrease the heat to medium or medium-low. Add the mushrooms and cook for a few seconds, while stirring, then add the elk with any juices and cook briefly, continuing to stir, just until the meat is heated through. Serve immediately.

———⟶◆⟵———

"Wood is now very scarce, but 'buffalo chips' are excellent—they kindle quick and retain heat surprisingly. We had this evening buffalo steaks broiled upon them that had the same flavor they would have had on hickory coals."

—Tamsen Donner, 1846, along the banks of the Platte River

———⟶◆⟵———

Venison Chili with Singapore Hot Sauce

• Yield: 6 servings •

This is a colorful and spicy chili with flecks of green and red in a reddish brown sauce. The hot sauce I use is made in Singapore, hence the recipe's name. Buffalo meat is equally good in this dish.

2½ pounds venison stew meat, trimmed and cut into ¾-inch cubes

2 tablespoons corn oil

1 cup chopped red bell pepper

1 cup chopped green bell pepper

½ cup chopped, seeded poblano chiles

2 cups chopped sweet yellow onions

6 cloves garlic, finely chopped

1 teaspoon sweet paprika

1 teaspoon ground coriander

1½ teaspoons ground cumin

1 tablespoon chile powder

1 teaspoon fennel seed

½ teaspoon salt

1 teaspoon freshly ground black pepper

1 (14½- to 16-ounce) can peeled crushed tomatoes with juices

12 ounces dark beer

¼ to ½ cup Yeo's Hot Chili Sauce

Pat the venison dry with paper towels. Heat the oil in a 12-inch-wide, 3-inch-deep sauté pan over medium-high heat. Add the venison and brown on all sides, about 5 minutes. Add the red and green bell peppers, poblano chiles, onions, and garlic. Stir well, cover, and cook 10 minutes, stirring occasionally. Add the paprika, coriander, cumin, chile powder, fennel, salt, and pepper and cook 1 minute, stirring continuously. Add the tomatoes and juices, beer, and hot sauce (use ½ cup if you like spicy chili). Bring the mixture to a simmer and cover the pan. Reduce heat to low and cook slowly until the meat is very tender and the sauce is slightly thickened, 1½ to 2 hours. If the sauce seems too thin, cook, uncovered, 10 to 15 minutes more. Serve hot.

Buffalo Burgers with Thyme
in Tarragon Cream Sauce

• *Yield: 6 servings* •

This may be gilding the lily, but it works. The creamy tarragon-flavored sauce makes this dish suitable for company.

3 tablespoons corn oil

2 cups finely chopped sweet yellow onions

2 pounds ground buffalo

1 teaspoon salt

1 teaspoon freshly ground black pepper

2 teaspoons minced fresh thyme

2 eggs

Unbleached all-purpose flour, for coating

⅓ cup dry white French vermouth

½ cup rich beef stock (page 12)

1 cup heavy cream

3 tablespoons minced fresh tarragon leaves

½ teaspoon freshly squeezed lemon juice, plus more if needed

Salt and freshly ground black pepper

Heat 1 tablespoon of the oil in a heavy 12-inch skillet over medium-high heat. Add the onion and stir to coat well with the oil. Cover the pan and reduce the heat to medium-low. Cook 5 to 8 minutes, until the onion is tender but not browned. Transfer onion to a large bowl, and set aside to cool slightly. Do not wash the skillet.

Add the buffalo, salt, pepper, thyme, and eggs to the onion and mix well with a wooden spoon. Shape the mixture into 6 patties about 3½ inches in diameter and 1 inch thick. Place the flour on a large sheet of waxed paper and lightly coat 3 of the patties, dusting off any excess. (Do this just before cooking or the flour will become gummy.) Add 1 tablespoon of the oil to the pan used to cook the onion and set it over medium-high heat. When it is hot, add the coated patties, leaving 1 inch or so between them, and cook for 3 to 5 minutes per side. (Medium-rare patties take about 6 minutes total cooking time.) Transfer the cooked patties to a platter, cover and keep warm. Coat the remaining 3 patties in the flour and cook in remaining 1 tablespoon oil. Cover and keep warm.

Pour off the cooking fat, but leave any browned bits of meat in the skillet. Add the vermouth and stock to the pan and set it over high heat. Bring to a boil, scraping the bottom of the pan with a wooden spoon to dislodge the browned bits. Boil rapidly until the liquid is reduced by about half. Add the cream and tarragon and continue boiling another minute or so, stirring continuously, until the sauce is thick enough to lightly coat a spoon. Remove the pan from the heat and stir in the lemon juice. Adjust seasoning with more lemon juice and salt and pepper, if desired. Spoon the sauce over the patties and serve immediately.

PAUNCH COOKING

Before emigrants came to the Great Plains with their metal pots, and began to trade with the Native Americans, the tribes used makeshift cooking vessels. They had an ingenious system of using the stomachs of buffalo and other large game animals for this purpose. After washing out the stomach, they created a scaffold for it by driving sticks into the ground. The stomach was supported on this structure and water and chunks of raw meat were added to it.

Meanwhile, clean, smooth stream-bed rocks were heated in a fire. When the rocks were sizzling hot, they were carefully added, one by one, to the paunch. After a half dozen or so of these rocks were in the paunch, the heat was sufficient to begin cooking the meat. As the rocks in the paunch cooled, they were removed and replaced with hot rocks from the fire. Wild onions, turnips, dried corn, or other vegetables were also added if available. In this way, soups and stews were cooked for hours, until the meat was very tender. After the contents of the paunch were consumed, the stomach was cut up and eaten as well. According to Western food historian Sam Arnold, eating the paunch meat was "rather like chewing on a tough car inner tube."

POULTRY

In the Old West, chickens were raised on every homestead or farm. The animals took care of themselves, roaming around the yard scratching for seeds and insects. Their eggs provided the household with a ready source of protein, and the Sunday supper of roasted chicken was something the whole family looked forward to.

Today, most commercial chickens are grown in crowded cages in huge buildings and never see the light of day. Fortunately, free-range chickens, which are often available in health food stores and at some supermarket butcher counters, offer an alternative to these "factory" farm birds. Many people believe the free-range birds are juicier and taste better than their cage-raised counterparts, but I think a more important consideration is showing respect for the animals that feed us by raising them humanely.

More than top-quality chickens are raised in the West. In this chapter, you'll also find recipes for ostrich, duck, turkey, and quail. In general, poultry dishes can be flavored with delicate or robust ingredients without overpowering the distinctive taste of the meats. It's this versatility that has helped make all kinds of poultry favorites with Western cooks and their families.

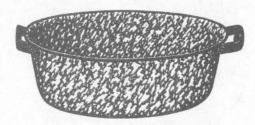

Ostrich Steaks with Green Peppercorn Sauce, Shiitakes, and Braised Shallots

· *Yield: 6 servings* ·

Ostriches are raised in many states and they are justly praised for their great-tasting meat. When I first tried ostrich, I couldn't believe I was eating a bird: it tasted like prime-quality beef. The raw flesh has a deep purple-red color, similar in appearance to venison or bear. The meat is lean and extremely low in fat, yet it cooks up so tender you can cut it with a fork.

Ostrich is commonly sold frozen by a number that corresponds to particular muscles (see page 143). I use number 11, which is about the same size as a large turkey breast. Any piece of meat will release blood as it thaws. Consequently, when you drain and pat the meat dry, it will weigh several ounces less. You'll need close to 1¾ pounds of thawed ostrich for this recipe. It needs no trimming, except for removing a thin membrane on the outside, and is ideally suited to cutting into thin steaks (see page 249 for mail-order sources). Or ask your butcher for large muscles that can be cut into tender steaks.

Serve small portions with full-flavored sauce made from rich beef stock (page 12) accented by a fine wine. The green peppercorns add a piquancy that round out the meat's sweet, clean taste.

Braised Shallots

1 tablespoon butter

12 large shallots, peeled

Salt and freshly ground black pepper

¼ cup rich beef stock (page 12)

¼ cup dry white French vermouth

4 fresh thyme sprigs

Shiitake Mushrooms

½ pound fresh shiitake mushrooms

1 tablespoon butter

Salt and freshly ground black pepper to taste

Ostrich Steaks with Green Peppercorn Sauce

2 pounds (frozen weight) ostrich meat, thawed

Salt and freshly ground black pepper

3 tablespoons corn oil

3 tablespoons finely chopped shallots

1 cup rich beef stock (see page 12)

½ cup pinot noir

2 tablespoons water-packed green peppercorns, drained and patted dry

3 tablespoons butter

1 tablespoon chopped fresh thyme

For the shallots, adjust an oven rack to the center position and preheat the oven to 350°. Melt the butter in an ovenproof 10-inch skillet over medium-high heat and add the shallots. Cook, shaking the pan frequently, until the shallots are golden brown in a few spots, about 8 minutes. Season with salt and pepper and add the beef stock and vermouth. Bring the mixture to a boil and cook for 1 minute, shaking the pan occasionally. Add the thyme sprigs and cover the pan. Bake for about 45 minutes, or until the shallots are very tender. (The shallots may be made hours ahead and set aside. Reheat in the oven or over low heat before serving.)

To prepare the mushrooms, remove the stems and save them to flavor soups or stocks. Slice the caps thinly. Melt the butter in a 10-inch skillet over medium-high heat. Add the mushrooms, salt, and pepper. Toss and cook until the mushrooms are lightly browned and tender, 2 to 3 minutes. Set aside.

Pat the meat dry with paper towels and cut it at an angle to make steaks about ½ inch thick. You should have about 18 small steaks or scallops. Cover and refrigerate until ready to cook. Just before cooking, pat the steaks dry again with paper towels and sprinkle both sides lightly with salt and pepper. Heat the corn oil in a 12-inch skillet over medium-high heat and add half of the ostrich steaks. Cook briefly, 1 minute on each side. Set the cooked meat aside while you cook the remaining ostrich, then cover loosely and keep warm while you make the sauce.

Pour off the fat remaining in the skillet, leaving the browned bits in the pan. Add the chopped shallots to the pan and stir with a wooden spoon, scraping the bottom of the pan to dislodge any browned bits. Return the pan to medium-high heat and add the beef stock and wine. Cook briskly to reduce the sauce by about one-third. Strain the sauce and discard the chopped shallots.

Return the sauce to the skillet and add the green peppercorns. Mash the peppercorns into the sauce and return the pan to medium heat. Add any juices that have drained from the ostrich to the pan. Bring the sauce to a boil and swirl in the butter. When the butter is incorporated, add the mushrooms. Adjust the seasoning to taste with salt and pepper. Add the ostrich to the pan to reheat and baste it with the sauce. Sprinkle the chopped thyme over the ostrich. Serve immediately on heated dinner plates with two baked shallots accompanying each serving.

Roasted Hazelnut~Marinated Ostrich with Garlic Chive Sauce

• *Yield: 4 servings* •

Make this for a special meal. You'll need a large, tender muscle, with no fibers or membrane, preferably the tenderloin or top loin. The meat marinates in a mixture of hazelnut and corn oils and vermouth for several hours. It is roasted quickly in a very hot oven and served with a sauce made from the browned bits in the roasting pan, rich beef stock, vermouth, and garlic chives. Be sure not to overcook the meat. It should be a nice reddish pink, or medium-rare, throughout. Tomatoes Stuffed with Fresh Herbs and Bread Crumbs (page 201) and steamed asparagus are perfect accompaniments.

1 ¾ to 2 pounds (frozen weight) ostrich roast, thawed

¼ cup plus 1 tablespoon hazelnut oil

¼ cup corn oil

3 cloves garlic, finely chopped

1 sweet yellow onion, thinly sliced

½ plus ⅓ cup dry white French vermouth

½ teaspoon salt

½ teaspoon freshly ground black pepper

1 tablespoon finely chopped fresh rosemary

⅔ cup rich beef stock (page 12)

2 tablespoons butter

3 tablespoons finely chopped fresh garlic chives

Salt and freshly ground black pepper to taste

Drain the roast and pat dry with paper towels. Combine ¼ cup of the hazelnut oil, the corn oil, garlic, onion, ½ cup of the vermouth, the salt, pepper, and rosemary in an airtight plastic bag. Add the ostrich, seal the bag, and marinate for 6 to 8 hours in the refrigerator. While it marinates, turn the bag 3 or 4 times to redistribute the marinade. When ready to cook, adjust an oven rack to the center position and preheat the oven to 450°. Remove the ostrich from the marinade and pat it dry with paper towels. Place the ostrich in a small roasting pan and rub the roast all over with the remaining 1 tablespoon of hazelnut oil. Roast for 20 to 25 minutes, or until the meat reaches an internal temperature of 130°. Transfer the ostrich to a platter, cover, and keep warm while you make the sauce.

Add the beef stock and the remaining ⅓ cup vermouth to the roasting pan. Set the pan over medium-high heat and scrape the bottom of the pan with a wooden spoon to dislodge any browned bits. Boil the mixture until it is reduced by almost half. Swirl in the butter. When the butter is melted, remove the pan from heat and add the garlic chives and salt and pepper to taste. Slice the ostrich into ¼-inch slices, arrange it on heated plates, and spoon the sauce over the meat. Serve immediately.

BIG BIRD RANCHING

Ostrich—the largest bird on earth—is the West's newest livestock species. It is being bred and raised for meat, leather, and feathers all over the United States. In 1995 there were over 10,000 ostrich ranches and over 1 million birds in this country. In Montana alone there are more than 100 ostrich ranches. The ranch industry is in what is known as the breeding phase, meaning that breeding birds sell for thousands of dollars and ostrich meat is very pricey. The birds grow quickly and are slaughtered when they are 12 to 14 months old. They weigh between 230 and 275 pounds at processing, and each bird yields about 75 pounds of meat.

The ostrich has 16 muscles that come from the leg, thigh, and back. Ostriches are flightless and have undeveloped breast muscles. Until recently, some suppliers labeled the muscle cuts from 1 to 16 according to tenderness. Numbers 15 and 16 are the most tender and can be cut with a fork; those numbered 7 through 14 are also tender and can be used for steaks, medallions, scallopini, and roasts. Muscle numbers 1 through 6 are good for ostrich burgers, marinated and grilled as kabobs, or cut into thin strips and used in stir-fry dishes.

The American Ostrich Association has recently introduced a more descriptive system for ostrich muscles. The tenderest ones, called the tenderlion cuts, are from the back, and the oyster, top loin, fan, and strip cuts come from the muscles of the leg. These cuts correspond to muscles 15 and 16. Medium tender muscles include other leg muscles and the tip and round muscles of the thigh. They are equivalent to muscles 7 through 14. Other less tender parts of the thigh, comparable to muscles 1 through 6, can be used as described above. When ordering ostrich, be sure to tell the supplier what you are going to use the meat for. That way, you'll get what you need.

Twice-Moreled Chicken Breasts with Sage

• Yield: 4 servings •

This recipe confirms the theory that there can never be too much of a good thing. If morels are unavailable, chanterelles or porcini mushrooms would also be terrific.

2 tablespoons butter

1 yellow onion, coarsely chopped

2 cloves garlic, coarsely chopped

¾ pound fresh morel mushrooms

2 large whole boneless and skinless chicken breasts (about 1½ pounds total)

Salt and freshly ground black pepper

24 fresh sage leaves

Unbleached all-purpose flour, for coating

1 egg

1 tablespoon water

1 cup fresh fine bread crumbs, made from day-old
    French or Italian bread, trimmed of crusts

½ cup freshly grated Parmesan cheese

3 tablespoons clarified butter (page 7)

2 tablespoons extra virgin olive oil

¼ cup minced shallots

⅓ cup dry white French vermouth

½ cup rich chicken stock (page 11)

1 tablespoon finely chopped fresh sage leaves

½ teaspoon freshly squeezed lemon juice, plus more if needed

Melt the 2 tablespoons of butter in a 10-inch skillet over medium heat. Stir in the onion and garlic and cook for 5 minutes, or until they are tender but not browned. Coarsely chop one-third of the morels and add them to the skillet. Continue cooking about 5 minutes, stirring occasionally, until the mushrooms are completely tender and almost no liquid remains in the pan. Set aside to cool.

Divide each whole chicken breast into halves and remove the thin strip of breast meat from each half. Cut away and discard the tough white tendon from each piece. Cut the strips of chicken into 1-inch pieces and place in the work bowl of a food processor with the metal blade in place. Pulse 4 times. Add the cooled morel mixture, ½ teaspoon salt, and ¼ teaspoon pepper. Pulse about 6 times to chop everything evenly and combine well.

Place each chicken breast half between sheets of plastic wrap and flatten the thicker parts slightly so that the meat is of uniform thickness, about ½ to ¾ inches throughout. Lightly salt and pepper both sides of the chicken and place the side that the skin was attached to down on plastic wrap. Arrange 6 sage leaves along the length of each piece of chicken and cover each with one-quarter of the mushroom mixture, flattening it into a thin even layer with your fingertips. Press firmly so the mixture adheres to the chicken. Cover loosely with plastic wrap and refrigerate 30 minutes.

Place the flour on a sheet of waxed paper and lightly coat the chicken with a thin layer of flour. Dust off excess. Beat the egg and water together in a shallow dish to combine well. In another shallow dish, mix together the bread crumbs and Parmesan cheese. Dip each piece of chicken into the egg mixture then coat with a thin layer of the crumb mixture, patting the crumbs gently to help them adhere. Place the chicken, mushroom side up, onto a rack set over a tray and refrigerate, uncovered, until ready to cook. (The recipe may be made several hours ahead up to this point.)

Melt the clarified butter in a 12-inch skillet over medium-high heat. When the butter is hot, add the chicken breasts, mushroom side down, and cook 3 to 4 minutes. Turn and cook the second side until the chicken is cooked and feels springy when pressed, about another 3 or 4 minutes. Transfer to a plate. Cover and keep warm while you make the morel sauce.

If the remaining morels are large, cut them into 1-inch pieces. If they are small, leave them whole. Heat the olive oil over medium-high heat in the same skillet the chicken was cooked in. Add the shallots and cook, stirring, about 30 seconds. Add the morels and cook, stirring, about 5 minutes, until tender. Add ½ teaspoon salt, ⅛ teaspoon pepper, and the vermouth. Cook and stir until the liquid has almost completely evaporated. Add the chicken stock and chopped sage and cook briefly until the sauce is slightly reduced and has thickened a bit. Add the lemon juice and taste the sauce. Add more lemon juice, salt, or pepper, if desired. To serve, place the chicken, mushroom side up, on dinner plates, and spoon the morels and sauce on top.

Chanterelle-Stuffed Chicken Breasts

• Yield: 4 servings •

This is a favorite when the first chanterelles make their appearance in spring. If there is an abundant supply of them, I cook and freeze the golden mushrooms (page 18) to use later in the year. Perfect accompaniments are crisp fried potatoes and steamed spinach.

4 tablespoons butter

2 large shallots, minced

½ pound chanterelle mushrooms, minced

½ teaspoon salt

¼ teaspoon freshly ground black pepper

5 tablespoons cognac

½ cup chicken stock (page 11)

2 tablespoons minced fresh parsley

4 boneless and skinless chicken breast halves (5 to 6 ounces each)

2 tablespoons vegetable oil

Unbleached all-purpose flour, for coating

½ teaspoon freshly squeezed lemon juice, or more to taste

Additional salt and freshly ground pepper to taste

Melt 2 tablespoons of the butter in a large skillet over medium-high heat. When the butter is hot, add the shallots and mushrooms. Toss and stir the mixture almost continuously with a wooden spoon for several minutes until the chanterelles are cooked and lightly browned. The mixture will be pasty; use the spoon to break it up. Add the salt and pepper, 3 tablespoons of the cognac, and 2 tablespoons of the chicken stock. Cook 1 to 2 minutes over medium-high heat, stirring with the wooden spoon until the liquid evaporates. Remove the pan from the heat and stir in 1 tablespoon of the parsley. The mushroom mixture should hold together.

Using a sharp knife, make deep horizontal cuts in the breast halves, and stuff each with the mushroom mixture. Cover and refrigerate. (The recipe may be made hours ahead up to this point.)

When ready to cook, adjust an oven rack to the center position and preheat the oven to 400°. Heat the remaining 2 tablespoons butter and the oil in an ovenproof 12-inch skillet over medium-high heat. Place the flour on a sheet of waxed paper and lightly coat each piece of chicken with flour, dusting off the excess. When the butter foam begins to subside, add the chicken to the skillet and cook over high heat for about

1 minute on each side to brown lightly. Cover the chicken loosely with a round piece of waxed paper that just fits inside of the skillet and place the pan in the oven. Bake 8 to 10 minutes, or until the chicken is just springy to the touch. Don't overcook. Remove the chicken from the pan, cover, and keep warm while you make the sauce.

To make the sauce, add the remaining 6 tablespoons chicken stock and 2 tablespoons cognac to the skillet and boil over high heat while swirling the mixture until it is syrupy. (This happens quickly.) Remove the pan from the heat and add the lemon juice and remaining 1 tablespoon of parsley. Adjust seasoning to taste with more lemon juice and salt and pepper, if desired. The sauce should not have a pronounced lemon taste; it should just have an edge of tanginess. To serve, place chicken on heated dinner plates and spoon the sauce over. There will just be enough sauce to coat the chicken lightly. Serve immediately.

PIONEER POULTRY HUSBANDRY

Making a living was not easy once emigrants reached their destinations at the end of the Oregon Trail. Here Arabella Clemens Fulton describes how she started a chicken business in Idaho Territory during the mid-1860s:

Early that fall Frank [Arabella's husband]…bought twenty-three pullets and one rooster, paying three dollars each for them. I had raised three pullets that summer by hand, so I had twenty-six hens to start the next season.

The men built a nice, warm chicken house of logs. A small opening was left for a window, over which they securely tacked a piece of white cloth. A wheat stack near the door gave the chickens a handy feeding place, and a little covered place in front afforded a dry scratching pen. We were greatly astonished when in mid-winter our pullets began to lay.

By the middle of March I had sold enough eggs to pay for my chickens, and now I began saving eggs for setting. When the snow went off, we opened up the hen house and let the chickens out during the day, but shut them up securely at night because of the cold and the varmints.

Although I could get a dollar and a half a dozen for eggs, I would not sell any, for I was intent on raising as many chickens as I could that season, as I knew they would bring me a fine price on the market. I brought off sixty fine, little chicks my first hatch and put them into a box and brought them into the house to keep them from chilling.

Hickory-Smoked Chickens

· *Yield: 8 servings* ·

Smoking foods has always been popular in the West, especially before modern refrigeration became an everyday convenience. Before then, many foods were cold-smoked to preserve them. Foods to be smoked were first treated with a brine solution or rubbed with a mixture of salt, sugar, and spices. Over a period of several hours, smoke passed to the food chamber, which was considerably cooler than the smokehouse. Food preserved by cold-smoking wasn't cooked; it was stored and cooked later. Nowadays, foods are hot-smoked, meaning that they are permeated with a delicious woodsy flavor as they are cooked. You can hot-smoke just about anything, and the food is ready to eat as soon as it's cooked. Chicken is particularly tender, moist, and tasty when rubbed with a mixture of spices and smoked this way. I like to eat it warm, and I love using the leftovers in salads or in sandwiches. Hot-smoked foods can be refrigerated for about a week. Freeze them for longer storage.

Despite the variety of spices in the following rub, the flavor imparted to the chicken is fairly subtle. It's terrific on turkey, too.

1 tablespoon freshly ground black pepper

2 teaspoons salt

1 tablespoon ground cardamom

1 tablespoon ground ginger

2 teaspoons ground cinnamon

2 tablespoons sweet paprika

1 tablespoon ground cumin

2 teaspoons ground allspice

1 teaspoon ground cayenne pepper

1 teaspoon ground cloves

1 tablespoon ground coriander

2 large chickens (4 to 4½ pounds each)

12 hickory chunks, or 3 cups hickory chips

Combine all the ingredients except the chickens and hickory chunks thoroughly. If your smoker is large enough, you may want to double the spice mixture and smoke four chickens. Rinse the chickens inside and out and pat them dry with paper towels. Without tearing the skin, carefully separate it from the breast and thighs with your fingers. Rub some of the spice mixture onto the meat and press the skin back in place.

Rub the remaining spice mixture over the outside of the chickens and in the cavities. Cover and refrigerate for 1 hour or longer.

Soak the hickory chunks or chips in water for at least 30 minutes. Prepare a charcoal grill or an electric smoker according to the manufacturer's directions. (Although some foods such as fish fillets can be smoked in a conventional large charcoal grill, I don't recommend smoking large food items this way. You'll spend so much time adding preheated briquets to the fire and lowering the temperature of the cooking chamber that the project won't be any fun.) When the smoker is ready, drain the hickory chunks and add half or, if using the chips, add one-third of the chips. Place the chickens on one of the cooking racks, cover the smoker and smoke for about 4 hours, or until the chickens are completely cooked. Test by wiggling a leg; it should move freely in its socket. Add more hickory chunks about halfway during cooking or add wood chips after 1 hour or so. Add the remaining drained wood chips about 1 hour before the chickens are cooked.

When done, the chickens will have a dark mahogany color. Remove the skin after carving the birds. Serve hot or warm. Cover and refrigerate if not serving within 1 hour.

Note: When the chickens are set on a platter and refrigerated, you'll notice some jelled chicken juices sticking to the skin the next day. Save this and use to flavor salad dressings or soups.

*Enjoying two rare luxuries—watermelon and
a break from the grind of pioneer life (circa 1900).*

Spaghetti with Smoked Chicken
and Wild Mushroom Sauce

• Yield: 4 servings •

Smoked chicken and wild mushrooms were made for each other. The first time I prepared this dish, I used fairy ring mushrooms, *Marasmius oreades*, which pop up in June all over lawns in Missoula. It's too bad most people don't know how tasty fairy ring mushrooms are or they wouldn't waste so much time treating them as pests and trying to rid their lawns of them. Since this mushroom species has such a short season, and since it takes an experienced mushroom hunter to identify it, I've suggested using morels instead.

1 pound fairy ring mushrooms or morels

2 tablespoons butter

¼ cup finely chopped shallots

½ teaspoon salt

¼ teaspoon freshly ground black pepper

¼ cup calvados

⅔ cup rich chicken stock (page 11)

1 cup whipping cream

3 tablespoons finely chopped fresh thyme

1½ cups (8 ounces) diced smoked chicken (page 148)

1 pound uncooked spaghetti

Freshly squeezed lemon juice to taste

Freshly grated Parmesan cheese

Rinse the fairy ring mushrooms well in a basin of cold water, stirring them with your hands to remove any grasses. Carefully remove the cleaned mushrooms from the water and squeeze them gently to remove excess water. Wrap the mushrooms in paper towels to absorb excess moisture. If using morels, look over them carefully and brush away any dirt. If morels are 1 inch or so big, use them whole; if they are larger, cut them into 1-inch pieces.

Heat the butter in a large skillet over medium-high heat. Add the shallots and stir for a few seconds. Add the mushrooms and stir well, cooking a few minutes until mushrooms release their juices. Add the ½ teaspoon salt and ¼ teaspoon pepper and continue cooking until most of the mushroom juices have evaporated. Add the calvados and cook 1 minute more. Stir in the chicken stock and boil the mixture until the liquid is reduced by about half. Add the cream, thyme, and chicken. Stir the sauce well and remove it from the heat. Cook the spaghetti according to package directions. While the spaghetti cooks, return the sauce to high heat and cook, stirring frequently, until it is slightly reduced and has thickened a bit. Remove the pan from heat.

When the spaghetti is al dente, drain it well and add it to the skillet with the sauce. Stir to coat well. Add lemon juice, salt, and pepper to taste. Divide among four pasta bowls and serve immediately, passing the Parmesan at the table.

Roasted Duck with Sweet Marsala and Balsamic Vinegar

· *Yield: 4 servings* ·

Duck is a delicious but fatty meat. The best way to coax the fat out of a duck is to steam the bird before roasting. When brushed with a sweet-sour mixture of sweet marsala, balsamic vinegar, sugar, and herbs, the duck takes on a beautiful mahogany color and its skin will be crisp and virtually fat-free. The meat will be so succulent that no sauce is necessary. Serve it with Roasted Garlic Mashed Potatoes (page 205) and lightly buttered steamed green beans with summer savory. You will need a large canning kettle or an oval roasting pan with a lid.

1 (5-pound) Pekin duck

1 lemon, cut in half

1 teaspoon kosher salt

¼ cup sweet marsala wine

½ cup balsamic vinegar

2 tablespoons sugar

½ teaspoon dried whole oregano leaves

¼ teaspoon dried whole thyme leaves

¼ teaspoon salt

¼ teaspoon freshly ground black pepper

2 unpeeled cloves garlic, cut into ¼-inch slices

1 tablespoon olive oil

8 sprigs fresh oregano

8 sprigs fresh thyme

Remove excess fat from the body cavity and under the neck skin of the duck with your fingers. If there is a large flap of neck skin, leave it attached. Chop off the wing joints so that there is only one attached to each side of the body. Save the bones for duck stock (page 14). To make carving the bird easier, there are three simple steps to perform. Remove the wishbone with a small sharp knife and add it to the wing bones. Locate the joints at which the wings join the body and sever the tendons. Finally, grasp the thighs and bend them both toward the backbone until you hear a "snap," indicating that you have freed them from their joints. At this point, the duck will look quite floppy. Rinse the bird inside and out under running water. Shake off excess water and pat the skin and cavity dry with paper towels. Squeeze a cut half of lemon all over the skin, rubbing the juice in, and squeeze some juice into the cavity. Sprinkle the skin and cavity with kosher salt and insert both lemon halves in the cavity.

To prepare the steamer, place about 2 inches of water into a canning kettle or oval roaster. Set the ring of a springform pan into the kettle or use several empty cans opened at both ends to act as support for a rack. Set a wire rack directly on the springform ring or cans. Place the duck breast side up on the rack, cover the pan, and bring the water to a boil over high heat. Cook for 30 minutes. Carefully turn over the duck, allowing the juices in the body cavity to drain into the liquid below, and steam for another 30 minutes. You'll notice the bird has firmed up and can be turned easily with potholders. Try not to tear the skin. During steaming, fat will melt out of the duck skin and some duck juices will flavor the boiling water; when defatted, this liquid can be used as a base for duck stock or soup.

While the duck is steaming, prepare the basting mixture. In a small saucepan, combine the marsala, balsamic vinegar, sugar, herbs, salt, pepper, and garlic. Bring to a boil and cook, stirring occasionally, for several minutes, until the liquid is reduced to about ½ cup. You can tell when that point is reached because the mixture will bubble up near the top of the pan. Strain and discard solids. Stir in the olive oil and set the mixture aside to cool. When the duck is ready, remove it from the steamer and let it cool for a few minutes.

Adjust an oven rack to the lower-third position and preheat the oven to 375°. Remove the lemon from the duck and insert the oregano and thyme sprigs in the cavity. Place the duck, breast side down, in a 13 × 9 × 2-inch pan and baste it all over with some of the marsala mixture. Cook for 20 minutes, brushing the back and sides with a little more of the mixture after 10 minutes. Turn the duck breast side up and brush it with the basting liquid. Return the duck to the oven and cook for another 30 minutes, brushing it with the marsala mixture two more times at 10-minute intervals, using up the basting mixture. When cooked, the duck will be a rich mahogany color. The meat will be juicy and practically fall off the bone. Let the duck rest in the roasting pan 10 minutes before carving.

Note: Although the duck needs no sauce, you could spoon some of the defatted duck juices over the portions before serving. Save all bones, including the carcass, and add them to the bones you've already saved for duck stock. Leftover duck is excellent in salads.

———◆◆◆———

George L. Curry traveled on the Oregon Trail in 1846. When his party came upon wild game birds, they savored their good fortune:

We supped last night on curlew, snipe, plover and duck—that's a prairie bill of fare for you! Don't your mouths water?—but they need not, if you let your minds take in the idea of the number of mornings and nights that plain middling meat, crackers and heavy biscuit comprise our fare.

———◆◆◆———

Asian-Style Marinated Smoked Duck

• *Yield: 8 servings* •

In this recipe, duck breasts and thighs are given a dry rub with a homemade version of Chinese five-spice powder and refrigerated overnight. The next day, the duck is steamed to partially cook it and to remove excess fat. After cooling, the duck is marinated in a hoisin sauce mixture and then roasted in the oven over a water bath to make it tender and moist. The cooked marinade is excellent spooned over the duck and it is especially good with steamed broccoli. All of the Asian ingredients are available in most supermarkets and in Chinese markets.

Dry Rub

2 tablespoons Szechwan peppercorns

4 whole star anise

2 teaspoons fennel seed

1 teaspoon ground ginger

1 teaspoon ground cinnamon

½ teaspoon ground cloves

2 teaspoons salt

4 Pekin duck breasts, with skin

4 Pekin duck thighs, with skin

Marinade

¾ cup strained freshly squeezed orange juice

¾ cup dry sherry wine

2 tablespoons coarsely chopped garlic

2 tablespoons dark sesame oil

2 tablespoons corn oil

⅔ cup hoisin sauce

⅓ cup water

Place the Szechwan peppercorns in a small, heavy skillet (cast iron or enamelware is ideal) and set the pan over medium heat. Stir occasionally for about 5 minutes, until the peppercorns are aromatic. Do not burn them. Cool the peppercorns and pulverize them in a spice mill or with a mortar and pestle. Pass the peppercorns through a coarse strainer to remove the larger pieces; set aside. Place the strained peppercorns in a small bowl. Crush the star anise with a mortar and pestle and add them to the Szechwan pepper. Crush the fennel seed and combine it with the peppercorns and star anise. Stir in the ginger, cinnamon, cloves, and salt. You will have about 3 tablespoons of spice rub. Use all of it to coat both sides of the duck breasts and thighs. Rub the spice into the skin and flesh with your fingertips. Cover and refrigerate overnight.

The next day, set up a steamer and rack as described on page 153. Steam the duck pieces, skin side down, by placing the thighs on the rack about 2 inches above boiling water. After about 15 minutes, add the breast pieces and steam 30 minutes. Remove the duck and let the pieces cool.

For the marinade, combine all of the ingredients in a medium-sized bowl. Place the steamed duck in a glass dish measuring 12 × 8 × 2 inches and pour in the marinade. Turn the pieces of duck to coat well and marinate, covered, for 2 to 4 hours in the refrigerator. Turn the pieces two or three times during the marination. If you're not going to cook the duck directly after marinating, remove the pieces from the marinade and refrigerate, covered, for up to 2 days. Refrigerate the marinade.

When ready to serve the duck, adjust an oven rack to the center position and preheat the oven to 375°. Pour about ½ inch of boiling water into a 13 × 9 × 2-inch baking dish and set a rack over the top. Arrange the duck pieces skin side up on the rack and carefully transfer the pan to the oven. Bake for 1 hour, or until the skin is a deep brown color and the duck is very tender. While the duck cooks, strain the marinade and boil it in a small saucepan for 5 minutes, until it has reduced in volume and is slightly thickened. Pour into a small bowl and serve with the duck.

Roasted Almost Boneless Turkey with Pork, Turkey, and Pine Nut Stuffing

• Yield: 10 to 12 servings •

Years ago I watched Julia Child bone a turkey, stuff it with a savory filling, and roast it. When she served it, there was no hassle carving the bird. She simply cut it crosswise and placed gorgeous slices on dinner plates. Years later I decided to do a similar recipe on my local television show, "Big Sky Cooking," as a Thanksgiving special. I had the camera aimed over my shoulder so that viewers would get a cook's eye view of the procedure. I also opted to do the boning in one continuous step without stopping. Since this was a half-hour show, I had about 10 minutes to accomplish what I needed to. We worked with only one camera, so cutting to different views was not possible. The producer kept a close eye on the time and kept signaling me to speed up. I was out of breath by the time I finished, but the deed was done and the viewers saw that it was possible to bone a turkey without spending a lot of time. I received more comments from that program than any other I have ever done. Men were particularly enchanted with the idea, and many stopped me in grocery stores and on the street to tell me how they adapted the recipe to suit their tastes.

If you can get a farm-raised turkey, your results will be superior to a commercial bird. When prepared in the following way, the turkey and stuffing are so juicy you don't really need a sauce, except perhaps for some lightly seasoned rich chicken or turkey stock flavored with a bit of wine. If you've never done something like this before, think of it as a culinary adventure and proceed with courage and confidence. Leftovers are excellent thinly sliced and served cold with mustard and cornichons (small pickles).

1 (10-pound) turkey

Salt and freshly ground black pepper

1½ pounds ground pork

1½ pounds lean ground turkey

2 teaspoons salt

1 teaspoon freshly ground black pepper

1 tablespoon chopped fresh thyme

2 tablespoons chopped fresh oregano

2 tablespoons chopped fresh garlic chives

½ teaspoon ground allspice

3 eggs

⅓ cup cognac

1 teaspoon olive oil

½ cup pine nuts

2 cups cooked diced carrots

2 cups rich chicken or turkey stock (page 11)

⅓ cup dry white French vermouth

Salt and freshly ground black pepper, to taste

Remove the giblets from the turkey and pull away any lumps of fat from the body cavity. If using a frozen turkey, thaw it in its wrapping in the refrigerator for 2 or 3 days before proceeding with the recipe.

Turn the turkey so that its back is facing up. With a sharp boning knife (it's very important that your knife is sharp and has a fairly short, stiff blade), make a slit down the back of the turkey from the neck to the tail to expose the backbone (step 1). Cut away the turkey meat on both sides of the backbone so that the rib cage is stripped of meat. Working on one side at a time, scrape and cut the flesh away from the carcass of the bird, always scraping against the bone to avoid tearing the flesh. As the meat comes away from the carcass, pull it aside with your fingers. Eventually you will reach the point where the upper wing bone is joined to the carcass by a ball joint (step 2). Cut through the joint and continue scraping the breast meat away from the breast bone until you reach the ridge of the breast where skin and bone meet. Stop here, and proceed to sever the thigh bone from its ball joint on the carcass. (This part always seems to take the longest, since the thigh bone is well connected to the carcass. Just take your time and be patient.) At this point, you've deboned half the bird. Repeat the steps on the other side, being careful not to cut through the skin at any point.

When you're done with the second side, the carcass frame will still be connected to the ridge of the breast bone. To sever this connection, lift the carcass frame from the tail end of the bird and place your knife edge tightly against the ridge of the breast bone. Moving the knife slowly in a forward direction toward the head end of the turkey, cut the carcass away from the turkey's flesh (step 3). You now have a turkey with wings and legs attached to a mass of flesh, which consists mostly of breast meat. With a large sharp knife, chop off the tips of the wings. Save them and the carcass to make a turkey stock. (Substitute turkey for chicken in the chicken stock recipe on page 11.) Wash and dry the deboned turkey and set it flesh side up in front of you. Remove the strips of meat that had been attached to the rib cage (step 4) and carefully cut away the white tendon running through each. Set these meat strips (fillets) aside. Season the turkey lightly with salt and pepper.

To make the stuffing, place the ground pork and ground turkey, salt, pepper, thyme, oregano, garlic chives, allspice, eggs, and cognac in a large bowl. Beat well with a wooden spoon or mix together with your hands until the ingredients are thoroughly combined. Heat the olive oil in a small heavy skillet over medium heat. Add the pine nuts and stir constantly until they turn a toasty brown color. Transfer them to a small

(continued)

bowl and set aside to cool. Mix the pine nuts and carrots into the stuffing. Pile about half the stuffing onto the center of the turkey and arrange the turkey strips on top. Cover with the remaining stuffing and pat the whole mass with your hands to form a loaf (step 5). Bring the turkey sides up over the loaf to cover the filling completely. Sew the two edges of skin together with a sharp needle and white twine or string (step 6). The best way to do this is to work from the tail toward the neck, looping the string through the skin as you move up the length of the bird. When you reach the end, secure the string to the skin with a tight knot. Turn the bird right side up. Push and pat the whole thing back into turkey shape. Secure the wings and legs to the turkey by encircling the bird 3 or 4 times with kitchen twine (step 7). The turkey is now ready to be roasted. (You can bone the turkey and prepare the stuffing a day ahead. Simply stuff the bird when you plan to roast it.)

Adjust an oven rack to the lower-third position and preheat the oven to 350°. Place the turkey on its side in a shallow roasting pan and cook for 30 minutes. Then turn the turkey onto its other side and roast another 30 minutes. Place the turkey breast side up and reduce the oven temperature to 325°. Continue roasting the turkey, basting it with the pan drippings every half hour or so, until an instant-read thermometer registers 180° when inserted in the center of the turkey. Total roasting time will be 4 to 4½ hours. When done, the turkey will be a beautiful rich brown color. Transfer the turkey to a serving platter and cover it loosely with aluminum foil to keep warm. Let the turkey rest 15 minutes before slicing into it. Meanwhile, pour off any fat remaining in the roasting pan, but do not discard the browned bits. Add the chicken or turkey broth to the pan along with the vermouth and set the pan over medium-high heat. Bring the mixture to a boil, scraping the bottom of the pan with a wooden spoon to dislodge any browned bits, and boil for 1 to 2 minutes. Adjust the seasoning with salt and pepper, if desired. Pass through a fine strainer and serve with the turkey.

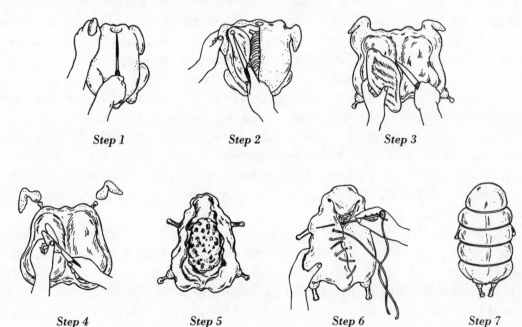

Step 1   *Step 2*   *Step 3*

Step 4   *Step 5*   *Step 6*   *Step 7*

THANKSGIVING IN THE PROMISED LAND

Pioneers carried on the pilgrims' and Native Americans' tradition of celebrating Thanksgiving Day when they arrived in the new land. Eliza Frances Cook was five years old when her family traveled the Oregon Trail and settled in Washington Territory. This is how she remembered her family's first Thanksgiving in their new home:

Thanksgiving of 1870 on Put-chem-mee creek was a frost-tanged day, filled with the gay tinkling laughter of eight children. I was eight years old and instead of helping mother, I climbed trees and slid from amazing heights on wild clematis vines.

That seemed to be one of my happiest Thanksgivings...We knew mother would use her best linens and silver and the marvelous caster [turntable] would occupy the center of the table.

My, I remember how much salt and pepper we used to take just to turn that caster around. And such a dinner! By one o'clock we were considered prim enough to sit at the table. Our hair was combed straight back over our ears and we had on our short white aprons. I almost forgot—we wore home-made shoes. Father made them...

That Thanksgiving dinner was grand, though. We had three deliciously stuffed wild prairie chickens, baked a golden brown; mashed potatoes and lots of gravy, dried corn, for we had a very good garden that summer, and winter radishes. But the prize dish was mother's apple dumplings...Mother made those delicious dumplings from dried apples father brought from The Dalles in the spring. Mother's jelly cake put the finishing touches to a wonderful Thanksgiving.

I remember that evening as I lay in my bed thinking of the happy times we had that day, I quietly drifted into sleep to a lullaby of low weird howls of the many coyotes.

Turkey Scallopini
with Lemon and Vermouth

• Yield: 4 servings •

Veal of any kind is hard to come by where I live. But you don't have to use veal to get an almost identical taste. Craig Claiborne once called turkey "the great impostor," referring to its ability to trick the taste buds into thinking veal was being eaten. Now, whenever I make scallopini, I always use turkey. Fresh turkey is available year-round and is far cheaper than veal. If you can, buy farm-raised turkey from a local supplier. That way you'll get far better meat and you'll have the satisfaction of knowing the birds were not cooped up in small cages with hardly any room to move. Serve this dish with steamed fresh green beans and Tomatoes Stuffed with Fresh Herbs and Bread Crumbs (page 201).

1¼ pounds boneless, skinless turkey breast

Salt and freshly ground black pepper

⅔ cup flour

1 tablespoon olive oil

4 tablespoons butter

¼ cup dry white French vermouth

½ cup rich chicken stock (page 11)

2 tablespoons freshly squeezed lemon juice

Dash of Worcestershire sauce

1 tablespoon chopped flat-leaf parsley

1 lemon, thinly sliced, for garnish

With a sharp knife, cut the turkey crosswise into slices about ¼ inch thick at an angle. You should have 12 to 15 scallopini. Lightly season both sides of the turkey slices with salt and pepper. Place the flour on a piece of waxed paper or plastic wrap. Coat half the turkey slices on both sides with the flour. Do this just before cooking or the flour will get gummy. Leave the turkey resting in the flour while you heat the olive oil and 2 tablespoons of the butter in a 12-inch skillet over medium-high heat. When the butter foam begins to subside, quickly shake off the excess flour from the turkey slices and add them to the skillet without crowding. Cook about 1 minute on each side, until the turkey is very lightly browned and tender. While the first batch cooks, coat the remaining turkey with the flour. Transfer the cooked turkey to a plate, cover it loosely with foil, and set it aside in a warm place. Cook the remaining turkey and add it to the first batch. Cover and keep it warm while you make the sauce.

Pour off any fat remaining in the skillet, but leave the browned bits in the pan. Add the vermouth and chicken stock and set the pan over high heat; scrape the bottom of the pan with a wooden spoon to dislodge any browned bits as the liquid boils. When the liquid has reduced by about one-third, remove the pan from the heat and stir in the lemon juice, Worcestershire sauce, and the remaining 2 tablespoons of butter. Adjust the seasoning with salt and pepper, if desired. Place the turkey slices in the pan and set the pan over medium heat. Turn the scallopini and spoon sauce over them. When hot, sprinkle with the parsley and serve immediately. Garnish each serving with a few lemon slices.

"Christmas will be quite solitary, for our community is very small and we are so cut off from the rest of the world, that we have hard work to get materials for a plum-pudding. I suppose our turkey will be the everlasting piece of beef as that is the only thing we can get. We did hope to have a little eggnog but as far as I can find out, there is not an egg within twenty miles."

—Julia Gilliss, from a letter dated November 18, 1866
sent from Fort Stevens, on the Oregon Coast

Grilled Smoked Quail in
Port Wine and Huckleberry Sauce

• Yield: 4 servings •

The smokiness of the succulent quail and the sweetness of the port and huckleberries are a dream combination. If ever there was a dish for a seduction, this is it. A 1992 Bandol with this meal would be perfection.

½ cup plus 1 tablespoon port wine

¼ cup strained freshly squeezed orange juice

¼ cup extra virgin olive oil

⅓ cup red wine vinegar

2 tablespoons firmly packed dark brown sugar

¾ teaspoon salt

¼ teaspoon freshly ground black pepper

2 tablespoons finely chopped fresh rosemary needles

8 boneless quail

1½ cups hickory chips

½ teaspoon cornstarch

½ cup fresh or frozen huckleberries

In a small bowl, whisk together ½ cup of the port, the orange juice, olive oil, red wine vinegar, brown sugar, salt, pepper, and rosemary. Transfer the mixture to a 12 × 8 × 2-inch glass baking dish and add the quail. Turn the quail to coat it well with the marinade. Cover and marinate 2 to 4 hours or as long as overnight in the refrigerator, turning the quail occasionally.

Soak the hickory chips in cold water for about 1 hour. Prepare a charcoal grill with a hot fire on one side for direct cooking. Keep the opposite side free of coals for indirect cooking.

Combine the remaining 1 tablespoon port with the cornstarch in a small cup and set aside. Remove quail from the marinade and place them on the grill rack over the coals. Cover and cook 5 minutes.

While the quail are cooking, boil the marinade in a 2-quart saucepan until it is reduced to ½ cup. Add the huckleberries and return the sauce to a boil. Stir the port and cornstarch mixture and add it to the pan. Swirl the pan and cook briefly until the sauce is thickened. Remove the pan from the heat and keep warm.

Turn the quail and grill, covered, another 5 minutes on the other side. Move the quail to the side of the grill without the coals. Drain the hickory chips and place them on top of the coals. Cover the grill and smoke the quail 8 to 10 minutes, or until completely cooked and tender. Serve immediately, spooning about 1 tablespoon of the huckleberry sauce over each quail.

Broiled Quail with Dijon Mustard and Toasted Sourdough Bread Crumbs

• Yield: 4 servings •

Much of the quail eaten today is farm raised, and the quality is excellent. You can order boneless quail with metal skewers strategically inserted to keep the birds flat as they cook (page 249).

½ cup Dijon-style mustard

½ cup extra virgin olive oil

2 shallots, finely chopped

½ cup dry white French vermouth

2 tablespoons chopped fresh thyme

1 teaspoon salt

½ teaspoon freshly ground black pepper

8 boneless quail

1 cup fresh fine sourdough bread crumbs, made from day-old
    sourdough bread, trimmed of crusts

2 tablespoons melted butter

Whisk together the mustard and olive oil in a medium-sized bowl. Stir in the shallots, vermouth, thyme, salt, and pepper, and combine well. Transfer the mixture to a 9-inch square glass baking dish. Add the quail, turning it to coat both sides. Cover and marinate for 2 hours or as long as overnight in the refrigerator.

When ready to cook, bring the quail to room temperature. Position an oven rack 5 to 6 inches from the broiler element and preheat the broiler. Line a shallow roasting pan with aluminum foil. Remove the quail from the marinade, leaving any marinade clinging to the quail. Set the quail about 1 inch apart on the foil. Broil 5 minutes, then turn the quail and broil another 5 minutes. Remove the pan from the broiler. Turn the quail again and spoon half of the remaining marinade evenly over the birds. Combine the bread crumbs and butter in a small bowl. Sprinkle about 2 tablespoons of the bread crumb mixture over each quail. (The recipe may be prepared hours in advance to this point and refrigerated.) Return the pan to the broiler and broil 2 to 3 minutes, or until the crumbs are nicely toasted. Turn the birds over, spoon the remaining marinade over them, and sprinkle evenly with the remaining crumb mixture. Return the quail to the oven and broil for another 2 to 3 minutes, until the crumbs are well browned. Serve immediately.

FISH AND SEAFOOD

The Pacific Northwest states—Washington and Oregon—are well represented in this chapter not only because they are part of the Old West, but also for their abundant and varied seafood. The coastal regions of Washington, Oregon, and Northern California were prime Native American fishing grounds for centuries. Today, anglers come from all over the country to fish these states' waters for salmon and steelhead trout. Columbia River sturgeon fishing is carefully regulated by Native Americans, but the fish is also available from fish farms near Sacramento. Lake and river trout, whether wild or farm raised, are also excellent eating fish. Whitefish (see page 190) are thriving in inland western lakes and rivers. Their caviar is served in homes and restaurants all over the country.

Although the pleasures of fishing for one's own supper never diminish, farm-raised fish will most likely become the primary source for most of the fish we eat in the future. Washington, Oregon, and California fish and seafood farms now raise mussels, clams, oysters, striped bass, catfish, crayfish, salmon, trout, sturgeon, abalone, tilapia, and other species year-round to satisfy the rising demand for seafood. Some purists may scorn fish and shellfish raised by aquaculture, but I have found that they are raised under rigorously controlled conditions to ensure their tastiness and healthfulness.

When my wife and I were graduate students, our research often took us out on the Pacific. Whenever the otter trawl came up, we found not only the animals we needed for our studies, but many different edible fish and shrimp species. In one area, Dungeness crabs were abundant, and always became the main feature in a big crab feed at the end of the day. Our friend Dan Hoffman studied the giant shrimp, *Pandalus danae*, and because he almost always collected more than he needed, we carried the extras home along with oysters, clams, and any other of the ocean's prized offerings. We were able to get Julia Child's *The French Chef* on our black-and-white television, and I frequently cooked up the seafood recipes she demonstrated. I can remember, in particular, her version of Shrimp in Sauce Nantua, and flounder fillets steamed in white wine and served with a creamy, buttery sauce.

Salmon, trout, sturgeon, and halibut also figure prominently in Western cooking, and I have recipes for all of them in this chapter. I have focused on sturgeon for two reasons: It is one of the tastiest and most versatile of all edible fish, and it is now successfully farmed, enabling many fish markets to carry it on a regular basis.

Fish lends itself to a broad variety of preparations. Here are recipes for sautés, baked fillets, smoked fish, even a crab quiche. In selecting fish, make sure it is fresh and has no smell at all. Fresh ocean fish should smell of the sea, if anything, and nothing else.

Herbed Baked Halibut

• *Yield: 6 servings* •

Fresh Pacific halibut is plentiful in the spring and summer months. When I was a restaurant chef, this is how I most often prepared halibut. You can marinate the fillets and coat them with the herbed crumbs several hours before baking or even a day ahead. The fish always comes out moist and aromatic. The recipe may be multiplied any number of times. Feel free to vary the herbs; almost any combination of basil, parsley, thyme, and oregano will work. Go easy when using tarragon or rosemary, however, as they can be too assertive for halibut if used with abandon.

6 fresh skinless halibut fillets (6 to 8 ounces each)

½ cup extra virgin olive oil

¼ cup freshly squeezed lemon juice

2 ½ cups fresh fine bread crumbs, made from day-old
    French or Italian bread, trimmed of crusts

¾ cup loosely packed fresh basil leaves

½ cup loosely packed fresh flat-leaf parsley leaves

1 tablespoon lemon thyme leaves, or 2 tablespoons fresh oregano leaves

1 teaspoon salt

½ teaspoon freshly ground black pepper

Select fillets that are at least 1 inch thick, and check them carefully for bones. Remove any bones with tweezers. Combine the olive oil and lemon juice in a 9-inch glass or ceramic dish and add the halibut. Marinate the fish in the refrigerator for 2 to 4 hours, turning 3 or 4 times while it's marinating.

Meanwhile, prepare the herbed crumb mixture. In a food processor fitted with the metal blade, process the bread crumbs with all of the remaining ingredients for about 30 seconds to make a fine mixture. Transfer to a large sheet of waxed paper. One by one, remove each fillet from the marinade, allowing any excess marinade to drain back into the dish. Don't pat the fish dry. Roll each fillet in the crumb mixture to coat evenly, pressing the crumbs with your fingertips to help them stick to the fish. (It's fine if a few bare spots remain.)

If you aren't baking the halibut immediately after coating it with the crumbs, wrap each fillet separately in plastic wrap, securing the wrap tightly to hold the crumbs on the fish. Refrigerate the fish and the marinade, separately, several hours or overnight before baking. When ready to bake, unwrap the fillets and bake as directed. Since you will be baking the fish when it's cold, add a few minutes to the cooking time.

Adjust an oven rack to the center position and preheat the oven to 400°. Lightly coat a baking sheet with olive oil and place the halibut on the sheet, leaving a couple of inches between the fillets. Stir the marinade and drizzle about a tablespoon over each fillet. Place the pan in the oven and bake the fish for 10 to 20 minutes. The length of time depends on the thickness of the fillets. To test for doneness, squeeze the sides of the fillets gently; they should feel springy, not firm or mushy. Serve immediately.

THE COSMOPOLITAN PINE NUT

Although most of us have learned to cook with pine nuts when making basil pesto, the nut is used in many cuisines across the Northern Hemisphere. Pine nuts appear in recipes from Italy, Spain, Portugal, the South of France, Turkey, the Middle East, China, Korea, the Balkan countries, and Mexico. In Europe, the nuts are called pignoli and are grown primarily in Portugal, Spain, Turkey, and North Africa. The so-called "Chinese pine nut," grown in Asia, is the most common pine nut available commercially in the United States today. Its affordable price and wide availablity account for its dominance in the marketplace.

In the United States, pine nuts, or "piñons," are harvested from the Spanish scrub pine and other related species. The trees grow wild throughout the Southwest. Native Americans used pine nuts for centuries as a valuable food source in a variety of ways—including snacking on them raw or roasted, grinding them to thicken stews, or boiling them. Collecting and shelling the nuts is a labor-intensive process and accounts for their high price. It is rare to find shelled American pine nuts for sale. However, millions of acres of the trees do grow in the Southwest, and homegrown American pine nuts will someday find their way into our kitchens with more regularity.

Halibut Fillets with Pine Nut Sauce

• Yield: 4 servings •

Toasted pine nuts and halibut go extremely well together. I like to start cooking this dish on the stovetop and finish it in the oven, where the surrounding heat assures that the fish will be moist and tender.

1 tablespoon olive oil

1½ teaspoons freshly squeezed lemon juice

¼ teaspoon salt

¼ teaspoon freshly ground black pepper

4 (8-ounce) skinless halibut fillets, each 1 inch thick

2 tablespoons butter

¾ cup pine nuts

¼ cup dry white wine or dry white French vermouth

Salt and freshly ground black pepper to taste

1 lemon, cut into 4 wedges

Combine the olive oil, lemon juice, salt, and pepper in a small bowl. Rub the halibut fillets all over with a thin coating of the mixture. Cover and refrigerate 1 to 2 hours.

When ready to cook, adjust an oven rack to the center position and preheat the oven to 400°. Melt the butter in a large ovenproof nonstick skillet over medium heat and add the pine nuts. Stir to coat nuts well. Shake the pan to spread the nuts in a single layer. Place the halibut in the skillet on top of the nuts. Cook briefly until the nuts begin to turn golden brown. Watch carefully so they don't brown too much. Place the skillet, uncovered, in the oven for 5 minutes. Then, add the wine, cover the pan, and continue baking just until the halibut is cooked, about 10 minutes. The timing depends on the thickness of the fish, so begin checking a bit early if the fillets are thinner than recommended. When you gently squeeze the sides of the fillets, they should be slightly springy, not mushy. If the nuts are not toasty brown, place the pan under the broiler for a minute or so until the nuts begin to sizzle. Remove the pan from the oven and taste the sauce, adding salt and pepper, if desired. Carefully place halibut on dinner plates and spoon the pine nuts and sauce over the top. Serve immediately with the lemon wedges.

Sturgeon Provençal

· *Yield: 4 servings* ·

Sturgeon interacts well with many different flavors. In this dish, salty olives and capers work with sweet onions, tomatoes, and bell peppers to bring out the sturgeon's rich taste. The fish's firm texture is a nice contrast to the vegetables and other ingredients in the sauce.

1½ pounds skinless sturgeon fillet, about 1 inch thick

Salt and freshly ground black pepper, to taste

Unbleached all-purpose flour, for coating

3 tablespoons extra virgin olive oil

1 yellow bell pepper, cored, seeded, and cut into ½-inch pieces

½ cup thinly sliced sweet onion

3 firm, ripe tomatoes, peeled, seeded, and coarsely chopped

2 cloves garlic, minced

½ cup fish stock (page 16)

½ cup dry white French vermouth

¼ cup pitted kalamata olives, coarsely chopped

2 tablespoons capers, rinsed and drained

1 cup loosely packed fresh basil leaves

Slice the sturgeon crosswise into twelve ¾-inch-thick pieces (2 ounces each). Lightly season both sides of the sturgeon pieces with salt and pepper and lightly coat each with flour. Do not season or flour the sturgeon until just before cooking.

Heat 1 tablespoon of the olive oil in a large nonstick skillet over medium-high heat until hot. Add the sturgeon pieces, shaking off the excess flour, and cook 1 to 2 minutes on each side until the fish is golden brown and just cooked. You may have to do this in batches to avoid crowding the fish. Add more oil, if necessary. Remove fish pieces as they are cooked and set them aside, cover, and keep warm.

To make the sauce, add the remaining 2 tablespoons of olive oil to the skillet and place over medium heat. When hot, stir in the bell pepper and onion. Cook 3 to 5 minutes, until semisoft, stirring occasionally. Add the tomatoes and garlic and cook another 5 to 8 minutes, stirring occasionally, until the pepper and onion are tender. Add the fish stock and vermouth. Raise the heat to high and cook for 1 to 2 minutes, or until the mixture is thickened and saucelike. Stir in the olives, capers, and basil and cook 1 to 2 minutes more. Taste and add salt and pepper, if desired. Divide the fish among 4 dinner plates and spoon the sauce over.

Sturgeon with
Morel Mushrooms and Cognac

• Yield: 4 servings •

I ate sturgeon many times as a child growing up in Shanghai, where it was one of the favorite *zakuski*, or appetizers, of my father and his Russian friends. But the first time I had sturgeon in America was when Andre Soltner prepared a dish for my wife and me at his legendary restaurant, Lutece, in New York City. He had just received some wild sturgeon from the Columbia River. During our meal, he stopped by our table to see how we had enjoyed the sturgeon, and I told him it was great. I particularly wanted to know how he made the sauce, since it had fresh caviar in it. "The sauce?" he said surprised. "What about the fish? Wasn't it fantastic?" At that moment, I learned it wouldn't have mattered how terrific the sauce was if the fish it was designed to complement wasn't of the highest quality.

In the following dish, sturgeon plays the starring role. The sauce is a supporting player, helping to bring the fish's flavor to the fore. Oven-roasted potatoes are excellent with this.

1½ pounds skinless sturgeon fillet, preferably of even thickness

Salt and freshly ground black pepper, to taste

Unbleached all-purpose flour, for coating

2 tablespoons corn oil, plus more if needed

2 tablespoons finely chopped shallots

1 cup rich beef stock (page 12)

¼ cup cognac

¼ pound fresh morel mushrooms, left whole if small or cut into 1-inch pieces if large, or 1 ounce dried morel mushrooms, rehydrated in 2 cups warm water then rinsed and cut into 1-inch pieces

2 tablespoons butter

2 teaspoons chopped fresh thyme

Slice the sturgeon crosswise into twelve ¾-inch-thick pieces or 2-ounce sizes. Season the sturgeon pieces with salt and pepper lightly on both sides and coat each with a thin layer of flour. Do not season or flour the sturgeon until just before cooking.

In a large nonstick skillet, heat the oil over medium-high heat until hot. Add the sturgeon pieces, shaking off excess flour, and cook 1 to 2 minutes on each side until fish is golden brown and just cooked. Fry in batches to prevent crowding the pieces, adding more oil, if necessary. Remove the fish pieces from the pan and keep warm. Pour off any oil remaining in the skillet and remove from the heat.

Add the shallots and scrape the bottom of the pan with a wooden spoon to dislodge any browned bits. Return pan to medium heat and add the beef stock, cognac, and mushrooms. Cook briskly until the mushrooms are tender and the liquid is reduced by half. Add the butter and swirl the pan to combine it with the sauce. Stir in the thyme. Adjust the seasoning with salt and pepper, if desired. Return the sturgeon pieces to the pan and spoon the sauce over the fish. Cook very briefly, just to heat the fish through. There will only be about ⅔ cup sauce in the pan.

Serve immediately, placing 3 pieces of fish on each dinner plate, and spooning the mushrooms and sauce over the fish.

STURGEON

Sturgeon once flourished in the fresh waters of the Pacific Northwest and the Rocky Mountain West. This ancient species, unchanged for 100 to 200 million years, was practically fished to extinction by the late 1890s.

Sturgeon fishing is now severely restricted, with most wild ones coming from the Columbia River. But sturgeon is widely available from fish farms in California's Sacramento Valley. Sturgeon can grow to gargantuan size. According to *Sunset* magazine, the largest sturgeon on record was caught in 1912 in British Columbia and weighed 1,800 pounds! A sturgeon's lifespan is estimated at 100 years or more. It takes 3½ to 4 years for these fish to reach 20 pounds, which is the size of most sold for our consumption.

Although sturgeon flesh is firm, moist, and delicious, most people associate sturgeon with caviar. It takes about 18 years for a female sturgeon in the wild to produce eggs. Farm-raised females can produce eggs in about 8 years, after they've attained a weight of about 100 pounds. At that age, considerable time and money have been invested in rearing and caring for the sturgeon. The monetary rewards for the caviar, not to mention the fish's fine eating quality, more than compensate the fish farmer.

Sturgeon Burgers

• *Yield: 4 servings* •

If you want to try something different that will wake up your taste buds, try these burgers. Ground sturgeon makes excellent ones because the fish cooks up juicy and tender. This recipe may be doubled or tripled successfully.

Burgers

1¼ pounds skinless sturgeon fillet

1 clove garlic, minced

1 teaspoon dark sesame oil

1 tablespoon minced Japanese pickled ginger (beni shoga)

¾ teaspoon salt

¼ teaspoon freshly ground black pepper

1 tablespoon dry sherry

Hoisin Mayonnaise

¼ cup mayonnaise

2 tablespoons hoisin sauce

1 tablespoon Dijon-style mustard

½ teaspoon freshly squeezed lemon juice

4 kaiser rolls, split and toasted

2 tablespoons corn oil

Arugula leaves or mixed baby lettuces

Thinly sliced tomatoes

Thinly sliced sweet onion or English cucumber

Cut the sturgeon into 1-inch strips and pass it through the fine die of a meat grinder or cut the sturgeon into small pieces and chop it on a cutting board until it is "ground," using a large, heavy, sharp knife. Do not use a food processor. Place the sturgeon in a mixing bowl and add the garlic, sesame oil, pickled ginger, salt, pepper, and sherry. Mix gently with a wooden or rubber spatula until thoroughly combined. Divide the mixture into 4 mounds and shape each into a 4-inch diameter patty about ¾ inch thick. Wet your hands to shape the patties to prevent sticking, if necessary.

Whick together the mayonnaise, hoisin sauce, mustard, and lemon juice in a small bowl. Toast the kaiser rolls and keep them warm.

Heat the corn oil in a large skillet over medium-high heat. When hot, add the patties. Cook 2 to 3 minutes on each side, or just until the fish is cooked through. Remove from the pan.

Spread Hoisin Mayonnaise on the tops and bottoms of the rolls, using all of the mixture. Place a few arugula leaves on the bottom of each roll, followed by tomato slices, sturgeon patties, and onion slices. Cover with the tops of the rolls. Serve immediately.

A STARK LANDSCAPE

Julia Gilliss was a 22-year-old new bride when she moved with her Army captain husband, James, from Washington, D.C., to Oregon. Unlike most emigrants, however, they journeyed by sea from New York to the Isthmus of Panama, by rail over the isthmus, and continued their voyage by ship up the Pacific Coast. The trip took about six weeks. Julia, the eldest child of Charles and Eliza Stellwagen, missed her family deeply, and she kept in touch with frequent letters. Julia and her husband settled at Fort Dalles on the Columbia River Gorge. In a letter dated January 10, 1866, she evocatively described the area, which is as stark and grand today as it was then:

> In point of scenic beauty, I must say a word. You can imagine yourself transported to the crater of an extinct volcano, or as a Californian graphically observes, "to the infernal regions, after the fire has gone out." For miles nothing is visible but huge masses of rocks and stones, of every size, but of volcanic description, sown broadcast. Trees all seem to have forsaken the land, for with exception of the firs and cedars at the garrison, I don't believe there is as much as a blade of grass for miles. It will look better, however, when the snow melts.

Hickory-Smoked Sturgeon

• Yield: 1 to 1½ pounds •

Smoked sturgeon is succulent and delicious all by itself or may be used as an ingredient in quiches, omelets, sandwiches, or in the Smoked Sturgeon Frittata with Fried Beets (page 175). I use a charcoal grill and hot-smoke the fish, which cooks and smokes it simultaneously. The procedure is based on a description found in *Fish: The Complete Guide to Buying and Cooking* by Mark Bittman.

1½ cups hickory chips

1 (1½- to 2-pound) sturgeon fillet, with skin

¼ cup sugar

¼ cup kosher salt

Soak the hickory chips in cold water for at least 2 hours.

Place the sturgeon in a glass or ceramic dish slightly larger than the fish. Combine the sugar and salt well. Coat the sturgeon completely with the mixture, patting it in place. Let marinate for at least 30 minutes, but no longer than 1 hour. (The texture of the fish changes if it sits in the salt-sugar mixture too long.)

Prepare a charcoal grill, preferably using hardwood charcoal. When the coals are ready, remove the grill rack and pour the coals to one side in a pile. Cover the grill.

Wipe off any remaining sugar-salt mixture from the fish and place skin side down on a piece of heavy-duty aluminum foil slightly larger than the fish. Poke a few holes in the foil with a metal skewer before setting the fish on it. Quickly uncover the grill, drain the wood chips, and scatter them over the coals. Replace the grill rack, place the fish on the side of the rack where there are no coals, and cover the grill. Keep the holes on the grill cover closed and cook for 1 to 1½ hours. When smoked, the fish will be golden brown to light brown in color and look and feel juicy. Serve hot, or let it cool completely and serve at room temperature. To store, cover and refrigerate for up to 1 week or freeze in an airtight container for up to 3 months.

Smoked Sturgeon Frittata with Fried Beets

· *Yield: 4 to 6 servings* ·

This is a wonderful way to use smoked sturgeon. It's best to mix all of the frittata ingredients together and let them stand about 30 minutes before cooking, so that the smokiness permeates the eggs. Prepare the beets ahead of time.

3 beets

5 tablespoons butter

6 large eggs

½ teaspoon salt

¼ teaspoon freshly ground black pepper

4 ounces fresh mozzarella cheese, cut into small cubes

4 to 6 ounces smoked sturgeon, cut into small cubes

½ cup loosely packed fresh basil leaves, coarsely chopped

Preheat the oven to 350°. Wash the beets and wrap them in aluminum foil. Bake them in the preheated oven for about 1 hour 15 minutes, or until tender. Leave them wrapped in the foil and let cool slightly. Trim the ends and peel the beets with a small sharp knife, then slice ⅛ inch thick. Heat 2 tablespoons of the butter in a 12-inch ovenproof nonstick skillet over medium heat. When hot, place the beets in the skillet in a single layer. Cook the beets until golden brown and a crust develops on both sides, about 10 minutes. Remove and drain on paper towels. (This step may be done hours ahead.)

In a large bowl, whisk together the eggs, salt, and pepper until well combined. Stir in the mozzarella, sturgeon, and basil. Set aside for 30 minutes to 1 hour.

Melt the remaining 3 tablespoons of butter over medium heat in the same skillet used to cook the beets. When the butter is foamy, quickly arrange the browned beets in the pan in a single layer and add the egg mixture, spreading the sturgeon and cheese to distribute them evenly. Decrease the heat to the lowest setting.

Cook the frittata without disturbing the eggs until it is almost completely set. Only the top should be a bit runny. This takes about 15 minutes, but watch carefully to avoid overcooking. Meanwhile, place an oven rack 5 to 6 inches below the broiler, and preheat the broiler. To set the top of the frittata, place the skillet under the broiler until the top is set but not browned, usually 30 seconds to 1 minute. Remove immediately from the oven, cut into wedges, and serve.

REVERENCE FOR SALMON

Some Native Americans believed that the salmon were ancestors who swam back to them up the Columbia River from the Pacific Ocean. Phoebe Judson, a pioneer in the Washington Territory, described their reverence for the fish this way:

> The Indians carefully removed the spinal column, hanging them high in the dry house for safe keeping, as they have a superstition that the spirit of the fish dwells in the backbone and returns to the salt waters to lure other salmon to their traps. I have seen innumerable quantities of these backbones hanging in the dry houses, for they never destroy them.

Proudly displaying the catch of the day, 1910.

Smoked Sockeye Salmon Fillet

• *Yield: 6 servings* •

When we lived on San Juan Island in the Puget Sound, we always bought sockeye salmon practically as they came off the boat in the summer. Sockeye salmon has a particularly appealing bright orange color. It is less fatty than king salmon, but king salmon also tastes wonderful smoked. The instructions for smoking are the same as for sturgeon (page 174), the only differences are in the seasoning mixture and marinating time. The star anise gives the salmon an intriguing taste. Smoked sockeye is excellent in salads and sandwiches.

1½ cups hickory chips

2 whole star anise

¼ cup firmly packed light brown sugar

¼ cup kosher salt

1 teaspoon freshly ground black pepper

1 (2-pound) fresh salmon fillet

Soak the hickory chips in cold water for at least 2 hours.

Pulverize the star anise in a mortar with a pestle or in a spice grinder. Combine the ground star anise, the brown sugar, salt, and pepper in a small bowl. Look over the salmon fillet carefully and remove any bones with tweezers. Rub both sides of the salmon with the dry mixture, using less on the skin side and on the thin belly portion of the fillet. Wrap the salmon tightly in plastic wrap, and then in aluminum foil. Place in a large dish and refrigerate overnight.

Prepare a charcoal or electric smoker following manufacturer's instructions. Follow the instructions for smoking sturgeon (page 174), cooking the salmon until it is tender and just done. Test by separating the flesh with the tip of a small sharp knife at the thickest part of the fillet. It should be almost opaque. The time will depend on thickness of the salmon, but it should take about 1 hour. Serve hot, or let it cool completely and serve at room temperature. To store, cover and refrigerate for up to 1 week or freeze in an airtight container for up to 3 months.

❖

"Salmon we get in abundance from the Indians, from ten to fifty cents apiece. I wish you were near enough to say to them as I do, 'Sikhs Siwash nika ticky mika chako tomollo, iskum tenas salmon [Friend Indian I want you to come tomorrow to get (bring) a small salmon].'"

—Julia Gilliss, in a letter dated June 15, 1866

Grilled Tarragon~Flavored Marinated Salmon Steaks

• Makes 4 servings •

Marinated salmon steaks are excellent grilled. The mixture is like that used to make gravlax, a cured salmon that has a waxy texture similar to lox. In this case, however, the marination is brief, just long enough to flavor the fish and firm up its flesh a bit. When grilled, the salmon has a succulent texture and delicious taste that needs no adornment.

2 tablespoons firmly packed light brown sugar

2 tablespoons kosher salt

2 tablespoons chopped fresh tarragon leaves

4 skinless salmon fillet steaks, 6 to 8 ounces each

1 tablespoon olive oil

1 lemon, cut into 4 wedges

Combine the brown sugar, salt, and tarragon in a small bowl. Check the salmon carefully for bones and remove any with tweezers. Place the salmon in an 8-inch square glass dish and sprinkle the dry mixture on both sides. Gently rub the salmon so that the mixture evenly coats all surfaces. Cover the dish with plastic wrap and refrigerate for 4 to 6 hours, or up to 12 hours. Turn the salmon once while it marinates. At the end of marinating time, the salt and sugar mixture will have liquefied.

Prepare a charcoal or gas grill with a cover to make a hot fire. When the grill is ready, quickly rinse the salmon fillets under cold running water and pat them dry with paper towels. Rub lightly all over with the olive oil and place on the grill rack. Cover and cook about 3 minutes on each side, or until desired degree of doneness. If you like your salmon slightly undercooked, check it after 5 minutes. Salmon is ideal just before the interior is completely opaque. Test by inserting the tip of a sharp, small knife between the muscle masses. Serve hot with lemon wedges.

PLIGHT OF THE SALMON

The need for hydroelectric power is jeopardizing the future of salmon in the American Northwest. Their migration paths to and from the Snake, Columbia, and Salmon rivers and the Pacific Ocean have been in use for millenia, but now the many dams on the rivers prevent the fish from navigating their way hundreds of miles downriver to the ocean as smolts (young salmon only a few inches long) and upriver as adults to spawn after a few years of feeding and growing in the ocean. Salmon must return to their native spawning grounds to reproduce. But in 1994, only one adult salmon managed to make it back to Redfish Lake, Idaho. Ironically, the lake is named for the color of the salmon. Salmon return to spawn in other lakes and rivers in the Northwest, but in decreasing numbers year after year. If the migratory pathways of salmon continue to be seriously disrupted, they will eventually become extinct.

One solution is to shut off the dams for very brief periods as the adult fish migrate upstream to spawn, and again as the smolts make their way from freshwater to seawater. These movements of fish en masse can be carefully timed, so the periodic loss of hydroelectric power would not cause hardships on consumers. In fact, this would be a way for those of us who live in the region to pay tribute to the fish that have played such a significant role in our cuisine.

*A fish and meat market in Havre, MT,
open and ready for business in 1897.*

Salmon, Shaggy Mane Mushrooms, and Sorrel in Phyllo Rolls

• Yield: 8 servings •

I serve this in late spring, when shaggy mane mushrooms suddenly make their appearance after a warm rain, wild salmon is available in the markets, and my sorrel plants have full, tender leaves. The rolls may be assembled ahead and refrigerated a few hours before baking, or they may be shaped, frozen, and baked within a week. All you need with this is a large salad of tender garden greens tossed in a garlicky olive oil vinaigrette. If you can't get shaggy mane mushrooms, regular cultivated mushrooms will also work.

2 pounds shaggy mane mushrooms, cooked and drained (page 19),
  or 1 pound white mushrooms

2 tablespoons plus ½ cup butter

4 ounces sorrel leaves, stems removed

3 scallions, thinly sliced

¼ cup finely chopped flat-leaf parsley

1 cup finely shredded dry jack cheese

1 teaspoon salt

½ teaspoon freshly ground black pepper

1 pound boneless and skinless salmon, cut into ½-inch pieces

¼ cup mayonnaise

¼ cup extra virgin olive oil

16 sheets phyllo, thawed

In a large skillet over medium-high heat, sauté the cooked and drained fresh shaggy manes in 2 tablespoons of the butter until the mushroom juices have evaporated. (If using cooked and frozen shaggy mane mushrooms, you will need 2 cups. Thaw and drain them, then sauté in the butter. If using white mushrooms instead of shaggy manes, clean the mushrooms and cut into ¼-inch cubes.) Sauté in butter until tender, 4 to 5 minutes.

Starting at one end, roll up the sorrel leaves and cut into thin strips. Add to the mushrooms and cook, stirring, until the sorrel wilts and turns an olive drab color, about 1 minute. Set aside to cool completely.

In a large bowl, combine the scallions, parsley, cheese, salt, pepper, salmon, and mayonnaise until well mixed.

Melt the remaining ½ cup of butter in a small saucepan over low heat and stir in the olive oil. The mixture should be tepid. Unwrap the phyllo and cover the sheets with a dry towel and then a damp one to keep them from drying out during preparation. Remove one phyllo sheet and brush it lightly with the butter-oil mixture. Set another sheet of phyllo on top and brush it with the butter-oil mixture. Arrange ½ cup of the salmon mixture in a column about 6 to 7 inches long along the short side of the phyllo sheets, leaving about 3 inches of the pastry closest to you uncovered and 3 inches between the ends of the column and the edge of the long sides. Fold the long sides over the column of filling to cover it partially and brush the folded edge of the pastry with the butter-oil mixture. Then fold the uncovered pastry nearest you over the filling, and roll the pastry to enclose the filling completely. Brush all surfaces lightly with the butter-oil mixture and set the finished pastry on an ungreased 17 × 14-inch baking sheet. Repeat with the remaining phyllo and salmon mixture, making 8 pastries in all. (The prepared rolls may be covered and refrigerated for several hours before baking.)

Preheat the oven to 375°. Set the rolls about 1 inch apart on the baking sheet. Bake on the center rack of the oven for 30 to 35 minutes, or until golden brown. Serve hot.

Note: The shaped rolls may be frozen before baking. Arrange the rolls as they are shaped on waxed paper–lined baking sheets and freeze until firm. Remove from the freezer, and wrap each roll individually in plastic wrap. Store rolls together in an airtight freezer bag. They will freeze well for 1 week. To bake, remove plastic wrap and arrange frozen pastries about 1 inch apart on an ungreased baking sheet. Bake in the center of a preheated 375° oven for 45 to 50 minutes, or until cooked through and golden brown.

AN INDIAN FISHING CAMP

"The shattered bridge formed the half dozen beautiful little islands that fill the river here and the rocky missiles are now the cause of the succession of rapids and cascades which give name to the place [The Cascades]. Here in this perilous position the Indians stand and with a net, dip, dip from morning till night with commendable patience for salmon. Some days they catch hundreds but on others they are rewarded only by two or three. The [Indian] village consists of two or three large huts, in which are Indians of every 'sort, kind, class & description,' cleaning salmon. With a true eye for the picturesque they have pitched their summer camp here on this lovely spot."

—Julia Gilliss, in a letter dated May 13, 1866

Trout Scallops

· *Yield: 4 servings* ·

We have many varieties of cold water river trout in the Rocky Mountain West, and all make fine eating. But just about any kind of trout, including commercially available rainbow trout, is excellent in this dish. Just be sure to use large fish, so you'll be able to make "scallops" of the right size.

2 large whole trout, cleaned (about 1 pound each, dressed weight)

Unbleached all-purpose flour, for coating

3 tablespoons butter

2 tablespoons olive oil

⅓ cup finely chopped niçoise or kalamata olives

2 tablespoons small capers, rinsed and drained

½ cup dry white wine or dry white French vermouth

2 tablespoons finely chopped fresh flat-leaf parsley

Salt and freshly ground black pepper to taste

1 lemon, cut into 4 wedges

To fillet the trout, lay the fish on its side on a work surface. With a sharp knife, make a cut behind the gill opening from the backbone down toward the belly (step 1). Turn the fish so that its back faces you. Make a long cut along the back from the gill opening to the tail, following the backbone closely as you cut (step 2). Press the knife against the bone and lift the flesh as you cut to make sure you're always following the backbone (step 3). When you get to the tail, cut from the back toward the belly side to release the fillet at that end. Lift the fillet away, and repeat the procedure on the other side of trout.

Each fillet will contain tiny bones called pin bones. Remove them with tweezers or with your fingernails. To skin each fillet, grasp it by the tail and make a small horizontal cut to separate the flesh from the skin. Now you'll have a piece of skin you can hold onto. As you hold onto the skin, work your knife, keeping it almost horizontal, along the length of the fillet from the tail end toward the head end, moving the knife from left to right as you move the skin right to left (step 4). Before you know it, the flesh will be free from the skin. Reserve the bones and skin for a fish stock.

To cut the fish into scallops, place each fillet so that it runs lengthwise from left to right on the work surface. Holding a sharp knife at an angle, cut each fillet into 3 scallops. (If not ready to use right away, cover and refrigerate for up to 1 day.)

Place the flour on a sheet of waxed paper. Heat 1 tablespoon of the butter and 1 tablespoon of the olive oil in a 12-inch skillet over medium-high heat until the butter foam begins to subside and the fat is very hot. Quickly dust half the trout scallops with the flour to coat lightly, shaking off the excess, and place the fish in the skillet. Cook only 1 to 2 minutes per side, or until the fish is just done. Adjust the heat if necessary so the cooking fat does not burn. Remove fish from the pan and keep warm. Repeat with the remaining trout, adding 1 tablespoon each of butter and olive oil to the pan before flouring and adding the fish. Set aside the cooked second batch of fish and keep warm.

To make the sauce, add the olives, capers, and wine to the pan. Boil the mixture, stirring, for about 30 seconds to thicken slightly. Add the remaining 1 tablespoon of butter and the parsley. Swirl the pan to combine everything well, add salt and pepper to taste, and return the trout to the pan. Spoon the sauce over the scallops; there will be just enough to coat the fish. Serve immediately with the lemon wedges, which should be squeezed over the fish before eating.

Step 1

Step 2

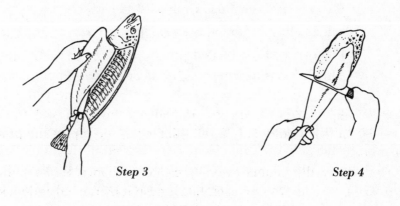

Step 3

Step 4

"There are several lakes in this vicinity of considerable size. They are curious for being high up among the mountains and keeping their waters pure and fresh by some agency down at the center of the globe for aught we know. They are full of trout, of which Jim only got fourteen when his bait was exhausted, but they were large enough for three breakfasts."

—Julia Gilliss, in a letter dated May 13, 1866

Dungeness Crab and
Matsutake Mushroom Kedgeree

• Yield: 4 servings •

Matsutake mushrooms, with their broad yellow caps, are highly prized and very expensive. The horseradishy aroma and taste of the mushrooms goes so well with the crab that I like to make this dish when both are available. Before buying the mushrooms, cut into a stem lengthwise to check for worms, or ask whether the market has already done this. If it has not been done, insist on it before buying. "Kedgeree" is the name of an East Indian concoction usually consisting of rice, lentils, and spices.

1 pound matsutake mushrooms

6 tablespoons butter

2 cups water

1 cup converted white rice or basmati rice

1 teaspoon salt

1 tablespoon olive oil

1 pound Dungeness crabmeat, shelled and cleaned

½ cup coarsely chopped fresh flat-leaf parsley

Salt and freshly ground black pepper, to taste

Finely grated zest of 1 lemon

4 tablespoons freshly squeezed lemon juice

Brush the mushrooms clean. The stems should be "peeled" by scraping away the surface layer with a sharp paring knife. Separate the stems from the caps and slice the stems thinly. Reserve the caps. Heat 1 tablespoon of the butter in a 3-quart saucepan over high heat. Add the stems. Stir and cook for several minutes, or until the stems begin to brown, release their juices, and are aromatic. Add the water and bring the mixture to a boil. Stir in the rice and salt and return the mixture to a boil. Cover the pan, reduce the heat to low, and cook until the rice is tender and the water is absorbed, about 20 minutes. Remove the pan from the heat and let it stand, covered, while you prepare and cook the mushroom caps.

Slice the caps ¼ inch thick. Heat 1 tablespoon of the butter and the olive oil in a 12-inch skillet over high heat. Add the sliced caps and stir and toss for several minutes, or until the mushrooms are cooked and lightly browned. Add the crabmeat, stirring very gently, just to heat through, then stir in the parsley. Add salt and pepper to taste. Add the remaining 4 tablespoons of butter and the lemon zest to the hot rice and stir until the butter is melted. Add the rice to the skillet and fold everything together gently, but thoroughly. Heat briefly over low heat just to be sure everything is hot. Divide among four dinner plates and sprinkle each portion with 1 tablespoon lemon juice before serving.

MATSUTAKE MUSHROOMS

This species, also known as the white matsutake (*Armillaria ponderosa*), is the American counterpart of the esteemed matsutake of Japan, *A. matsutake*. It grows throughout northern North America, but it particularly likes the conifer forests of the Pacific Northwest, where it is collected commercially. According to David Arora in his encyclopedic book, *Mushrooms Demystified*, the American matsutake has been placed in a new genus and is now known as *Tricholoma magnivelare*. Mushroom guidebooks may still list it under both names.

The mushrooms have a distinctive spicy aroma. Some people think of it as a cinnamon scent, others find it smells like horseradish. People go wild over the rich and meaty taste, which has a pronounced and appealing peppery undertone. The matsutake flesh is pure white. The entire mushroom is edible, but the stems are a bit tough. Slow cooking in butter or steaming with rice will soften the stems and make them extremely palatable. I have been told that the mushrooms are harvestable when the caps are small and tightly closed or when they are several inches in diameter and completely opened. The Japanese favor the smaller matsutakes. I have cooked with the small and large ones and love them both.

The future of the American matsutake is uncertain because of the willingness of some to pay exorbitant prices for freshly picked ones—as much as $500 a pound by one account. Because the mushroom is so coveted, collectors have emptied the forest floors in some areas, depriving the mushrooms of a chance to reproduce. Since the mushrooms yield only one crop a year, the matsutake may disappear forever from their habitats if conservation measures are not taken.

Dungeness Crab Quiche

• Yield: 6 to 8 servings •

This quiche is definitely elegant and indulgent. I make it for important occasions only, when Dungeness crab is fresh and the tarragon in our herb garden is tender and aromatic, with just a faint edge of licorice.

Pastry

1 ⅓ cups (6 ounces) unbleached all-purpose flour

¾ cup (3 ounces) cake flour

½ teaspoon salt

½ cup butter, chilled and cut into 6 pieces

¼ cup vegetable shortening, chilled

1 egg yolk

1 teaspoon cider vinegar

Filling

2 tablespoons butter

1 large sweet yellow onion, peeled and thinly sliced

¾ pound lump Dungeness crabmeat, shelled and cleaned

3 tablespoons dry sherry

2 tablespoons finely chopped fresh tarragon leaves

4 large eggs

1½ cups whipping cream

½ teaspoon salt

⅛ teaspoon freshly ground black pepper

⅛ teaspoon freshly ground nutmeg

3 tablespoons freshly grated Parmesan cheese

Measure flours for the pastry by spooning them into measuring cups, filling the cups to overflowing, and sweeping off the excess with a metal spatula.

To make pastry in a food processor, place the flours in the work bowl of a food processor fitted with the metal blade. Add the salt, butter, and shortening. Pulse the processor 4 times, about 1 second each. Combine the egg yolk, cider vinegar, and enough ice water to total ⅓ cup. While pulsing the food processor rapidly, gradually pour the egg mixture through the feed tube. Keep pulsing rapidly until the dough almost gathers into a ball. Remove the dough from the work bowl and place on a sheet of plastic wrap. Pat dough gently to form a 6-inch disc. Wrap and refrigerate for 1 hour or longer.

To make pastry by hand, place the flours in a large mixing bowl and stir in the salt. Add butter and shortening and cut in with a pastry blender until particles resemble small peas. Combine the egg yolk, cider vinegar, and enough ice water to total ⅓ cup. Sprinkle this mixture over the dry ingredients while gently tossing with a fork. Keep tossing until the mixture is moistened and gathers into a ball. Remove the dough from the bowl and pat it gently to form a 6-inch disc. Wrap in plastic and refrigerate for 1 hour or longer.

Adjust an oven rack to the center position and preheat the oven to 400°. Roll the chilled pastry into a 14-inch circle on a lightly floured surface. Fold the circle in half and place in an 11-inch tart pan 1-inch deep with fluted sides and a removable bottom. Carefully unfold the pastry and tuck it gently into the corners without stretching it. Trim the overhanging pastry to within ½ inch of the tart pan rim, then fold the overhang against the sides of the pastry in the pan, pressing firmly to make a double thickness. Shape and press the edge so that it is of even thickness and extends about ⅓ inch above the rim. Place the pan on a baking sheet and freeze until the pastry is firm, about 15 minutes. Line the pastry shell with foil, pressing the foil so that it fits snugly into the corners. Fill the shell with dried beans or rice. Place the pastry (still on baking sheet) in the oven and bake 15 to 20 minutes, until the edge of the pastry just begins to color. Remove from the oven and carefully lift away the foil and beans or rice. Prick the bottom of the pastry shell all over with a fork and return the pan to the oven for another 5 minutes, to dry out the bottom of the pastry shell. Remove the tart pan from the baking sheet, and cool the pastry shell on a wire rack while you prepare the filling. (The pastry may be baked hours in advance and left at room temperature, or you can make it a day or two ahead and freeze it; just thaw it before filling.)

Melt the butter in a 10-inch skillet over medium-low heat. Stir in the onion and cook slowly, for about 30 minutes, adjusting heat as necessary so that the onions become tender and golden but don't brown too much. Raise the heat to medium-high and stir in the crab and sherry. Cook, stirring occasionally, until the liquid has almost completely evaporated. Remove the pan from the heat and stir in the tarragon. Set aside to cool. (May be made hours in advance and refrigerated).

Preheat the oven to 325°. Whisk together the eggs in a medium bowl, just until they are well combined. Whisk in the cream, salt, pepper, and nutmeg. Stir in the cooled crab mixture. Carefully pour into the pastry shell in the tart pan (which should be again set on the baking sheet), distributing the crabmeat evenly. Sprinkle the Parmesan evenly over the top. Bake about 1 hour, or until the filling has puffed and set and the top is a rich golden brown. Remove from the oven and let the quiche stand 10 minutes. Set the quiche pan onto an inverted 8-inch round cake pan. The side of the quiche pan should fall away. Carefully slide the quiche onto a large round platter, cut into wedges, and serve.

Whitefish Fillet Roulades
with Watercress Sauce

· Yield: 4 servings ·

The firm texture and large size of whitefish fillets make them ideal for stuffing with a savory vegetable filling, but any firm-fleshed flatfish, such as sole, can be substituted as long as the fillets are 5 to 6 ounces. Peppery watercress leaves have been used in soups, salads, and sauces for centuries. Watercress grows wild in the damp spots of every state, including Alaska and Hawaii. (I find my watercress year-round alongside a nearby thermal spring.) To store, wash the leaves well, pat them dry, and keep in a plastic bag in the refrigerator, where they will keep for about 1 week. Serve steamed, lightly buttered small red potatoes or hot buttered rice with this dish.

4 (5- to 6-ounce) skinless, boneless whitefish fillets, thawed if frozen

1 large leek

1 large carrot, peeled

¼ cup butter

¼ teaspoon salt plus additional to taste

⅛ teaspoon freshly ground black pepper plus additional to taste

1 cup loosely packed watercress leaves, coarsely chopped

1 lemon, cut in half

2 large shallots, finely chopped

1 cup water

½ cup dry white French vermouth

1 tablespoon all-purpose flour

Rinse the whitefish fillets in cold water and pat them dry with paper towels. Remove any small bones and set the fillets aside.

Trim off the leek's root end and cut a 4-inch length, including the white part and some of the green. Cut the length crosswise into 2-inch pieces and then into ⅛-inch-thick strips (about 2 cups.) Cut the carrot into 2-inch-long julienne (about 1 cup). Melt 2 tablespoons of the butter in a heavy ovenproof 10-inch skillet over medium-low heat. Add the leek, carrot, salt, and pepper. Stir well, and cover the pan. Cook about 10 minutes, stirring occasionally, until the vegetables are almost tender but not browned. Transfer the vegetables to a small bowl and set aside.

In a small saucepan, melt 1 tablespoon of the butter over medium heat. Add the watercress. Cook 1 minute, stirring, just to wilt the watercress. Set aside.

Place the fish on a flat surface and squeeze lemon juice over both sides of the fillets, gently rubbing the juice into the fish with your fingertips. Season both sides of the fish with salt and pepper. With the side of the fillet that the skin was attached to facing you, spread each fillet with one-quarter of the leek-carrot mixture. Roll the fillets into cylinders. Sprinkle the shallots over the bottom of the skillet and set the fillets seam side down in the pan. (The recipe may be prepared hours ahead up to this point. Cover and refrigerate, then bring to room temperature about 1 hour before cooking.)

Adjust an oven rack to the lower-third position and preheat the oven to 350°. Pour the water and vermouth into the skillet. The liquid will come halfway up the fish rolls. Lightly butter a square of parchment paper and set the paper butter side down on the fish. Cover the pan and place it in the oven. Bake for 30 to 35 minutes, or until the fish is just cooked through and opaque when tested with the tip of a knife. Carefully remove the skillet lid and parchment paper. Slowly pour the liquid that has collected in the pan thorough a strainer set over a heavy 2- to 3-quart saucepan; there will be about 2 cups. Cover the fish in the skillet and keep warm.

Boil the fish cooking liquid over high heat until it is reduced to 1 cup. Melt the remaining 1 tablespoon butter in a small, heavy saucepan over medium heat. Whisk in the flour and stir continuously for 1 to 2 minutes, cooking the flour without browning it. Remove the pan from the heat and immediately add the reduced hot cooking liquid. Whisk well and return the sauce to medium-high heat. Cook, whisking continuously, for about 1 minute, or until the sauce is slightly thickened. Remove from the heat and stir in the watercress. Taste the sauce and adjust the seasoning with salt, pepper, and additional lemon juice, if necessary. Place the fillets on warm serving plates and spoon the watercress sauce over them, passing the remaining sauce at the table.

A WHITEFISH STORY

Whitefish are found throughout the West's mountain lakes and rivers and have always been popular, but not as popular as salmon. In an effort to please the sport fishermen and stimulate commercial salmon fishing, the Montana Department of Fish, Wildlife, and Parks attempted to increase the kokanee salmon population in the early 1980s by introducing mysis shrimp, a favorite kokanee food, into Montana's Flathead Lake, the largest freshwater lake west of the Mississippi. The theory was that if there were plenty of mysis shrimp for the kokanee to feed on, the salmon population would grown quickly. The plan didn't work. Instead, the kokanee population plummeted over a period of years and remains quite low today. No one knows exactly why the project was unsuccessful, but one possible explanation is that the mysis shrimp and kokanee have different periods of activity. Mysis are active the lake's surface at night. Kokanee, on the other hand, are active during the day.

In the mid-1980s, fishermen began landing lots of large whitefish in the lake. The fish weighed an average of 2 pounds, but some were almost 9 pounds, which was unheard of prior to that. Coincidentally, the hitch that prevented kokanee from feeding on the mysis shrimp may explain the whitefish boom. Whitefish are bottom feeders and typically eat small fry. As a result, the proliferation of mysis shrimp returning to the lake bottom every dawn was the equivalent of free food literally raining on the whitefish.

In 1991, Ron Mohn established Mountain Lake Fisheries at Columbia Falls, Montana, to process whitefish for sale to the public. Whitefish flesh is flavorful yet mild, but the bonus is the fish's caviar. The eggs have a beautiful apricot color and are mildly salty, with no fishy taste at all. The caviar has a surprisingly long freezer life of almost 2 years. Once thawed, the jars keep for 30 days in the refrigerator. Ron collects the fish in the Flathead River during their spawning run, which begins in late October or early November and lasts until mid-December. The fish is single-line caught by a crew of up to 70 fishermen. During a 6-week season, Mountain Lake Fisheries hauls in about 20,000 pounds of whitefish—roughly ⅓ of 1 percent of the 6 million whitefish population in Flathead Lake. Whitefish are virtually fat free and very high in protein. Mountain Lake Fisheries sells whitefish, caviar, and other products through the mail. See page 249 for ordering information.

VEGETABLES, GRAINS, AND SIDE DISHES

The moist, damp climate in the Pacific Northwest and the short growing season in the Rocky Mountains present challenges to the home gardener. Regardless, a remarkable variety of crops thrive throughout the West. Idaho potatoes are famous worldwide, and Colorado's San Luis Valley produces some of the best potatoes in the country. Washington State is known for its huge, sugary Walla Walla onions. Grains such as quinoa, black quinoa, and barley love the long, warm days and cool nights of the western high plains and mountain valleys. The mild climates in California and parts of Washington and Oregon provide westerners (and the rest of the country) with an array of produce that rounds out the offerings from the region's more severe climes.

If—and it can be a big *if*—we have been blessed with consistent, warm sunshine, abundant amounts of vine-ripened tomatoes, eggplant, corn, and peppers are available for the picking by the end of summer. Because these crops don't always succeed, we relish them all the more when they do, and western cooks like me get a special kick from finding new ways to use them.

In Montana, some of the most successful small farmers are new immigrants, such as the Hmong who moved to this country from Southeast Asia after the Vietnam War. They farm organically and offer crops such as broccoli and carrots at our local farmers market long before anyone else. And they've become expert huckleberry collectors. They inspire those of us who are less adroit kitchen gardeners, supplying the goods that enable western cooks to relish the gifts of our landscape.

Black Quinoa Dressing

• *Yield: about 12 cups* •

This is my version of a recipe from John McCamant of Denver. My wife and I spent a delightful afternoon with John and his wife one cold March day at his home, where we learned part of the fascinating quinoa story (see page 196). John says this stuffing—which can be used in turkey or chicken—is so good, he always prepares extra so that there'll be leftovers. He cooks the extra in a casserole dish and digs into it when the other stuffing runs out.

2 cups black quinoa

1 cup quinoa

5½ cups chicken stock (see page 11)

2 teaspoons salt

½ teaspoon freshly ground black pepper

¼ cup butter

1 large onion, finely chopped

1 large leek, washed well and diced

2 large celery stalks, washed and diced

½ pound oyster mushrooms, coarsely chopped

8 cloves garlic, finely chopped

½ cup chopped flat-leaf parsley

1 tablespoon chopped fresh thyme

1 tablespoon chopped fresh sage

1 tablespoon chopped fresh oregano

1 tablespoon chopped fresh tarragon

¾ cup pine nuts

Rinse both quinoas in a fine-mesh strainer under cold running water for about 1 minute. Shake to remove excess water. Combine both quinoas, the chicken stock, salt, and pepper in a 4- to 5-quart saucepan. Bring to a boil over medium-high heat, cover the pan, and reduce heat to low. Cook 15 to 20 minutes, until the liquid is absorbed. Remove the pan from the heat and let stand, covered, while you prepare the rest of the stuffing.

Preheat the oven to 350°.

Melt the butter in a 5-quart sauté pan over medium heat. When hot, add the onion, leek, and celery and cook until tender but not browned, 6 to 8 minutes. Add the mushrooms and garlic and cook 2 to 3 minutes, stirring occasionally, until the mushrooms are cooked. Add the remaining ingredients and the cooked quinoa and combine well. Taste and adjust seasoning with salt and pepper, if necessary. Use as a stuffing or transfer to a buttered 3- to 4-quart baking dish, cover with foil, and bake about 45 minutes.

Signs of culinary exchange between
Native Americans and settlers (circa 1900).

Black Quinoa and
Basmati Rice Pilaf

• Yield: 6 servings •

I first enjoyed this outstanding combination at The Fort, a fabulous restaurant near Denver, Colorado. It was Sam Arnold, the owner and proprietor, who first told us about black quinoa (page 196). The basmati rice and black quinoa pilaf he served us accompanied an impressive dish of musk ox, venison, and buffalo steaks. I added pine nuts for roastiness. The cardamom pods contribute an intriguing and exotic taste.

⅓ cup black quinoa

⅔ cup chicken stock (page 11)

1 cup basmati rice

1 quart cold water

1 tablespoon olive oil

1 onion, finely chopped

1 clove garlic, finely chopped

⅓ cup pine nuts

1¼ cups hot water

1 teaspoon salt

4 cardamom pods

Rinse the quinoa in a fine-mesh strainer under cold running water for about 1 minute. Shake the strainer to remove excess water. Bring the chicken stock to a boil in a small saucepan and stir in the quinoa. When the mixture returns to a boil, cover the pan, and decrease the heat to very low. Cook 15 to 20 minutes, or until the liquid is absorbed. Remove the pan from the heat and set aside, uncovered.

Rinse the basmati rice in a fine strainer under cold running water for about 1 minute. Combine the rice with the cold water in a bowl and let stand 30 minutes. Drain well and set aside. Both the quinoa and the rice may be prepared hours in advance.

Heat the olive oil in a 3-quart saucepan over medium heat. Add the onion, garlic, and pine nuts. Cook, stirring with a wooden spoon, until the pine nuts are lightly browned. Add the rice, raise the heat to high, and stir continuously to evaporate excess moisture, about 1 minute. Add the hot water, salt, and cardamom pods. Give the rice a stir and return the mixture to a boil. Cover the pan and decrease the heat to very low. Cook 20 minutes, or until the rice is tender. Add the quinoa to the rice and fluff with a fork. Cover and reheat over low heat. Serve hot.

Black Quinoa Tabbouleh

• Yield: 6 to 8 servings •

This recipe was created to help use up the mint forest growing outside our house where a dripping faucet waters the plants quite efficiently. One summer I made lots of mint juleps, convincing myself that the drink contained the four basic food groups. By fall, our mint supply appeared undiminished. Then a healthier idea struck. Why not make tabbouleh, the classic Lebanese salad? It uses lots of mint and parsley, which we also had in abundant supply. Tabbouleh is traditionally made with bulgur (cracked wheat). Here I've combined it with black quinoa, which has a nutty, slightly acid taste, for a different texture. Because cooked quinoa is slightly moist, this tabbouleh is wetter than most.

½ cup black quinoa

¾ cup plus 2 tablespoons water

⅓ cup fine bulgur

3 cups cold water

1 bunch scallions, thinly sliced

2 cups chopped fresh flat-leaf parsley

¾ cup chopped fresh mint

1 cucumber, peeled, cut in half, seeded, and finely diced

1 teaspoon salt

½ teaspoon freshly ground black pepper

¼ cup freshly squeezed lemon juice

¼ cup extra virgin olive oil

4 plum tomatoes, preferably 2 red and 2 yellow,
    cut in half crosswise, seeded, and diced

6 to 8 large red lettuce leaves, washed and dried

Rinse the quinoa in a fine-mesh strainer under cold running water for about 1 minute. Shake the strainer to remove excess water. Bring the ¾ cup and 2 tablespoons of water to a boil in a small saucepan and stir in the quinoa. When the mixture returns to a boil, cover the pan and decrease the heat to very low. Cook 20 minutes, or until the liquid is absorbed. Remove from the heat and set aside, uncovered, to cool.

Soak the bulgur in the 3 cups of cold water for 15 minutes. Drain well and squeeze the bulgur dry in washed cheesecloth. Combine the bulgur, cooled quinoa, scallions, parsley, mint, cucumber, salt, pepper, lemon juice, and olive oil in a large bowl, tossing with a fork. Mix in the tomatoes. Cover and refrigerate 1 or 2 hours before serving. Place one lettuce leaf on each salad plate. Divide the tabbouleh among the lettuce leaves and serve cold.

QUINOA

Quinoa (pronounced KEEN-wah) is an annual plant that has been cultivated for thousands of years in the Andes. The tiny grains, about the size of millet, were a staple food of the ancient Incas. In fact, quinoa was so important to the diet of the Incas that they called it the "Mother Grain." Quinoa is exceptionally high in protein and in the amino acids lysine, methionine, and cystine, which are especially important for vegetarian diets. Quinoa is so nutritious that it helped sustain Thor Heyerdahl and his crew on their trans-Pacific voyage on the Kon Tiki. Quinoa's appeal stems from its rich, nutty taste and its ability to be substituted for almost any grain. Quinoa can also be processed into flour and used in a variety of pastries and bread recipes for a unique flavor and a protein boost.

Quinoa seedheads grow atop stalks 3 to 7 feet tall. They are dazzlingly beautiful in the field when they turn brilliant shades of red, white, yellow, or black. The leaves of the plant are also edible; quinoa is closely related to spinach and beets and even more closely to a worldwide weed known as lamb's-quarters. Each summer our underweeded garden is overrun with this delicious green, and the lamb's-quarters leaves looked remarkably like the quinoa leaves. Quinoa, along with amaranth and buckwheat, is probably best referred to as a leafy grain.

Until the mid-1980s, all quinoa came from South America. Since then, quinoa has been grown commercially in various parts of North America, including Washington, Oregon, Colorado, and western Canada. John McCamant has worked extensively with quinoa at the White Mountain Farm in the San Luis Valley. He prepared several dishes for my wife and I, including black quinoa patties and crispy black quinoa crackers. Black quinoa is crunchier than white quinoa and its taste is unlike regular white quinoa. John says that black quinoa is to regular quinoa what wild rice is to white rice—wild and chewy as opposed to bland and soft.

Black quinoa is really a mixture of colors. Before the outside coat is taken off, an important step for all quinoas as it removes most of the bitter-tasting substances known as saponins, the quinoa is black, dark brown, tan, purple, and red. (Although most of the saponins are removed during processing, you should still rinse quinoa in water before using to wash away any adhering molecules.) When processed, the colors change to brown, tan, and off-white. Black quinoa is a relatively new variety of quinoa. It didn't exist until South American quinoa was hybridized with its North American wild relatives in 1983. After many years of genetic experiments and various crop disasters, enough black quinoa became available in 1994 for national distribution on a small scale. Chances are you won't find it in a local store, but it can be ordered (see page 250).

Fettuccine with Butternut Squash, Swiss Chard, Wild Mushrooms, and Garlic

• *Yield: 4 servings* •

This is a perfect fall dish. I made it for the first time when we had an abundance of butternut squashes ripening in our garden. Our Swiss chard was also at its peak, so I decided to combine the two. Fresh shiitake mushrooms are a good addition. You could also use oyster mushrooms.

1 bunch red Swiss chard, stems and ribs removed

2 cups peeled and diced butternut squash

¼ pound fresh shiitake mushrooms

1 pound dried fettuccine

3 tablespoons extra virgin olive oil

4 cloves garlic, minced

1 ½ cups chicken stock (page 11)

Salt and freshly ground black pepper

Rinse the chard well in cold water to remove any dirt and drain briefly. Place the chard in a 4-quart saucepan with about ½ cup water. Cover the pan and set over high heat. Boil, covered, 2 to 3 minutes, or until the chard is wilted. Drain and plunge the chard into a large bowl of cold water. Let stand several minutes or until cool. Transfer the chard to a colander and allow it to drain further, then gently squeeze it to remove most of the remaining moisture. Chop the chard coarsely and set aside. (The chard may be prepared several hours ahead and refrigerated.)

Place the squash in 2 quarts of rapidly boiling water. Cover and cook about 5 minutes, or until just tender. The tip of a sharp knife should meet a little resistance when inserted in the center. Drain in a wire strainer and set aside.

Remove the stems from the shiitake mushrooms and slice the caps into ¼-inch strips. Cook the fettuccine according to the directions on the package. The pasta should be al dente when the sauce in finished.

Heat the olive oil in a large skillet over medium-high heat. Add the mushrooms, squash, and garlic. Stir and cook 1 to 2 minutes, or until the mushrooms are almost tender and the squash is hot. Add the chard, chicken stock, salt, and pepper. Stir well and cook another minute or so to be sure the sauce is hot. Adjust the seasoning, if desired.

Drain the fettuccine and add it to the skillet. Toss to combine well and divide the pasta among four warmed pasta bowls. Serve immediately.

Oyster Mushroom, Asparagus, and Sweet Onion Sauté

· *Yield: 4 servings* ·

In late spring or early summer in the inland Mountain West, we get our first shipments of Walla Walla sweet onions from Washington. If we've had a good rain, the oyster mushrooms suddenly pop up at about the same time. And the asparagus, whether homegrown or bought, is in abundance. When all are cooked together, you have a major hit on your hands. The dish goes well with just about any poultry, fish, or meat.

1 pound asparagus

2 tablespoons extra virgin olive oil

1 large sweet yellow onion, thinly sliced

½ pound oyster mushrooms, sliced ¼ inch thick

Salt and freshly ground black pepper to taste

If the asparagus spears are thin, use only their tips. About 4 inches from the tip, slice the asparagus into 2 pieces at an angle. Save the rest of the stalk for another use. If you have thick spears, peel the stalks and cut them at an angle into 2-inch lengths. You should have about ½ pound of prepared asparagus whether using whole spears or tips. Place the asparagus in a large pot of lightly salted boiling water and cook for 1 minute. Drain, then plunge the asparagus into a large bowl of cold water. Let stand a few minutes until cool, and drain well in a colander until needed. (The recipe may be prepared hours ahead up to this point and refrigerated.)

Heat 1 tablespoon of the olive oil in the 10-inch skillet over medium heat. Add the onion and cook, stirring occasionally, until the onion is tender and lightly browned, about 10 minutes. Transfer the onion to a bowl and set aside.

Heat the remaining 1 tablespoon of oil in the skillet over medium heat and add the mushrooms. Sauté until the mushrooms are cooked and lightly browned, about 5 minutes. Add the asparagus and onions and cook briefly to heat through. Add salt and pepper to taste. Serve hot or warm.

Green Bean, Sweet Onion, and Yellow Beet Sauté with Vinegar

• Yield: 4 servings •

In late summer, my wife and I harvest our green beans. Besides simply steaming them and enjoying them with butter, here is another way we like to eat them. This is a sweet-sour dish that tastes both homey and sophisticated. Yellow beets do not "bleed" and I like using them in sautés for both their sweetness and color. Summer savory is the herb of choice, but if you don't have any you may substitute fresh thyme.

1 pound (4 medium) yellow beets

½ pound green beans (3- to 4-inch-long pods)

2 tablespoons extra virgin olive oil

1 large sweet yellow onion, thinly sliced

2 tablespoons red wine vinegar

1 tablespoon sugar

1 tablespoon chopped fresh summer savory or chopped fresh thyme

Salt and freshly ground black pepper

Preheat the oven to 350°.

Wash the beets and wrap them in aluminum foil. Bake them for 1 hour 15 minutes in the preheated oven, or until tender. (Test by piercing a beet through the foil with the tip of a sharp knife. Remove the beets from the oven and let cool for 30 minutes. Trim the ends and peel the beets, and cut them into strips about 1½ inches long and ¼ inch wide. Set aside. (The beets may be made hours ahead and refrigerated.)

Snap the ends off the beans, leaving the beans whole. Place them in a large pot of lightly salted boiling water. Cover and return the water to a boil, then cook, uncovered, until the beans are slightly tender but still have a bit of crunch, about 3 minutes. Drain and plunge beans into a large bowl of cold water. Let stand several minutes until the beans are completely cool. Drain well in a colander, pat dry with paper towels, and set aside. (The beans also may be made hours ahead and refrigerated.)

Heat 1 tablespoon of the oil in a 12-inch skillet over medium heat. Add the beets and sauté for several minutes to brown lightly on all sides, then remove the beets and set aside. Heat the remaining 1 tablespoon oil in the skillet over medium heat and add the onion. Cook, stirring occasionally, until the onion is tender and lightly browned, about 10 minutes. Add the beans and continue cooking and stirring for several minutes until the beans are tender. Add the beets and cook briefly to heat them through. In a small bowl, combine the vinegar with the sugar and add it to the skillet, stirring well. Add the summer savory, salt, and pepper. Toss well and continue cooking 1 minute, or until the vinegar is absorbed. Serve hot or warm.

Beans with Fried Sweet Onions

• Yield: 6 to 8 servings •

In mid- to late August, depending on how much of a summer we've had, green beans, yellow wax beans, and sweet Walla Walla onions mature at about the same time. I like to pair the beans with the fried onions; frying brings out a caramel taste in the onion that helps the sweetness of the beans to shine through. I like using a mixture of the yellow and green beans not only because the combination is pretty, but because they have slightly different tastes—the yellow wax beans being milder and less assertive than the green. Use slim pods about 4 inches long or slightly longer. You can serve this with just about anything, or eat a plateful all by itself, as I do. Incidentally, do not be alarmed by the large amount of oil used to fry the onions; if the temperature is right, hardly any oil is absorbed.

2 pounds green beans or a mixture of green and yellow wax beans

2 large Walla Walla or Vidalia onions

1 cup olive oil

3 tablespoons butter

2 teaspoons chopped fresh summer savory or fresh thyme

Salt and freshly ground black pepper

Snap both ends off the beans, discard, and rinse the beans in a colander. In a large pot, bring about 8 quarts water and 2 tablespoons salt to a boil over high heat. Drop in the beans, cover the pan, and return the water to a rapid boil as quickly as possible. Immediately uncover the pan and let the beans boil for about 3 minutes, until they're cooked but still have a bit of crunch. Taste frequently during the cooking to test. Drain the beans in a colander, then plunge them into a large bowl of cold water for a few minutes to stop the cooking process. Drain well and pat the beans dry on paper towels. This step is also important to maintain a fresh taste if you are going to refrigerate the beans for several hours or overnight.

Peel the onions and slice off the stem and root ends. Cut the onions into circles between ⅛ and ¼ inch thick. Separate the circles into rings and pat them dry on paper towels. Heat the oil in a large skillet over medium-high heat. When the oil begins to smoke, drop in a few onion rings at a time, stirring, until about half have been added. Cook until the onions are a deep golden brown. Remove with a slotted spoon and transfer to paper towels to drain. Repeat with the remaining onion. (These may be prepared hours, or up to 1 day ahead.) Wrap and refrigerate when cool.

When ready to serve, melt the butter in a large skillet over medium-high heat. Add the beans and summer savory, toss and cook to heat the beans through. Add salt and pepper. Add the browned onions and stir briefly to heat. Serve hot.

Tomatoes Stuffed with Fresh Herbs and Bread Crumbs

• Yield: 4 to 8 servings •

These stuffed tomatoes are delicious summer fare, when the vine-ripened globes fill the markets. Although you will have 8 tomato halves, one is often not enough for a serving. To be on the safe side, I recommend serving one whole tomato per person.

4 ripe but slightly firm tomatoes

¾ teaspoon salt

½ cup fresh fine bread crumbs, made from day-old
   French or Italian bread, trimmed of crusts

⅛ teaspoon freshly ground black pepper

1 clove garlic, minced

1 scallion, finely chopped

2 tablespoons finely chopped fresh oregano

2 tablespoons finely chopped fresh flat-leaf parsley

2 tablespoons melted butter

Remove the stems from the tomatoes and cut the tomatoes in half crosswise. Carefully remove the seeds with a small spoon or with the tip of your pinky finger and squeeze the halves gently to expel some of the juices. Sprinkle the cavities lightly with ½ teaspoon of the salt and set the tomatoes cut side down on a large plate for about 30 minutes to help draw out even more juice.

Meanwhile, combine the remaining ¼ teaspoon salt and remaining ingredients in a small bowl. Divide the filling evenly among the tomatoes and pack it down gently into the crevices. Place the tomatoes on a baking sheet; cover and refrigerate until ready to bake. (The tomatoes may be prepared several hours ahead.)

When ready to bake, adjust an oven rack to the upper-third position and preheat the oven to 400°. Bake, uncovered, 15 to 20 minutes, or until the crumbs are lightly browned and the tomatoes are thoroughly heated. Do not overbake or the tomatoes will lose their shape. Serve immediately.

Russian Beet, Potato, and Green Pea Salad with Horseradish Dressing

• *Yield: 6 to 8 servings* •

As part of Easter celebrations, my Russian grandmother made a salad called "vinigrette." Although the name is similar to the French "vinaigrette," there is no other similarity. This salad typically contains red beets, but it is wonderful with yellow beets. The yellow beets don't bleed like the red ones do, so the colors of the vegetables remain distinct. All the vegetables may be cooked a day ahead, wrapped separately, and refrigerated. The dressing may also be made a day ahead and refrigerated. Simply assemble everything about 1 hour before serving. Be sure to buy the freshest, salmonella-free eggs from a reliable vender when making this dish or any other that uses raw eggs.

4 yellow beets

1 pound yellow Finn or Yukon gold potatoes,
    peeled and cut into ½-inch cubes

1 tablespoon plus ½ teaspoon salt

2 carrots, peeled and cut into ½-inch cubes

2 cups fresh shelled peas, or 1 (10-ounce) package frozen peas

1 large egg

3 tablespoons corn oil

1 tablespoon freshly squeezed lemon juice

2 teaspoons Dijon-style mustard

1 teaspoon prepared horseradish

¼ teaspoon freshly ground black pepper

3 tablespoons olive oil

⅓ cup sour cream

2 tablespoons chopped fresh dill, for garnish

Preheat the oven to 350°.

Wash the beets and wrap them in aluminum foil. Bake for about 1 hour 15 minutes, or until tender. Test by piercing a beet through the foil with the tip of a sharp knife. Remove from the oven and let cool in the foil for 30 minutes. Trim the ends of the beets, peel, and cut them into ½-inch cubes. Set aside. (The beets may be prepared hours ahead and refrigerated.)

Place the potatoes and 1 tablespoon salt in 2 quarts of rapidly boiling water. Cook until the potatoes are just tender when pierced with the tip of a sharp knife, about 5 minutes. With a slotted spoon, transfer the potatoes to a large bowl of cold water to stop the cooking process; let stand 5 minutes, then drain well and set aside. Add the carrots to the boiling water and cook until just tender, about 5 minutes. With a slotted spoon, transfer the carrots to a bowl of cold water and let them stand 5 minutes. Drain well and set aside.

Add the fresh or frozen peas to the boiling water. If using fresh peas, cook them for 3 minutes. Cook frozen peas only until thawed, about 1 minute. Using a slotted spoon, transfer the peas to a bowl of cold water to stop the cooking process; let stand for 5 minutes, then drain well and set aside.

To make the dressing, combine the egg, 1 tablespoon of the corn oil, the lemon juice, mustard, horseradish, ½ teaspoon salt, and pepper in a food processor fitted with the metal blade for 1 minute. With the machine running, gradually add the remaining 2 tablespoons corn oil and the olive oil through the feed tube in a fine stream. Scrape down the inside of the work bowl and add the sour cream. Process 10 seconds, then transfer to a mixing bowl. Cover and refrigerate until needed.

To assemble the salad, place the beets, potatoes, carrots, and peas in a 3-quart bowl. Add the dressing and gently fold together. Adjust the seasoning as desired. Cover and refrigerate 1 hour. Transfer to a serving dish and sprinkle with the dill.

"One day while my brother-in-law Tom was making a garden, I gave him a bucketful of potato peelings, and told him to plant them. I had left the eyes pretty deep and had been saving them for that purpose. Sister Addie spoke up and said she had some, too. Frank had put the idea into our heads to save potato peels. I was peeling potatoes one day and throwing away the peels. Frank said, 'Don't do that. It is a sin to throw away even one potatoe eye, because, if you plant it, it might raise half a dozen potatoes.'

"Tom planted the peels, and when he dug his potatoes that fall he sold one hundred fifty dollars worth—all grown from peels that ordinarily would have been thrown away."

—Arabella Clemens Fulton, Boise Valley settler in Idaho Territory, 1865

Bull's Eye Beets and Beet Greens with Fennel Tops

• Yield: 6 servings •

My wife, Dorothy, found these "bull's eye" beets at our local farmers market. The vendor had cut open a couple of them to reveal pink and white concentric circles. Hence, my name for them. (The beets are commonly known as striped beets and are a cross between Detroit red and sugar beets, which makes them extra sweet.) As we paid and turned to leave, the vendor said, "Here, take some fennel tops, too. They're great with beets." She was right. I've added a bit of balsamic vinegar to them so that the sweet beet taste doesn't overwhelm the mild greens. For the optimal taste, eat a bite of beet with a bit of greens.

2 bunches striped beets with greens

¼ cup butter

1 tablespoon chopped fresh fennel tops

2 teaspoons balsamic vinegar

Salt and freshly ground black pepper

Preheat the oven to 350°.

Cut the beets off the greens, leaving about an inch of stems attached. Wash the beets and arrange them in a single layer on a sheet of aluminum foil. Wrap the beets tightly in the foil and bake for 1 hour 15 minutes, or until beets are tender. Test by piercing a beet through the foil with the tip of a sharp knife. Remove from the oven and cool in the foil for 30 minutes. Trim the ends of the beets, peel, and slice them into ¼-inch-thick circles. Pat the beets dry with paper towels and set aside. (The beets may be prepared hours ahead and refrigerated.)

Strip away any tough stems from the beet greens and rinse the leaves in a colander under cold running water. Bring a large pot of water to a boil and add the greens. Boil the greens, partially covered, for 2 minutes. Drain well and plunge the greens into a large bowl of cold water to stop the cooking process. Drain in a colander and set aside.

Melt 2 tablespoons of the butter in a 12-inch nonstick skillet over medium-high heat. When the butter is hot, add the beets in a single layer and cook until the slices are lightly browned on both sides. When all the beets are cooked, sprinkle the fennel tops over them. Remove the beets from the pan. Cover and keep warm.

Melt the remaining 2 tablespoons butter in the same skillet and set the pan over medium-high heat. Gently squeeze the beet greens to remove most of the water and add them to the pan. Season with the balsamic vinegar, salt, and pepper. Stir and cook until the greens are hot. To serve, pile the greens onto a serving platter and encircle with the beet slices or arrange them on individual dinner plates.

Roasted Garlic Mashed Potatoes

• *Yield: 6 servings* •

The best potato for mashing, in my opinion, is a variety called Caribe. They grow well in our climate and mature early. The skin is purple but the flesh is pure white. The potato is rich tasting and has a very smooth texture. Because of that, you can dispense with the cream and use milk or buttermilk instead. I use a combination.

2 heads garlic, separated into cloves and peeled

⅓ cup extra virgin olive oil

1 tablespoon plus 1 teaspoon salt

3 pounds Caribe or russet potatoes, peeled and cut into 2-inch pieces

½ cup milk

½ cup buttermilk

¼ teaspoon freshly ground white pepper

⅛ teaspoon freshly grated nutmeg

Salt to taste

¼ cup snipped fresh chives (optional)

Adjust an oven rack to the center position and preheat the oven to 325°.

Combine the garlic with the olive oil in a baking dish small enough so that the garlic is completely covered with oil. Cover the dish and bake about 1 hour, or until garlic is very soft. Cool slightly, then transfer the garlic and oil to a small wire strainer placed over a bowl. Set aside to drain. Save the oil for sautés or salad dressings.

Bring 2 quarts of water and the 1 tablespoon of salt to a rolling boil in a 4-quart saucepan over high heat. Add the potatoes and return the water to a boil. Cover the pan and cook over medium-high heat until the potatoes are tender when pierced with the tip of a sharp knife, 15 to 20 minutes. Be sure to cook the potatoes completely; slightly underdone potatoes do not mash well. Cut and taste one to test.

Drain the potatoes and return them to the pan. Stir 1 minute over medium heat to break up the potatoes and drive off excess moisture. Combine the milk and buttermilk in a small saucepan and set it over low heat. Do not allow the milk to boil. To mash the potatoes, pass them through a ricer and return them to the saucepan for the smoothest results. Or mash them in the pan with a handheld electric mixer or a conventional potato masher. When the potatoes are mashed, add the cooked, drained garlic, 1 teaspoon salt, the white pepper, nutmeg, and about half the milk mixture. Beat together well with a heavy wooden spatula or handheld electric mixer. Add more of the milk mixture to reach the consistency you like. Adjust the seasoning with salt and white pepper, if desired. Stir in the chives and serve immediately.

Sweet Onion Tart

• Yield: 6 to 8 servings •

For this tart, slices of Walla Walla onions are dipped in flour and sautéed. The onions are arranged in a tart shell, bathed with a custard, and baked until golden brown. This serves 6 as a luncheon entrée or makes 8 appetizer portions.

Pastry

1½ cups (6¾ ounces) unbleached all-purpose flour

½ cup (1¾ ounces) cake flour

½ teaspoon salt

¾ cup cold butter, cut into 8 pieces

⅓ cup ice water

Filling

3 large sweet yellow onions

Unbleached all-purpose flour, for coating

3 tablespoons butter

3 tablespoons olive oil

3 eggs

1 cup half-and-half

½ teaspoon salt

¼ teaspoon freshly ground black pepper

⅛ teaspoon freshly grated nutmeg

1 tablespoon chopped fresh oregano

5 tablespoons freshly grated Parmesan cheese

Measure the flours for the pastry by spooning them into metal measuring cups, filling the cups to overflowing, and sweeping off the excess with a metal spatula.

To make the pastry in a food processor, place the flours, salt, and butter in the work bowl of a food processor fitted with the metal blade. Pulse 4 times to chop the butter coarsely. Then, while pulsing very rapidly, gradually add the ice water through the feed tube in a steady stream. Pulse 20 to 30 times, or until the dough almost gathers into a ball. Carefully remove the dough from the work bowl and shape it into a 6-inch disc on waxed paper. Dust the dough lightly with flour if it is sticky. Wrap and refrigerate the dough 1 hour or longer.

To make the pastry by hand, place the flours, salt, and butter in a medium-sized bowl. Cut in the butter with a pastry blender until the particles resemble coarse meal. Sprinkle the ice water over the dry ingredients while gently tossing the mixture with a fork. Continue mixing until the dough gathers into a ball. Shape, wrap, and refrigerate as directed.

Roll out the pastry on a lightly floured surface to form a 13-inch circle. Fit the dough loosely into a 10-inch tart pan 1-inch deep with a removable bottom. Gently work the pastry into the corners, but do not stretch it. Use scissors to trim the overhanging pastry to ½ inch beyond the edge of the pan. Fold the pastry onto itself, making the sides a double thickness by pressing the pastry firmly into place. While doing so, raise the edge of the pastry so that it extends about ¼ inch above the pan rim. Place the tart pan on a baking sheet and freeze, uncovered, for 20 to 30 minutes.

Meanwhile, adjust an oven rack to the center position and preheat the oven to 400°. Line the pastry shell with aluminum foil and fill it with dry beans or rice. Bake 20 minutes, or until the edge of the pastry is lightly colored. Remove the foil and beans and return the pastry to the oven for 5 minutes, or until it appears set and is only very lightly browned. If the pastry puffs up during baking, prick it gently with a fork in a couple of places. Cool until ready to use.

To make the filling, peel the onions and slice them into circles about ⅓ inch thick. You should have 15 to 16 slices. Spread the flour on a large sheet of waxed paper and dip the onion slices in the flour to lightly coat both sides. Combine 1½ tablespoons of the butter and 1½ tablespoons of the olive oil in a 12-inch skillet over medium heat. When the butter is hot, add half the onion slices in a single layer and cook until nicely browned on both sides, about 10 minutes. Turn the onions carefully with a wide metal spatula to keep the slices intact. Transfer the onions to paper towels and set aside to drain. Repeat with the remaining 1½ tablespoons butter and oil and the onions.

When ready to bake, adjust the oven rack to the center position and preheat the oven to 325°. In a medium-sized bowl, whisk together the eggs, half-and-half, salt, pepper, nutmeg, and oregano until well combined. Sprinkle the bottom of the pastry shell with 3 tablespoons of Parmesan. Arrange the onion slices, slightly overlapping, in the shell to cover the bottom. Pour in the egg mixture and sprinkle with the remaining 2 tablespoons of Parmesan. Bake the tart for 45 to 50 minutes, or until it is puffed and browned and the filling is set. Cool 5 minutes. Set the tart on an inverted 8-inch round cake pan. The sides should drop away easily. Slip a wide metal spatula between the tart and the base of the pan to remove the pastry, and slide it onto a serving platter. Serve hot or warm.

Twice-Baked Potatoes with Parsnips and Goat Cheese

• *Yield: 6 servings* •

Although goat cheese is not normally associated with the Mountain West, it has become very popular here in recent years. Several local dairies make wonderful goat cheeses, as excellent as any I've tried. In this recipe, the goat cheese gives a richness to the filling while adding a tanginess that accentuates the sweetness of the parsnip. You can prepare this dish a day ahead and bake it just before serving.

3 large russet potatoes

1 large parsnip, peeled and cut in ½-inch pieces

1 small carrot, peeled and cut in ½-inch pieces

3 cloves garlic, peeled and thinly sliced

2 ounces goat cheese

¼ teaspoon Tabasco sauce

½ cup buttermilk

¾ teaspoon salt

¼ teaspoon freshly ground black pepper

⅛ teaspoon freshly grated nutmeg

1 egg white

2 scallions, thinly sliced

2 tablespoons grated Romano cheese

¼ teaspoon sweet paprika

Adjust an oven rack to the center position and preheat the oven to 450°. Wash the potatoes, pierce them well with a fork, and place them on the oven rack. Bake until tender, about 50 minutes. Remove from the oven and let cool 30 minutes.

Meanwhile, bring 2 quarts of water to a boil in a 4-quart saucepan over high heat. Add the parsnip, carrot, and garlic. Cook, uncovered, about 20 minutes, or until the vegetables are tender. Drain well. Transfer the vegetables to the work bowl of a food processor fitted with the metal blade. Process until smooth, about 1 minute. Scrape down the inside of the work bowl. Crumble the goat cheese into the bowl and add the Tabasco. Process again until smooth and set aside.

Cut the warm potatoes in half lengthwise and scoop out the pulp, leaving a ¼-inch-thick shell. Place the pulp in a medium-sized bowl and mash with a potato masher or handheld electric mixer. Add the buttermilk, salt, pepper, nutmeg, and egg white and beat together well. Stir in the scallions, then add the parsnip mixture. Stir well and adjust the seasoning, if necessary. Spoon the potato mixture into the shells, mounding the filling slightly in the center. Combine the Romano cheese and paprika in a small bowl and sprinkle about ½ teaspoon over each potato.

To bake, preheat the oven to 400°. Place the potatoes on a baking sheet and bake, uncovered, 15 to 20 minutes, or until the filling is very hot and the tops are lightly browned.

FESTIVITIES AT FORT LARAMIE

The emigrants pulled out all stops when celebrating Independence Day. By July 4, they would have arrived at Fort Laramie in Wyoming, where they could purchase all manner of provisions, including eggs, butter, and whiskey. The wagon train would rest for a day or two to allow a long and proper celebration. Women baked many kinds of cakes and cooked game. Yeast breads took up the space in Dutch ovens usually occupied by saleratus-leavened varieties. Baked beans simmered for hours over hot coals. Cooked dried fruits found their way into flaky pie crusts. Hot coffee, tea, and chocolate were passed around. And sometimes, even mint juleps were prepared with snow, wild mint leaves, and whiskey.

POTATOES

When I first started cooking, only two kinds of potatoes were commonly sold in the market: baking and boiling varieties. Today, the selection in many markets is still limited to these two kinds, but there are literally thousands of potato varieties, many with unique tastes and textures. I buy and try any new type I happen to find at our local farmers market. My wife, Dorothy, tries to grow different kinds all the time, but the deer in our neighborhood have such aggressive appetites that they gobble up the beautiful potato foliage earlier and earlier in the season, resulting in small or poorly formed tubers.

The Mountain West is an ideal potato-growing area because of the summer's long warm days and cool nights. I had always thought Idaho produced the nation's premier potatoes, but Colorado's San Luis Valley is where the best potatoes are grown. The high altitude (7,600 feet), abundant sunshine, and southern latitude (bordering northern New Mexico) are conditions potatoes love. White Mountain Farm, in San Luis Valley, cultivates about 100 different kinds of organic potatoes, some for experimental purposes, and some of which are for sale to consumers (for ordering information, see page 249). My favorite potato for mashing is called Caribe, and the potatoes I love to use for salads or for roasting are either yellow Finn or Yukon gold. Potatoes for mashing should be mealy or starchy, which results in a fluffy texture. Potato salads, or roasted potatoes, however, need to have a compact texture so that their shape holds together during cooking. If your market doesn't carry these varieties, ask the grocer to order them for you.

Scalloped Potatoes with Leeks and Garlic

Yield: 6 to 8 servings

Leeks add a richness of flavor to an old favorite. This is delicious with anything, or on its own.

1¾ pounds boiling potatoes, such as yellow Finn

1 tablespoon butter

2 cloves garlic, minced

2 cups thinly sliced leeks, including some of the tender green part

1⅔ cups milk

¾ teaspoon salt

¼ teaspoon freshly ground black pepper

⅛ teaspoon freshly grated nutmeg

1 egg

¼ cup grated Swiss, Gruyère, or Emmenthaler cheese

Adjust an oven rack to the center position and preheat the oven to 425°. Lightly butter a 12 × 8 × 1¾-inch ovenproof baking dish; set aside. Peel the potatoes and slice them thinly. (I like to use the 2mm slicing disc of a food processor.)

Melt the butter in a 2-quart saucepan over medium heat. Stir in the garlic and leeks. Cover the pan and cook 5 minutes, then set aside. In a medium-sized bowl, whisk together the milk, salt, pepper, nutmeg, and egg to combine well. Arrange one-third of the potatoes in a single layer on the bottom of the prepared dish. Spoon half the leek mixture over the potatoes. Repeat the layering with half the remaining potatoes, the remainder of the leeks, and finish with the last of the potatoes. Carefully pour in the milk mixture, which should just come to the top of the potatoes. Place the dish in the oven. After 30 minutes, remove the dish and press the top layer firmly with a large metal spatula to immerse the potatoes in the milk mixture. Sprinkle with the cheese and return the dish to the oven. Bake 15 to 20 minutes longer, or until browned on top and the potatoes are tender. Cut into squares and serve hot.

Barley, Corn, and Dry Jack Cheese Bake

· *Yield: 6 to 8 servings* ·

This is my version of a barley and corn side dish that I devoured in Red Lodge, Montana, at the Pollard Hotel. The chef, Scott Greenlee, served it with ostrich steaks (for more information about ostrich meat, see page 143), and the combination was sensational. Barley is so tasty, it deserves more attention. The two most common forms of barley available are whole hulled barley, which you are most likely to find in health food stores, and pearl barley, which is available in supermarkets and in health food stores. Whole hulled barley needs to be soaked overnight in water before cooking; but even pearl barley, which can be cooked without soaking, will have a fluffier texture if presoaked. I believe it is improper cooking that has limited the appeal of this tasty, nutritious grain. According to Bert Greene in *The Grains Cookbook*, heating the cooking liquid to boiling before adding the barley will prevent the grains from sticking to each other. Another of his recommendations to achieve a fluffy texture is to parboil the barley and then steam it. This dish may be made several hours ahead and refrigerated before baking.

1 cup whole hulled or pearl barley

2 tablespoons plus 1 teaspoon salt

2 tablespoons butter

1 large sweet yellow onion, chopped

2 ears sweet yellow corn, kernels cut off the cob

1 small red bell pepper, cored, seeded, and diced

¼ teaspoon freshly ground black pepper

3 tablespoons chopped fresh flat-leaf parsley

1 tablespoon chopped fresh thyme leaves

1 cup grated dry Monterey jack cheese

If using whole hulled barley, soak it overnight in 5 cups cold water. It isn't necessary to soak the pearl barley, but you can if you want to. The next day, bring 4 quarts of water and the 2 tablespoons of salt to a rolling boil in an 8-quart pot. If presoaked, drain the barley in a wire strainer. Add the barley to the pot and stir once or twice to prevent it from sticking. Cover briefly until the water returns to a boil, then uncover and boil the whole hulled barley for 1 hour. Or boil the pearl barley for 20 minutes. Drain in a colander.

Fill a steamer with several inches of boiling water and bring the water to a boil. Add the barley to the top of the steamer, cover it loosely with a damp kitchen towel, and steam for 30 minutes. (Presoaked pearl barley will probably be ready in 15 minutes.) The barley should be fluffy and tender. Set aside until ready to use.

Butter a 12 × 8 × 2-inch ovenproof dish.

Melt the butter in a large skillet over medium heat. When hot, add the onion and corn. Cook, stirring often, until the onion and corn are almost tender, 6 to 8 minutes. Do not brown the vegetables. Add the red bell pepper and cook 2 to 3 minutes. Stir in the steamed barley, remaining 1 teaspoon of salt, the pepper, parsley, and thyme. Transfer half of the mixture to the prepared pan. Sprinkle with ½ cup of the cheese and spread the remaining barley mixture over the cheese. Sprinkle the remaining cheese over the top.

Adjust an oven rack to the center position and preheat the oven to 350°. Cover the dish tightly with aluminum foil and bake for 45 minutes, or until the barley is very hot. Serve immediately.

Variations:

- Remove and discard stems from ¼ pound fresh shiitake mushrooms. Slice the mushroom caps thin and sauté them in 1 tablespoon butter until tender; season with salt and freshly ground black pepper and stir into barley-corn mixture. Proceed with the recipe as described above.

- For a smoky taste, cook 4 slices of bacon until crisp. Drain well and crumble the bacon or chop it into small pieces. Stir it into the barley-corn mixture and proceed with the recipe as described above.

- For a Southwestern flavor with a bit of heat, roast, peel, seed, and dice 2 poblano chiles and add them to the barley-corn mixture. You can also add red bell pepper both for color and for its sweet taste. Proceed with the recipe as described above.

TOO MUCH OF A GOOD THING

At the peak of travel on the Oregon Trail, about 6,000 emigrants a day stopped at Fort Laramie. Thousands of pounds of salt pork found their final resting place on the grounds surrounding the fort. Many guidebooks recommended far too much of this foodstuff, and at Fort Laramie the emigrants dumped what they didn't need and left it to scavengers.

Gratin of Winter Squash with Parsnips

• Yield: 8 servings •

This is definitely a dish to serve on a cold winter's day. Cubes of winter squash and parsnips are tossed with seasoned bread crumbs, topped with Cheddar cheese, and baked. I like to use Cougar Gold or Natural American Cheddar made at Washington State University in Pullman, Washington. These cheeses have robust flavors and crumbly textures and make fine eating. (For ordering information, see the mail-order sources on page 249.) I've also had good results with English Double Gloucester and aged Wisconsin or Vermont white Cheddar.

⅓ cup dry unseasoned fine bread crumbs

½ teaspoon dried oregano leaves, crumbled

½ teaspoon dried whole thyme, crumbled

1 teaspoon salt

¼ teaspoon freshly ground black pepper

½ cup finely chopped fresh flat-leaf parsley

6 cups peeled, cubed winter squash, such as Hubbard

2 cups peeled, cubed parsnips

3 tablespoons extra virgin olive oil

1 cup shredded sharp Cheddar cheese

Adjust an oven rack to the center position and preheat the oven to 325°. Lightly butter a shallow 2-quart ovenproof baking dish. (I use a 10-inch glass dish that is 2 inches deep).

In a large bowl, combine the bread crumbs, oregano, thyme, salt, pepper, and parsley. Add the squash and parsnips and toss to coat well. Add the olive oil and toss to combine well. Transfer to the prepared dish and cover tightly with foil. Bake 1½ hours. Uncover the pan and sprinkle evenly with the cheese. Return the pan to the oven and bake, uncovered, another 15 minutes. Serve hot or warm.

DESSERTS

In the Mountain West, fresh fruits take center stage in desserts. We lavish attention on wild huckleberries, strawberries, and raspberries. Our locally grown cherries, especially the sour Montmorency variety, are used in pies, tarts, and turnovers. The sweet cherries are mostly eaten as is, preserved whole in brandy, or stewed into a sauce for game. Every year, we eagerly await the arrival of Oregon blueberries, blackberries, and Marion berries as well as the many varieties of Washington apples. In summer, Washington's glorious peaches and nectarines ripen and reach their peak near the end of August.

Rhubarb, which thrives in the cool mountain air, is especially appreciated here, where the warm weather takes its time to come; it is the first of summer's "fruit," ready to be picked in early May. Rhubarb, which is really a vegetable, needs a lot of sugar to temper its acidity. When using rhubarb, I do not skimp on sugar, but I also try to avoid overwhelming its natural taste. Vanilla, for example, adds a sweetness of its own, which allows me to use less sugar. You'll find recipes here for unusual uses of rhubarb—such as rhubarb ice cream and rhubarb curd.

In July, the strawberries ripen (provided the robins and voles haven't claimed them first), followed by raspberries, blueberries, and huckleberries. I am inspired by nature's bounty to make pies, tarts, sorbets, ice creams, sauces, chutneys, and jams. So much fruit, and so little time!

I've worked on the pastry recipes for the pies and tarts in this chapter over many years, until I felt I couldn't make them any better. During this process, I've come to prefer making pastry dough with the food processor. The food processor gives me excellent results quickly, and I can make batch after batch if I'm pressed for time.

I have not included chocolate recipes because I wanted to celebrate the foods that grow in the region. For surefire success with these recipes, use the freshest ingredients of the highest quality, and follow the instructions closely. You will be delighted with your results.

"Mrs. Steele and I have been tramping over the hills through the deep snow all morning, then I came home and made a custard for dessert, a batch of ginger cakes, and a jelly cake for tomorrow's tea, and I feel sort of finished up for today, especially as I did my Saturday's cleaning before going out."

—Julia Gilliss, Fort Dalles settler in Oregon Territory,
in a letter dated March 2, 1866

Bitterroot Valley Strawberry Pie

• *Yield: 8 servings* •

The Bitterroot Valley, just south of my home in Missoula, is one of the best strawberry-growing areas in the country. The berries are small, tender, juicy, and loaded with flavor. Besides eating them plain with a bit of sugar, they are excellent baked in this pie. This recipe is based on a prizewinner from the Tenth Pillsbury Bake-Off. I was a teenage finalist in the same contest and only recently made the pie. The small amount of pineapple in the filling works wonderfully with the strawberries. This pie is delicious plain or with whipped cream, ice cream, or vanilla frozen yogurt.

Pastry

1¼ cups (5½ ounces) unbleached all-purpose flour

⅓ cup (1¼ ounces) cake flour

½ teaspoon salt

½ cup butter, chilled and cut into 6 pieces

¼ cup vegetable shortening, chilled

¼ cup ice water

Strawberry-Pineapple Filling

1 cup plus 1 tablespoon sugar

5 tablespoons cornstarch

¼ teaspoon salt

5 cups hulled and sliced strawberries

1 (8-ounce) can pineapple tidbits in juice, very well drained

2 tablespoons butter, chilled and cut into small pieces

Measure the flours for the pastry by spooning them into measuring cups, filling the cups to overflowing, and sweeping off the excess with a metal spatula.

To make the pastry in a food processor, place both flours in the work bowl of a food processor fitted with the metal blade. Add the salt, butter, and shortening. Pulse the machine 4 times, about 1 second each. Then, while pulsing rapidly, gradually add the ice water through the feed tube. Keep pulsing very rapidly until the dough almost gathers into a ball. Remove the dough from the work bowl and place it on a sheet of plastic wrap. Pat the dough gently to form a 6-inch disc.

To make the pastry by hand, place both flours in a large mixing bowl and stir in the salt. Add the butter and shortening and cut them in with a pastry blender until the particles resemble small peas. Sprinkle in the ice water while tossing the mixture lightly with a fork. Keep tossing until the mixture is moistened and gathers into a ball. Remove the dough from the bowl, place it on a sheet of plastic wrap, and pat it gently to form a 6-inch disc.

Cut one-quarter of the pastry circle away and bring the cut ends of the larger piece together to form a new, smaller circle. Wrap both pieces of pastry in plastic and refrigerate at least 1 hour.

Adjust two oven racks with one rack in the lowest position and one rack in the center. Place a heavy baking sheet on the lower rack and preheat the oven to 450°. On a lightly floured surface, roll the larger piece of pastry into a 13-inch circle. Fit it loosely into a 9-inch pie pan. Trim away excess pastry with scissors, leaving ½ inch of overhang. Reserve the pastry scraps. Fold the pastry edge back on itself and press together to form a high-standing rim. Flute the edge. (Even with a high rim, the filling may bubble over if the berries are especially juicy.) Place the crust in the freezer while you prepare the filling.

In a large mixing bowl, combine the 1 cup sugar, the cornstarch, and salt. Add the strawberries and pineapple and fold them in until the mixture is moistened. Add the pastry scraps to the wedge of pastry and roll it into an 8-inch circle on a lightly floured surface. Prick the pastry generously with a fork and cut it into 8 wedges.

Remove the crust from the freezer and pour the filling into it. Dot the top with the butter and set the pastry wedges over the filling, leaving a little space between the wedges. Lightly brush cold water over the pastry and sprinkle it with the remaining 1 tablespoon sugar. Immediately place the pie on the baking sheet on the lower shelf and bake for 15 minutes. Transfer the pie, still on the baking sheet, to the center shelf, reduce the oven temperature to 350°, and continue baking 50 to 60 minutes, or until the filling is very bubbly and the top crust is golden brown. Cool completely, cut into wedges, and serve.

Rhubarb Purée

• Yield: 2½ cups •

Rhubarb is like zucchini—one plant will give you more than you can use in a season. Rhubarb grows exceptionally well in the Pacific Northwest and in the Rocky Mountain West. The cool nights and long days provide us with luxuriant rhubarb plants with bright red stalks from early May through August. Spring rhubarb is less fibrous and more tart than summer rhubarb, and I prefer it in this rhubarb purée. Rhubarb Ice Cream (page 220), and Rhubarb Curd (page 219) are just a couple uses of this versatile preparation.

> 2 pounds trimmed rhubarb stalks
>
> 2⅔ cups sugar

Cut the rhubarb stalks into 1-inch pieces. Combine the rhubarb and sugar in a heavy 4-quart stainless steel or enamelware saucepan. Cover and cook over medium-low heat, stirring occasionally, until the rhubarb is very tender and falling apart, about 1 hour. Let it cool slightly, then either pass the mixture through the finest holes of a food mill or through the power strainer attachment of a food processor. If using early season rhubarb, you should have about 4 cups of purée; late-season rhubarb will give you about 3 cups purée. In either case, return the purée to the saucepan and cook, stirring frequently over medium-low heat, until thickened and reduced to 2½ cups. Remove from the heat, and cool completely; cover and refrigerate. This keeps well in the refrigerator for about 1 week.

———⊳•⊲———

"Rhubarb stalks or the Persian Apple is the earliest ingredient for pies, which the Spring offers. Strip the skin and cut the stalk into small bits, and stew very tender. These are dear pies for they take an enormous quantity of sugar."

—Mrs. Child, *The American Frugal Housewife*, 1844

———⊳•⊲———

Rhubarb Curd

• *Yield: 1 cups* •

This is a tart and delicious spread to use on toast, English muffins, crumpets, hot biscuits, pancakes, or waffles. You can also use it to fill tart shells or as a base for a filling in cream puffs, cakes, or pies. It keeps well in the refrigerator for 2 weeks. The color is a bit odd, almost like coffee with a small amount of cream added. But don't be put off by its looks. The beauty, in this case, is very definitely in the taste.

3 eggs

¼ cup butter

1 cup rhubarb purée (page 218)

Whisk the eggs in a small bowl to combine well. Melt the butter in a heavy 2-quart saucepan over medium heat. Stir in the rhubarb purée. Cook, stirring continuously with a rubber spatula, until the mixture is warm. Remove the pan from the heat and quickly whisk in the eggs. Return the pan to the heat and cook, stirring continuously with the rubber spatula, until the mixture thickens to the consistency of lightly whipped cream, 8 to 10 minutes. Draw the flat tip of the spatula from side to side over the bottom of the pan. You should be able to see the bottom of the pan briefly before the curd flows together. When ready, the curd should register 180° on an instant-read thermometer.

Place the saucepan in a large shallow pan filled with ice cubes and water, and stir occasionally with the rubber spatula until the curd reaches room temperature. Transfer to a container, cover tightly, and refrigerate. The curd will thicken further and become like a soft pudding when chilled.

"We hardly ever got any eggs, but when we did, if I had some extra, I'd make cream puffs for dessert after dinner. I'd mix flour, salt, and egg whites together until the mixture was right. Then I'd drop spoonfuls of it in a Dutch oven, cover and bake them until they got puffy and browned. We never had any real cream, so for a filling I made a custard out of sugar, evaporated milk, flour, egg yolks, and flavoring. Those cream puffs were sure a big hit!"

—Tony Grace, turn-of-the-century chuck wagon cook, beginning in 1913

Rhubarb Ice Cream

• *Yield: 6 cups* •

This is velvety smooth, rich, and creamy, much like a gelato. The addition of strawberry liqueur prevents the ice cream from becoming rock hard. This is excellent by itself or served with Rhubarb Pie (page 230), Gingered Apple Pie (page 234), or Rhubarb, Strawberry, and Hazelnut Crisp (page 242).

4 egg yolks

2 cups heavy cream

⅛ teaspoon salt

¼ cup sugar (optional)

1½ cups strained rhubarb purée (page 218)

¼ cup strawberry liqueur

Whisk the yolks in a small bowl, just well enough to blend. Place the cream in a heavy 2-quart saucepan and set over medium-high heat until tiny bubbles form around the edges and steam rises from the surface. Very gradually, whisk about ½ cup of the cream into the egg yolks to warm them. Then, off heat, whisk the egg yolk mixture into the remaining cream in the saucepan. Stir in the salt and sugar. The amount of sugar you use, if any, will depend on the tartness of the rhubarb. Taste carefully and adjust the sweetness accordingly.

Return the pan to medium heat and stir continuously with a rubber spatula, going all around the side of the pan and along the bottom until the mixture thickens into a custard and is very hot. The temperature should be 175° to 180°. Do not allow it to boil. Place the pan in a large shallow pan filled with ice cubes and water, and stir occasionally with the rubber spatula until the mixture reaches room temperature. Stir in the rhubarb purée and liqueur. Chill well, about 2 hours. Freeze in an ice cream maker according to the manufacturer's directions.

MOUNTAIN SNOW ICE CREAM

Ingenious cooks on the Oregon Trail even made ice cream. They took advantage of mountain snow in the summertime at high elevations and used it to freeze milk sweetened with sugar. Charles Parke gave this description of making ice cream on Independence Day in the South Pass area of Wyoming, where the Oregon Trail crosses the Rocky Mountains:

> After crossing Sweetwater for the last time, we traveled up the valley 10 miles and camped on a small brook, arriving at 1:00 P.M., where we laid over all afternoon. This being the nation's birthday and our under clothing not as clean as we could wish, we commenced our celebration by "washing dirty linen" or rather woolens, as we all wore woolen shirts. Washing done and shirts hung out to dry—we never iron—all hands set about enjoying themselves as best they could. Some visited two large banks of snow about half a mile from the ford on Sweetwater. Having plenty of milk from two cows we had with us, I determined to [do] something no other living man ever did in this place and on this sacred day of the year, and that was to make *Ice Cream at the South Pass of the Rockies*.

> I procured a small tin bucket which held about 2 quarts. This I sweetened and flavored with *peppermint*—had nothing else. This bucket was placed inside a wooden bucket, or Yankee Pale, and the top put on. Nature had supplied a huge bank of coarse snow, or hail, nearby, which was just the thing for this *new factory*. With alternate layers of this, and salt between the two buckets and aid of a *clean* stick to stir with, I soon produced the most delicious ice cream tasted in this place. In fact, the whole company so decided, and as a compliment drew up in front of our Tent and fired a Salute, bursting one gun but injuring no one.

Rhubarb, Strawberry, and Hazelnut Crisp

• Yield: 8 servings •

The tartness of rhubarb and the sweetness of strawberries are a classic duo. Luckily, the two appear in markets at about the same time. But I have made this crisp without strawberries and think it is just as delicious, maybe because the hazelnuts add their own sweetness. Serve with Rhubarb Ice Cream (page 220), whipped cream, vanilla ice cream, or frozen vanilla yogurt.

Filling

¼ cup (1¼ ounces) unbleached all-purpose flour

½ cup granulated sugar

½ cup firmly packed dark brown sugar

½ teaspoon ground cinnamon

¼ teaspoon freshly grated nutmeg

⅛ teaspoon mace

½ pound ripe, juicy strawberries

1½ pounds trimmed rhubarb stalks, cut in ½-inch pieces (6 cups)

1 teaspoon pure vanilla extract

Topping

1 cup (5 ounces) unbleached all-purpose flour

⅓ cup firmly packed dark brown sugar

2 tablespoons granulated sugar

1 teaspoon ground cinnamon

½ cup chilled unsalted butter, cut into 6 pieces

½ cup toasted, skinned hazelnuts (see page 10).

Adjust an oven rack to the center position and preheat the oven to 375°.

Measure the flour for the pastry by scooping a measuring cup into the flour container, filling the cup to overflowing, and sweeping off the excess with a metal spatula. In a large bowl, combine both sugars, the cinnamon, nutmeg, mace, and flour. Use your fingertips to break up any lumps of brown sugar. Rinse the strawberries and pat them dry on paper towels. Remove the hulls and cut the berries into ¼- to ½-inch-thick slices. (You should have about 2 cups.) Add the rhubarb, strawberries, and vanilla to the sugar mixture and fold gently with a rubber spatula until the mixture is well moistened. Turn into an ungreased 9 × 9 × 2-inch baking pan or a 10-inch round baking dish 2 inches deep.

Measure the flour for the topping by scooping a measuring cup into the flour container, filling the cup to overflowing, and sweeping off the excess with a metal spatula.

To make the topping in a food processor, place the flour in the work bowl of a food processor fitted with the metal blade. Add both sugars, the cinnamon, and butter. Pulse 3 or 4 times to begin breaking the butter up into smaller pieces. Add the hazelnuts and pulse rapidly about 10 times until both the butter and the nuts are finely chopped.

To make topping by hand, combine the flour, both sugars, and the cinnamon in a large bowl. Use your fingertips to break up any lumps in the brown sugar. Add the butter and cut it in with a pastry blender until the particles resemble small peas. Chop the hazelnuts medium-fine with a large knife and stir them in.

Turn mixture over the rhubarb filling and spread it gently with your hands, without packing it down, to cover the filling completely. Place the pan in the oven and bake 40 to 50 minutes, or until the filling is very bubbly and the topping is a rich brown color. Remove from the oven, cool, and serve warm or at room temperature.

RHUBARB IN THE ROCKIES

Silverton, Colorado, a small mining town situated 9,300 feet above sea level in the San Juan Mountains, is an unlikely place to find any crop growing. Horseradish and dandelions do well there—and so does rhubarb. European miners brought rhubarb to Silverton in the late 1800s and considered it to have valuable nutrition and medicinal qualities. The climate in Silverton turned out to be ideal for rhubarb, and plants are found all over town today. By one account, 390 plants, one for each resident, are scattered throughout the small community.

Each Independence Day, the Silverton Public Library sponsors a rhubarb festival, which features a parade—complete with a brass band and baton twirlers—and a cooking competition. Dozens of recipes are submitted each year. Lemon Rhubarb Mousse and Smoky Chinese Ribs with Rhubarb Glaze won top awards one year, while one recipe, called Rhubarbudweiser, won the distinction of Absolutely No-Place Winner. The library publishes the winners in *The Silverton Public Library's International Rhubarb Cookbook and Other Little Gems*, which contains over 100 rhubarb recipes and anecdotes about the town's history. You can order a copy by calling (970) 387-5770 or writing to the library at P.O. Box 68, Silverton, CO 81433.

Sour Cherry Streusel Tart

• *Yield: 8 to 10 servings* •

Fresh sour pie cherries are as precious as rubies. Bright and shiny like the gems they resemble, the sour Montmorency cherries have a short season where I live—only 2 to 3 weeks in July—so I always buy some to use fresh and some to freeze. A true luxury is popping a just-picked warm fresh cherry into my mouth, pulling away the stem, and eating the flesh off its pit. I shiver from the tartness, but I know summer is here at last.

This recipe is one of the best ways I know to celebrate the pie cherry. Please note that the filling mixture needs to sit at room temperature about 5 hours, so prepare it first. You could even start it the night before and leave it in the refrigerator. And be careful when eating this mouthwatering treat: even though the cherries are pitted, I always warn people to beware of renegade pits. One or two often manage to escape the pitter.

Filling

2 pounds fresh sour pie cherries, stemmed and pitted (4 cups)

1 cup sugar

3 tablespoons cornstarch

¼ teaspoon salt

Finely grated zest of 1 lemon

Pastry

1¼ cups (6¼ ounces) unbleached all-purpose flour

⅓ cup (1½ ounces) cake flour

¼ teaspoon salt

1 tablespoon sugar

½ cup chilled unsalted butter, cut into 6 pieces

2 tablespoons chilled vegetable shortening

⅓ cup ice water

Streusel Topping

½ cup (2½ ounces) unbleached all-purpose flour

½ cup firmly packed light brown sugar

1 teaspoon ground cinnamon

¼ teaspoon mace

6 tablespoons chilled unsalted butter, cut into 6 pieces

To make the filling, combine the cherries with the sugar in a large bowl and let the mixture stand for about 5 hours at room temperature, stirring occasionally, until the sugar is dissolved and the cherry juices are released. Drain well in a wire strainer set over a bowl. Transfer the juice to a 2-cup glass measure and add enough water to reach 1¼ cups. In a heavy-bottomed 2-quart saucepan, whisk together the liquid, cornstarch, and salt. Bring to a boil over medium heat, stirring gently but continuously with a rubber spatula, and cook 2 to 3 minutes, or until the mixture is thick and translucent. Remove from the heat and stir in the grated lemon zest and the drained cherries. Set aside to cool.

Measure the flours by scooping a measuring cup into the flour containers, filling the cup to overflowing, and sweeping off the excess with a metal spatula.

To make the pastry in a food processor, place both flours, the salt, sugar, butter, and shortening in the work bowl of a food processor fitted with the metal blade. Pulse rapidly 4 times to begin breaking up the fat. While pulsing very rapidly, gradually pour the ice water through the feed tube. Pulse 20 to 30 more times, or until the dough almost gathers into a ball. Carefully remove the dough from the work bowl, lightly dust it with flour, and shape it into a 6-inch disc. Wrap securely in plastic wrap and refrigerate at least 1 hour.

To make the pastry by hand, place both flours, the salt, sugar, butter, and shortening in a large mixing bowl. Cut in the fats with a pastry blender until the particles resemble small peas. While tossing with a fork, gradually sprinkle in the ice water until the dough gathers into a ball. Continue as directed above.

Roll out the pastry on a lightly floured surface into a 14-inch circle. Loosely fit it into an 11-inch tart pan 1 inch deep with a removable bottom and a fluted edge. Trim the overhanging pastry to within ½ inch of the tart pan rim, then fold the overhang against the sides of the pastry in the pan, pressing firmly to join the two. There should be about ¼ inch of pastry extending above the tart rim. Place the tart pan in the freezer for 15 minutes.

Meanwhile, adjust an oven rack to the center position, place a heavy baking sheet on the rack, and preheat the oven to 400°. Remove the pastry from the freezer and line it with a square of aluminum foil, pressing the foil into the corners and allowing the excess to extend upright above the rim. Fill the tart pan with dried beans or rice, place the pan on the baking sheet, and bake for about 20 minutes, or until pastry is lightly colored. Remove the pan from the oven, carefully remove the foil and beans or rice, and return the tart shell to the oven for 5 more minutes. Watch carefully to see if the pastry puffs; if it does, prick it in a few places with a cake tester or a narrow wooden skewer. Remove the pan from the oven and set aside to cool. (The crust may be made hours ahead.)

Measure the flour for the topping by scooping a measuring cup into the flour container, filling the cup to overflowing, and sweeping off the excess with a metal spatula.

To make the topping in a food processor, place the flour, brown sugar, cinnamon, mace, and butter in the work bowl of a food processor fitted with a metal blade. Pulse several times, or until the mixture is crumbly.

(continued)

To make the topping by hand, combine the flour, brown sugar, cinnamon, and mace in a medium-sized bowl, breaking up any lumps in the brown sugar with your fingertips. Add the butter and cut it in with a pastry blender until the mixture resembles coarse crumbs.

Preheat the oven to 400°.

Turn the cherry filling into the cooled partially baked crust, and spread it level. Sprinkle the topping evenly over the filling, patting it very gently in place without packing it down. The tart shell should be full. Place the tart pan on the baking sheet and place in the oven. Bake for 30 minutes, or until the filling is bubbly and the topping is nicely browned. Remove from the oven and place on a rack to cool. When the tart has cooled to room temperature, remove the side of the pan, cut the tart into wedges, and serve.

Note: To prepare pie cherries for freezing, combine 4 cups pitted cherries with 1 cup sugar and 4 level teaspoons of Fruit Fresh, stirring to mix well. Transfer to airtight freezer containers, seal, date, and freeze. The cherries will keep well for up to 1 year, but you'll probably want them during the winter to revive summer memories. To use, thaw thoroughly in a wire strainer set over a bowl to collect all the juices. Measure the juice and add enough water to reach 1¼ cups. Proceed as the recipe directs.

Packing cherries at the 8-mile Cherry Orchard
in western Montana (circa 1915).

Huckleberry Ice Cream

• Yield: 1 quart •

The first dessert I make with the season's first huckleberries is Huckleberry Pie (page 230). I make this ice cream to serve with it. It may be overkill, but nothing succeeds like excess. This ice cream does not freeze brick hard.

>   3 cups huckleberries
>
>   1 cup sugar
>
>   2 cups heavy whipping cream
>
>   4 egg yolks
>
>   ¼ teaspoon salt

Combine the huckleberries and sugar in a heavy-bottomed 3-quart nonreactive saucepan. Cover and cook over medium-low heat, stirring occasionally, until the berries are cooked and very soft and the sugar is dissolved, about 20 minutes. Uncover the pan, increase the heat to medium-high, and boil the mixture for 5 minutes, stirring often. Remove from the heat and break up the berries in the pan with a potato masher. Pass through a fine strainer, pressing on the pulp to extract as much liquid as possible. You should have about 1½ cups of huckleberry syrup.

Heat the cream in a heavy 1-quart saucepan over medium heat until bubbles form around the edges and the cream is very hot but not boiling. Set aside. Meanwhile, whisk the yolks and salt together in a medium-sized bowl just to combine well. Very gradually whisk in the hot cream, adding droplets at first then adding it in a thin stream as the yolks warm up. Transfer the mixture to the 3-quart saucepan and cook over medium-low to low heat, stirring continuously with a rubber spatula until the mixture thickens into a custard and coats the spatula with a thin layer. When cooked, the mixture should register between 175° and 180° on an instant-read thermometer. Remove from the heat and stir in the huckleberry syrup.

Place the saucepan in a larger pan filled with ice cubes and water and stir occasionally until the mixture feels cold. It will thicken as it chills. Freeze in an ice cream maker according to the manufacturer's directions. Transfer to an airtight container and freeze. It keeps well for about 1 week.

Blueberry-Rhubarb Pie

• *Yield: 8 servings* •

In midsummer, when blueberries make their welcome appearance, I like to make this pie. Blueberries or huckleberries and rhubarb are an excellent combination.

Pie Crust Pastry

1¾ cups (8¾ ounces) unbleached all-purpose flour

¾ cup (3¼ ounces) cake flour

½ teaspoon salt

1 cup chilled butter, cut into 8 pieces

1 egg yolk

1 teaspoon cider vinegar

Ice water

Blueberry-Rhubarb Filling

¾ pound trimmed rhubarb stalks, cut into ½-inch pieces (3 cups)

1½ cups sugar

4 to 5 tablespoons quick-cooking tapioca

¼ teaspoon salt

¼ teaspoon ground cinnamon

¼ teaspoon mace

Finely grated zest of 1 orange

1½ pounds (5 cups) blueberries, picked over

2 tablespoons cold butter, cut into small pieces

Additional sugar for sprinkling

Measure the flours by scooping a measuring cup into the flour containers, filling the cup to overflowing, and sweeping off the excess with a metal spatula.

To make the pastry in a food processor, place both flours in the work bowl of a food processor fitted with the metal blade. Add the salt and butter. Pulse 4 times to break up the butter. In a glass measuring cup, combine the egg yolk, cider vinegar, and enough ice water to total ½ cup. Start pulsing very rapidly while adding the liquid in a steady stream through the feed tube. It will take 25 to 30 quick pulses to thoroughly mix the pastry, but do not process until dough gathers into a ball; stop just before that happens. Remove the dough from the work bowl, press it gently into one mass and divide it in two, with one piece slightly larger than the other. (If you have a scale, one portion should weigh about 12 ounces and the other 10 ounces.) Shape each portion into a 6-inch disc, dusting it lightly with flour if necessary, and wrap securely in plastic wrap. Refrigerate 1 hour or longer.

To make the pastry by hand, place both flours in a large mixing bowl. Stir in the salt and add the butter, cutting it in with a pastry blender until the mixture resembles coarse meal or small peas. In a glass measuring cup, combine the egg yolk, cider vinegar, and enough ice water to total ½ cup. Gradually add the wet ingredients to the flour and butter mixture while gently tossing with a fork. Continue tossing until the mixture gathers into a ball. Shape and chill as directed above.

To prepare the filling, combine the rhubarb and ½ cup of the sugar in a 2- to 3-quart saucepan. Cover and cook over low heat, stirring occasionally, until the rhubarb begins to soften and its juices are released, about 20 minutes. Transfer to a wire strainer set over a bowl and set aside to cool. (You will not use the juice in this recipe, however, it makes an excellent drink when combined with mineral water or dry white wine.) In a large bowl, combine the remaining 1 cup sugar, the tapioca, salt, cinnamon, mace, and orange zest. Add the blueberries and rhubarb and fold together gently but thoroughly. Let the mixture stand for 15 minutes.

Meanwhile, adjust two oven racks so that one is on the lowest shelf and the other is in the center. Place a heavy baking sheet on the lower rack and preheat the oven to 450°.

On a lightly floured surface, roll the larger pastry disc into a 13-inch circle. Fit the dough loosely into a 9-inch glass or metal pie pan, leaving excess pastry hanging over the edge. Spread the filling in the crust, mounding it slightly in the center, then pat it gently in place with your hands. Scatter the butter pieces over the blueberries and rhubarb.

On a lightly floured surface, roll the second pastry disc into a 12- to 13-inch circle. Brush the edge of the bottom crust lightly with water and cover it with the top crust, pressing the edges to seal. Trim away excess pastry with scissors, leaving ½ inch of overhang. Fold the pastry edge back on itself to make a standing rim and flute. Brush the top of the pastry lightly with cold water and sprinkle it evenly with sugar (about 1 tablespoon). Make 4 slits at right angles about 1½ inches long in the top crust to allow steam to escape during baking, and place the pie on the baking sheet on the lower rack. Bake for 15 minutes. Transfer the pie, still on the baking sheet, to the center shelf, reduce the temperature to 350°, and continue baking for 1 hour, or until the crust is well browned and you can see the juices bubbling away in the slits. Cool for several hours before serving. (If you cut the pie too soon, the filling may run.) Refrigerate any leftovers.

Huckleberry Pie

• *Yield: 8 servings* •

I've struggled over the years with huckleberry pies, attempting to find the best thickener and figuring out how much of it to use. I've tried quick-cooking tapioca, flour, cornstarch, or a combination of flour and cornstarch. Each batch of berries seemed to require a different amount of thickener and I never knew what to expect until I cut into the pie. Sometimes the berries would be perfectly set; other times, the filling would run all over. Lately, I've been getting fairly consistent results with quick-cooking tapioca. But even if your filling turns out runny, don't lose heart; the pie will still be delicious. If you can't get Rocky Mountain huckleberries, use ready-made huckleberry filling (see the mail-order sources on page 249) or blueberries and follow the directions for the variation that follows this recipe.

Pie crust pastry (page 228)

Huckleberry Filling

1 cup plus 1 tablespoon granulated sugar

¼ cup firmly packed light brown sugar

4 to 5 tablespoons quick-cooking tapioca

1 teaspoon ground cinnamon

½ teaspoon freshly grated nutmeg

1¾ pounds huckleberries, picked over (5 cups)

1 tablespoon freshly squeezed lemon juice

2 tablespoons butter, chilled and cut into small pieces

Refrigerate the pastry dough for at least 1 hour.

On a lightly floured surface, roll out the larger disc into a 13-inch circle. Fit the dough loosely into a 9-inch glass or metal pie pan, leaving excess pastry hanging over the edge. Refrigerate until ready to fill.

Adjust two oven racks, placing one on the lowest shelf and the other in the center. Place a heavy baking sheet on the lower shelf. Preheat the oven to 450°.

In a large bowl, combine 1 cup of the granulated sugar, the brown sugar, tapioca, cinnamon, and nutmeg. Break up any brown sugar lumps with your fingertips and mix everything together thoroughly. Fold in the huckleberries and lemon juice and let the mixture stand for 15 minutes.

Remove the pie shell from the refrigerator and pour the filling into the crust, mounding it slightly in the center. Dot with the butter and set aside. On a lightly floured surface, roll out the top crust into a 12-inch circle. Brush the edge of the lower crust lightly with water and place the top crust over the berries. Press the edges firmly to seal and trim away excess pastry to within ½ inch of the rim of the pan. Fold the pastry back on itself to form a standing rim and flute. Make four slits at right angles about 1½ inches long in the top crust with the tip of a small sharp knife. Brush the top lightly with water and sprinkle with the remaining 1 tablespoon sugar. Place the pie in the oven on the baking sheet and bake for 15 minutes. Transfer the baking sheet to the center shelf, reduce the temperature to 350°, and continue baking for 45 to 60 minutes, or until the juices are thickened and bubbly and the crust is a rich brown color. Cool completely for several hours before cutting. Or refrigerate the cooled pie for a few hours before serving. Refrigerate any leftovers.

Note: If you use frozen berries, use them unthawed and increase the baking time by about 15 minutes.

Blueberry Pie Variation: Combine 1 cup granulated sugar, 2 tablespoons firmly packed dark brown sugar, 1 teaspoon pumpkin pie spice, and 4 to 5 tablespoons quick-cooking tapioca in a large bowl. Add 2 pounds (6 cups) blueberries and 2 tablespoons freshly squeezed lime juice. Fold together gently with a rubber spatula and let stand for 15 minutes. Continue with the directions for Huckleberry Pie, baking for 60 to 70 minutes once the oven temperature is reduced to 350°.

HUCKLEBERRY HEAVEN

"Once in the mouth…there can be no doubt: this is something else entirely. And here the trouble begins, because for those who have tasted mountain huckleberries, no description is needed; and for those who haven't description is impossible."

—Asta Bowen, *The Huckleberry Book*

Rhubarb Pie

• Yield: 8 servings •

Most rhubarb pies turn out soft and runny. Not this one. Mixing the cut rhubarb with sugar and letting the mixture stand overnight draws out the excess moisture from the rhubarb. Some of the liquid is then thickened with cornstarch, folded into the rhubarb, and baked in the pie. After the pie has cooled, the filling stays put when you cut it. This double-crust pie makes a great visual presentation—as good to look at as it is to eat.

Pie Crust Pastry (page 228)

Rhubarb Filling

2 pounds trimmed rhubarb stalks, cut into ½-inch pieces (about 8 cups)

2 cups sugar

3 whole cloves

Finely grated zest of 1 lemon

3 tablespoons freshly squeezed lemon juice

¼ cup cornstarch

1½ teaspoons pure vanilla extract

2 tablespoons chilled butter, cut into small pieces

Refrigerate the pastry dough overnight.

Combine the rhubarb, sugar, and cloves in a large mixing bowl. Cover and let stand at room temperature overnight. (If your kitchen is warm, refrigerate the mixture then bring it to room temperature before proceeding.) The next morning, the rhubarb will be sitting in a pool of juice. Drain well for about 1 hour in a large strainer set over a bowl and discard the cloves.

Measure 1¼ cups rhubarb juice and stir in the lemon zest, lemon juice, and cornstarch. Place in a 2-quart saucepan and cook over medium heat, stirring gently and continuously with a rubber spatula until the mixture boils and thickens. Cook and stir gently for another 2 minutes, scraping the bottom of the pan well with the rubber spatula, then cool to room temperature and stir in the vanilla.

Prepare the oven and roll out the pastry as described in the Blueberry-Rhubarb Pie recipe (page 228).

Gently fold the drained rhubarb and cornstarch mixture together. Pour into the bottom crust and smooth the top, mounding it a bit in the center. Dot the filling with the chilled butter bits and cover with the top crust. Finish the crust and complete the baking as directed on page 229. Cool completely on a wire rack before serving. Refrigerate the pie for a few hours and serve it cold. Refrigerate any leftovers.

APPLE GROWING IN THE WEST

It's safe to say that the one crop Washington State is most famous for is apples. Who could have known that when Dr. John McLoughlin planted the first apple tree in the Pacific Northwest in 1826 that apples would become one of Washington's top cash crops? Today, Washington State produces more than half the country's apples, enough to supply every American with 15 apples a year.

Apple growers there have known for more than a hundred years that the warm summer days, cool nights, and volcanic soil, made it an ideal apple-growing environment. At least a dozen apple varieties are now grown in the Yakima and Wenatchee valleys. Because of modern storage facilities, certain varieties such as Red Delicious, Golden Delicious, Fuji, and Granny Smith are available year-round. Other popular varieties such as Gala, Elstar, Criterion, and Jonagold, are in stores September through March. The Newtown Pippin and Rome Beauty varieties, both excellent cooking apples, can be purchased from September through early summer.

Apples are also grown in parts of Idaho and Montana. At the turn of the century, apple growing lured many to come out West from the East. In Montana, most apple ranches didn't succeed because of the extreme climate and blight, and commercial apple production eventually fell by the wayside. However, many apple varieties can be grown in certain parts of the state if one perseveres. Art and Nancy Callan grow many types of apples in the Bitterroot Valley. They tend about 1,200 trees on 2½ acres, and they begin selling their apples at farmers markets in early August. Every week the selection changes, depending on what's been harvested. Apples that do particularly well here are the disease-resistant varieties such as the all-purpose Liberty and William's Pride. For some reason, blight is more prevalent in Montana than in Idaho and Washington. If everything goes well, in a good year the annual crop may yield Vista Bella, Discovery, Jersey Mac, State Fair, Summer Red, William's Pride, Lyman's Large, Jonamac, MacIntosh, Gala, Liberty, Kidd Orange, Sweet Sixteen, and Honey Crisp. Jonamac is their most dependable variety. It is a delicious all-purpose cooking and eating apple that can be harvested from early September to mid-October. Many of these varieties do not store well, so they must be used soon after picking.

In Idaho, apple farming is less of a gamble than in Montana. The conditions there are not as extreme, so the growing season is longer. Many of the same apple varieties that are grown in Montana can be grown in Idaho. My wife's family, the Hinshaws, settled in Greenleaf, Idaho, in the early 1900s. The apple orchards started by her grandfather are still thriving.

Gingered Apple Pie

• Yield: 8 servings •

This makes a huge, gorgeous pie. Be sure to use a firm cooking apple in this recipe. You can't go wrong with Golden Delicious, but if you live in an apple-growing region, do ask about local varieties that are good to bake with.

Pie crust pastry (page 228)

Apple-Ginger Filling

Juice of 1 lemon

4 pounds firm cooking apples, peeled, cored, and cut in quarters

¾ cup plus 1 tablespoon granulated sugar

2 tablespoons dry unseasoned bread crumbs

¼ cup (1¼ ounces) unbleached all-purpose flour

½ cup firmly packed light brown sugar

1 teaspoon ground cinnamon

¼ teaspoon mace

¼ cup finely chopped crystallized ginger

3 tablespoons butter, chilled and cut into small pieces

1 egg

2 teaspoons water

Refrigerate the pastry dough for at least 1 hour.

Strain the lemon juice into a large mixing bowl. Slice each apple quarter into 3 or 4 wedges. Add to the lemon juice, tossing well as you go along. Add ½ cup of the granulated sugar and toss to combine thoroughly. Let stand 1 hour or longer to draw out excess juices. Drain well. (You will not need the juice.)

Adjust two oven racks with one on the lowest shelf and the other in the center. Place a heavy baking sheet on the lower shelf and preheat the oven to 450°.

On a lightly floured surface, roll out the larger pastry disc into a 13-inch circle. Place the dough loosely in a 9-inch glass or metal pie pan, leaving the excess pastry hanging over the edge. Sprinkle the bread crumbs over the bottom of the pie shell.

Measure the flour by scooping a measuring cup into the flour container, filling the cup to overflowing, and sweeping off the excess with a metal spatula.

In a large bowl combine the flour, brown sugar, ¼ cup of the granulated sugar, the cinnamon, mace, and ginger. Add the apples and fold together until the mixture is moistened. Transfer the filling to the pie shell and dot the top with the butter. On a lightly floured surface, roll out the second pastry disc into a 12- to 13-inch circle. In a small bowl, beat the egg and water together with a fork just to combine well, and brush some onto the edge of the bottom crust. Place the second circle of pastry on top and press the edges firmly to seal. Trim away excess pastry to within ½ inch of the edge of the pie plate. Fold the pastry back on itself to form a standing rim and flute. Cut four slits at right angles about 1½ inches long in the top of the pie and brush the crust with the egg wash. Sprinkle with the remaining 1 tablespoon sugar and place the pie on the baking sheet. Bake 15 minutes, then transfer the baking sheet to the center rack. Reduce the temperature to 350° and continue baking for 60 to 70 minutes, or until the crust is well browned, the apples are tender (insert a sharp knife through one of the slits in the top crust to test), and the filling is bubbly. Cool completely before serving. Refrigerate any leftovers.

Harvesting apples in Montana's Bitterroot Valley (circa 1910).

Raspberry Cobbler

• Yield: 8 servings •

The entire Rocky Mountain West and Pacific Northwest are great raspberry-growing areas. The cool nights and long days make for exceptionally juicy and flavorful berries. In our garden, we grow thornless varieties of red and yellow berries, which are easy to pick. I've made this cobbler with both kinds, either combined or separately, and I can't tell which one I like best. Just use the plumpest and freshest berries you can find.

½ cup firmly packed dark brown sugar

4 teaspoons cornstarch

½ teaspoon ground cinnamon

¼ teaspoon freshly grated nutmeg

½ cup water

2 teaspoons pure vanilla extract

3 pints raspberries (6 cups)

1 cup (4½ ounces) unbleached all-purpose flour

¼ cup granulated sugar

1 teaspoon baking powder

¼ teaspoon baking soda

¼ teaspoon salt

6 tablespoons butter, chilled and cut into 6 pieces

⅔ cup buttermilk

Adjust an oven rack to the center position and preheat the oven to 400°.

In a large bowl, combine the brown sugar, cornstarch, cinnamon, nutmeg, water, and vanilla. Press the mixture against the side of the bowl with the flat side of a rubber spatula to break up any sugar lumps and dissolve the cornstarch; set aside. Pick over the raspberries and set them aside.

Measure the flour by spooning it into a measuring cup, filling the cup to overflowing, and sweeping off the excess with a metal spatula. In a medium-sized bowl, sift together the flour, granulated sugar, baking powder, baking soda, and salt. Cut in the butter with a pastry blender until the mixture resembles coarse meal. Add the buttermilk and stir with a fork just until the mixture gathers together to form a soft dough. Gently fold the raspberries into the cornstarch mixture with a rubber spatula. Pour the mixture into a shallow 2-quart baking dish. (I use a round ovenproof glass dish

10 inches in diameter and 2 inches deep.) Place spoonfuls of batter over the raspberries in 8 mounds, leaving a bit of space between the mounds. Bake for about 35 minutes, or until the cobbler is well browned and the juices are thickened and bubbly. Serve warm or cool. Refrigerate any leftovers.

———◆———

"The berry-picking season brings back some of the happiest times in my life. I loved to get them. Straight up the mountain-side in front of our house, was a small patch in the burned timber. I would take a five-pound lard pail and go after them…There is no finer sight than to see a wild raspberry bush from below, hanging full of ripe berries. Then the climbing over rocks and logs, squatting near each bush, the sun warm on your back, everything so still and peaceful— how you could dream and enjoy it!…Mama makes a cobbler of them, and, oh, the smell when the oven door is opened! The odor of raspberries cooking…can take me in a moment back forty years…"

—Anne Ellis, recalling her family's experiences after settling
in the gold fields of the Colorado Rockies in 1879

———◆———

DESSERTS

237

Hazelnut Praline Angel Food Cake

· *Yield: 12 to 16 servings* ·

Hazelnuts, or filberts as they are sometimes called, grow abundantly in Oregon. I decided to see how they'd work in an angel food cake, and this is the result. For years I had problems baking egg white–based cakes where I live. The altitude, about 3,500 feet, is not exceptionally high, but it is just high enough above sea level to make trouble. I found that putting the cake pan into a cold oven and then setting the thermostat to the desired temperature was the way to avoid disaster. The cakes always rose beautifully and stayed that way—no last-minute collapse, which happened if the oven were preheated. The reason the cold oven works is simple: As the bubbles in the batter expand, the air pushes against a protein network. If the expansion happens too quickly, as it does in a preheated oven, the proteins don't have enough time to set properly and to trap the air. Instead, they break down, the air escapes, and the cake falls. I have become so fond of this method that I even use it at sea level, where it works just as well for me. You'll need a 10 × 4-inch angel food pan with a removable bottom but without a nonstick finish. Also handy is a large (8-quart) stainless steel mixing bowl. Mine measures 13½ inches across and 5 inches deep. An extra-wide rubber spatula helps speed the folding process. Be sure all bowls and utensils are grease-free.

The cake needs no accompaniment, but it goes particularly well with blackberries mixed with a bit of sugar and allowed to stand for an hour or so. Or serve it with heavy cream flavored with hazelnut liqueur (use about 1 tablespoon liqueur for each cup of cream) and whipped to soft peaks.

Hazelnut Praline

1 cup sugar

¼ cup water

¼ teaspoon cream of tartar

½ cup blanched, toasted hazelnuts (page 10)

Cake Batter

1 cup (4 to 4¼ ounces) sifted unbleached all-purpose flour

1 cup sifted confectioners' sugar

2 cups egg whites (14 to 16 large eggs)

½ teaspoon salt

1½ teaspoons cream of tartar

1½ teaspoons pure vanilla extract

⅔ cup granulated sugar

Line a 9-inch square baking pan with aluminum foil and set aside. To make the praline, combine the sugar, water, and cream of tartar in a heavy-bottomed 1-quart saucepan over high heat. Stir continuously with a wooden spatula until the sugar is dissolved and the mixture comes to a boil. Cover the pan and boil 3 minutes. (During this time, the condensing steam inside the pan will wash down any sugar crystals clinging to the side). Uncover the pan and keep boiling, without stirring, for several minutes until the syrup turns a deep caramel color. Swirl the pan occasionally to keep the color even. Remove the pan from the heat and quickly add the nuts, swirling the pan to combine them with the syrup. Immediately pour the mixture into the prepared pan. Do not scrape the pan clean, just pour out what will come. Cool the praline completely, about 30 minutes, then break it up into chunks and pulverize it into a powder in a food processor fitted with the metal blade. Store in an airtight container. The praline powder keeps very well in the freezer for months.

To make the cake batter, adjust an oven rack to the lower-third position, but do not preheat the oven. Sift the flour with the confectioners' sugar four times and set aside.

In the large bowl of an electric mixer, beat the egg whites with the whip attachment on medium speed until foamy, about 1 minute. Add the salt, cream of tartar, and vanilla. Increase the speed to medium-high and continue beating until the egg whites form soft peaks. Test by dipping the tip of a rubber spatula in the beaten whites; the whites should curl over, not form stiff peaks, when the spatula is pulled away. Beat again at medium speed and add the granulated sugar 1 rounded tablespoon at a time, beating for 15 seconds between additions. When all of the sugar has been incorporated, increase the speed to high and beat just until the whites are glossy and hold a firm peak when the whip is raised (the peaks should stand up straight). This happens quickly.

Transfer the whites to the large mixing bowl. Measure ¾ cup of the hazelnut praline powder, and set aside. Return the dry ingredients back to the sifter and sift about ¼ cup at a time over the surface of the whites as you fold gently with a large rubber spatula. Work quickly, and remember to be gentle but thorough. Sprinkle the praline evenly over the whites and fold it in quickly with a few broad strokes. Immediately spoon the mixture into a grease-free 10 × 4-inch angel food cake pan. The pan will be almost full. Run a table knife through the batter in concentric circles to remove large air pockets, and smooth the top with a rubber spatula.

Place the pan in a cold oven. Set the thermostat to 350° and turn the oven on. Bake for 45 to 55 minutes, or until the top of the cake is well browned and the cake springs back when gently pressed with a fingertip. The top of the cake may crack during baking.

Cool the cake in its pan, upside down, with plenty of air circulation underneath. Even if the pan has "feet," it must still be supported with more space. I use a metal funnel or a narrow-necked wine bottle. The cake must be completely cool before you remove it from the pan. To do that, use a sharp, serrated knife, with a long blade. Holding the knife vertically, insert it between the cake and the side of the pan. Use a slow up-and-down sawing motion as you rotate the pan and work your way all around it to release the cake from the sides. Lift the cake out of the pan by its central tube and run a small sharp knife under the cake to release it from the bottom of the pan. Carefully invert onto a rack, remove the pan bottom, and invert the cake again onto a dessert platter. Cut with a serrated knife to serve.

Calamity Jane, born Martha Jane Cannary, was a legendary frontierswoman. She had many talents, one of which happened to be cooking. She also had a highly developed imagination and kept a diary addressed to her imaginary daughter Janey. She was a generous, good-hearted woman, and this is her "receipt" or recipe for fruitcake, which she calls "20 Year Cake."

Mix together 25 eggs beaten separate, 2½ pounds each of sugar, flour and butter, 7½ pounds seeded raisins, 1½ pounds citron cut very fine, 5 pounds currants, ¼ ounce [ground] cloves, ½ ounce cinnamon, 2 ounces mace, 2 ounces nutmeg, 2 teaspoons yeast powder [baking powder], or 2 teaspoons soda & 3 cream tartar. Bake.

This will make 3 cakes 8 pounds each. Pour a pint of brandy over the cakes while still warm. Seal in tight crock. This cake is unexcelled & will keep good to the last crum 20 years.

Huckleberry Shake

• Yield: one 1-cup serving •

This shake is a gorgeous purple color with that special tang only real huckleberries have.

¼ cup milk

⅓ to ½ cup huckleberries, fresh or frozen

½ cup premium vanilla ice cream or frozen yogurt

Pour the milk into a blender and add the berries (if frozen, thaw first). Blend at high speed 1 minute. Add the ice cream and blend until smooth. Pour into a tall frosted glass and drink immediately.

When my wife and I moved to Montana in 1972, it was almost the beginning of huckleberry season. Our neighbors kept talking about whether it would be a good year for the wild berries and their plans for their harvest. We had never heard of huckleberries, but within a few weeks we knew what all the fuss was about. Rocky Mountain huckleberries have a taste all their own: similar to blueberries, but much tarter and richer in flavor.

Since then, we've also tasted huckleberries from the Cascade Mountains. The berries from the Cascades not only looked smaller and had larger seeds, they didn't have the depth of flavor of our Rocky Mountain berries. Botanically speaking, all huckleberries and blueberries belong to the genus *Vaccinium*, but sorting out the details of their relationships is very complicated.

What we call huckleberries in Montana may be referred to as whortleberries, bilberries, dewberries, or by some other name in another part of the country. The different varieties of huckleberries don't taste the same. The wild mountain huckleberries we eat range in color from light purple to almost black. One tiny specimen has a pronounced reddish tinge. If you can't get fresh huckleberries, the next best thing to do is to buy a jar of huckleberry jam, syrup, or pie filling made from wild Montana or Idaho berries. Then you will have some idea of what all the fuss is about.

Fresh Apricot-Blueberry Crisp

• Yield: 8 servings •

We have two beautiful apricot trees in our backyard. Every five years—if we're lucky—we get a crop. Each year, the trees bloom at the end of April. The bees come by the hundreds to pollinate the flowers, then we hold our breath, hoping a late frost won't kill our expectations. If we can just make it to the end of May, we're safe. The problem with apricots is that they do bloom early. In fact, the name "apricot," is derived like the word "precocious" from the Latin praecox. There is nothing like the taste of a homegrown apricot, warmed by the sun and bursting with flavor. Fortunately, store-bought apricots taste better baked than fresh and work perfectly well in this crisp. In supermarkets, apricot season is very short, lasting from late May to the beginning of July.

1 cup (4½ ounces) unbleached all-purpose flour

½ cup firmly packed dark brown sugar

1 teaspoon ground cinnamon

¼ teaspoon mace

¼ teaspoon freshly grated nutmeg

¼ teaspoon salt

½ cup butter, chilled and cut into 6 pieces

2 pounds fresh apricots, cut in half, pitted, and cut into 1-inch pieces

1 cup blueberries

½ cup granulated sugar

2 teaspoons pure vanilla extract

1 pint vanilla frozen yogurt (optional)

Adjust an oven rack to the center position and preheat the oven to 350°. Butter a 9 × 9 × 2-inch baking dish and set it aside.

Measure the flour by spooning it into a measuring cup, filling it to overflowing, and sweeping off the excess with a metal spatula.

In a medium-sized bowl, stir together the flour, brown sugar, cinnamon, mace, nutmeg, and salt. Add the butter and cut in with a pastry blender until the mixture resembles small peas. In a large bowl, combine the apricots, blueberries, granulated sugar, and vanilla until the mixture is moistened. Turn into the prepared pan and sprinkle with the crumb mixture, patting it gently in place without packing it down. Bake 40 to 45 minutes, or until the topping is browned, the filling is bubbly, and the apricots are tender. Cool. Serve warm or at room temperature with the frozen yogurt, if desired. Refrigerate any leftovers.

Huckleberry-Lime Sauce

• *Yield: 2 to 3 cups* •

I often freeze huckleberries and make this sauce throughout the winter to serve with sponge cake, cheesecakes, pancakes, waffles, or ice cream. It keeps in the refrigerator for 2 weeks.

4 to 5 cups huckleberries, fresh or frozen

1½ cups sugar

2 tablespoons freshly squeezed lime juice

2 teaspoons cornstarch

2 tablespoons water

Place 3 cups of the huckleberries (if frozen, measure the 3 cups first, then thaw) and the sugar in the work bowl of a food processor fitted with the metal blade. Process 2 minutes, then transfer to a 3-quart saucepan. Stir in the lime juice. Dissolve the cornstarch in the water and add it to the berry mixture. Cook over medium heat, stirring gently but continuously with a rubber spatula, until the mixture thickens and comes to a boil. Decrease heat to low and cook, stirring, 2 minutes more. Remove from the heat and pass through a fine-mesh strainer set over a large bowl, pressing to extract as much juice as possible. Discard the pulp. Stir the remaining 1 to 2 cups berries into the sauce (if frozen, add them unthawed). Cool completely, then cover and refrigerate. Serve cold.

Treasure State Tropical Cake

• *Yield: 12 to 16 servings* •

Montana is known as the Treasure State, and we who live in western Montana, where the climate is strongly influenced by Pacific coastal weather systems, tend to have milder winters compared to the rest of the state. Because of this, a very popular bumper sticker appeared several years ago, proclaiming "Native of Tropical Montana." Whenever I traveled by car to points south, people always commented on that message. Montana is, of course, far from tropical. But I make this cake to honor the sentiment on the bumper sticker and to use up all the egg yolks left over from the Hazelnut Praline Angel Food Cake (page 238).

Cake Batter

Unseasoned dry fine bread crumbs, for dusting

3 cups (13½ ounces) unbleached all-purpose flour

½ cup cornstarch

¼ teaspoon salt

1¼ cups egg yolks (about 14)

1½ cups butter, softened

4 cups (12 ounces) sifted confectioners' sugar

Grated zest of 1 lemon

Grated zest of 1 orange

Grated zest of 1 lime

2 teaspoons pure vanilla extract

3 tablespoons freshly squeezed lime juice

1 cup nonfat plain yogurt

1 teaspoon baking soda

Tropical Icing

1⅓ cups (4 ounces) sifted confectioners' sugar

1 tablespoon freshly squeezed lemon juice

½ teaspoon orange extract

1½ teaspoons hot water

For the cake, butter a 10-inch, 3½-inch-deep nonstick bundt pan and dust it generously with the bread crumbs. Tap out excess crumbs and set the pan aside. Adjust the oven rack to the lower-third position and preheat the oven to 350°.

Measure the flour by spooning it into a measuring cup, filling the cup to overflowing, and sweeping off the excess with a metal spatula. Transfer the flour to a sifter set over a square of waxed paper. To measure the cornstarch, place a ½-cup measure on waxed paper and pour cornstarch into the cup, filling it to overflowing and sweeping off the excess with a metal spatula. Sift the flour, cornstarch, and salt together 3 times and set aside.

In the large bowl of an electric mixer, beat the egg yolks at high speed with the whip attachment until they are more than triple in volume and are very pale and thick, about 5 minutes. Transfer the yolks to another bowl and set aside. In the first bowl, beat the butter on high speed about 1 minute until it is smooth and creamy. Add the confectioners' sugar, fruit zest, and vanilla. Beat several minutes on high speed until the mixture is fluffy and almost white. Scrape the side of the bowl once or twice. On medium or medium-high speed, beat in the lime juice, then add the beaten yolks. At first the mixture may appear curdled, but continued beating will make it smooth.

In a medium-sized bowl, stir together the yogurt and baking soda. The mixture will become very foamy. With the mixer set on the lowest speed, add the flour mixture in four additions, alternately adding the yogurt mixture in three additions, beginning and ending with the dry ingredients; stop periodically to scrape down the bowl well between additions. Pour the batter into the prepared pan and spread it level with a rubber spatula. The batter will fill the pan halfway. Bake for 50 to 60 minutes, or until the cake is a rich golden brown color and a cake tester or wooden skewer comes out clean when inserted in the center. When baked, the cake will fill the pan by three-fourths and may have a few cracks on the top.

Let the cake cool in the pan set on a rack for 30 minutes, then cover it with a cake rack, invert the two, and remove the pan. Cool completely.

Prepare the icing by whisking together all of the ingredients in a small bowl until smooth. The icing will be the consistency of medium-thick cream. Adjust the consistency with a little more sugar or hot water if necessary. Spoon and spread the icing on the top of the cake to cover it completely, letting some drip unevenly down the sides. When the icing has set, carefully transfer the cake with a wide metal spatula to a dessert platter. Cover and let the cake stand a few hours before serving. Store, covered, at room temperature for up to 4 days.

Nectarine Pie

• Yield: 8 servings •

In August, juicy and flavorful nectarines reach their peak in eastern Washington. Unlike peaches, nectarines do not have to be peeled before they are used in pies. Select fruit that feel firm but give a little when gently pressed. Nectarines should smell fruity when purchased and should be used as soon as possible. Serve the pie plain or with vanilla frozen yogurt, vanilla ice cream, or Huckleberry Ice Cream (page 227).

Pie crust pastry (page 228)

Filling

3½ pounds ripe nectarines

½ cup firmly packed light brown sugar

½ cup plus 1 tablespoon granulated sugar

4 to 5 tablespoons quick-cooking tapioca

1½ teaspoons pumpkin pie spice

¼ teaspoon salt

1 tablespoon freshly squeezed lime juice

2 tablespoons chilled butter, cut into small pieces

Refrigerate the pastry dough at least 1 hour.

Pit the nectarines and slice them about ½ inch thick. Combine the brown sugar, ½ cup of the granulated sugar, the tapioca, pumpkin pie spice, and salt in a large bowl. Add the nectarines and lime juice and fold everything together gently and thoroughly with a rubber spatula. Set aside 15 minutes.

Meanwhile, adjust two oven racks with one on the lowest shelf and the other in the center. Place a heavy baking sheet on the lower shelf and preheat the oven to 450°.

On a lightly floured surface, roll out the larger pastry disc into a 13-inch circle. Fit the dough loosely into a 9-inch glass or metal pie pan, leaving the excess pastry hanging over the edge. Mound the nectarine filling in the pastry, patting it down slightly with the rubber spatula. Scatter the butter pieces over the filling.

On a lightly floured surface, roll out the second pastry disc into a 12- to 13-inch circle. Brush the overhanging edge of pastry with water and place the top crust over the filling; press the edges of the top and bottom crusts together firmly to seal. Trim away excess pastry to within ½ inch from the rim of the pie pan. Fold over the pastry edge to form a standing rim and flute. Brush the top of the pastry lightly with water and sprinkle it with the remaining 1 tablespoon granulated sugar. Cut four 1½-inch-long slits at right angles in the top crust. Place the pie pan on the baking sheet and bake for 15 minutes. Transfer the baking sheet to the center shelf, reduce the oven temperature to 350°, and continue baking about 75 minutes, or until the pie is a deep golden brown color and the filling is bubbling up through the slits. Cool completely on a wire rack for several hours before serving. Refrigerate any leftovers.

Harvesting sugar beets (circa 1920).

Mail-Order Sources for
Specialty Ingredients and Equipment

Aux Delices des Bois
14 Leonard St.
New York, NY 10013
(800) 666-1232

*Many varieties of fresh, dried, and frozen
wild and cultivated mushrooms.*

Bear Creek Fisheries
358 Bear Creek Rd.
Libby, MT 59923
(800) 822-8478

*Ready-to-use huckleberry fillings for pies,
tarts, and cobblers as well as other
huckleberry, chokecherry, and raspberry
products.*

Dale's Exotic Meats
214 Denargo Market
Denver, CO 80216
(303) 297-9453

Large selection of game meats.

D'Artagnan
399-419 St. Paul Ave.
Jersey City, NJ 07306
(800) DARTAGNAN

*Huge selection of game meats, including New
Zealand venison and red deer (elk), ostrich,
duck, quail, and a variety of smoked and
cured meats. Also source for lamb.*

Denver Buffalo Company
1120 Lincoln St.
Denver, CO 80203-9790
(800) 289-2833

*Wide range of buffalo cuts, buffalo sausage,
leather products, and sauces.*

Eva Gates
P.O. Box 696
Bigfork, MT 59911-0696
(406) 837-4356

*Wide range of homemade preserves and
syrups, including huckleberry, raspberry,
black cap, and cherry.*

Fairé Game, Inc.
P.O. Box 7026
Loveland, CO 80537
(800) 889-6328

*Large variety of fresh and smoked game
meats, including pheasant, New Zealand red
deer (elk), and ducks. Also source for dried
wild mushrooms and dried berries.*

Game Sales International
P.O. Box 5314
Loveland, CO 80538
(800) 729-2090

*Large selection of game meats, dried wild
mushrooms, and other wild products.*

Giusto's Vita-Grain
241 E. Harris Ave.
South San Francisco, CA 94080
(415) 873-6566
(415) 873-2826 (fax)

High-performance organic baking flours.

Gourmet Mushrooms
P.O. Box 391
Sebastopol, CA 95472
(707) 823-1743

Fresh and dried cultivated mushrooms.

Indian Harvest Specialifoods, Inc.
P.O. Box 428
Bemidji, MN 56601
(800) 346-7032

*Specialty heirloom dried beans and other
hard-to-find items.*

Jamison Farms
171 Jamison Ln.
Latrobe, PA 15650
(800) 237-5262

*Lamb in all forms, including whole dressed
lambs. Most orders are shipped frozen, but
fresh shipments can be arranged.*

King Arthur Flour Company
P.O. Box 876
Norwich, VT 05055-0876
(800) 827-6836

An outstanding source for many kinds of organic and inorganic flours; baking equipment, including scales, baking stones, and specialty baking pans; high-quality bulk yeast; books, and much more.

Manchester Farms
P.O. Box 97
Dalzell, SC 29040
(800) 845-0421

Specializes in quail.

Meco Corporation
1500 Industrial Rd.
Greenville, TN 37743-8222
(800) 346-3256

Excellent electric water smokers, grills, grill accessories, and wood chunks and chips.

Mountain Lake Fisheries
P.O. Box 1067
Columbia Falls, MT 59912
(800) 809-0826

Whitefish, whitefish caviar, and smoked whitefish sausage, among other products.

Rocky Mountain Natural Meats, Inc.
P.O. Box 16668
Denver, CO 80216
(800) 327-2706

Wide range of buffalo cuts and sausages. Will do special orders.

Sur La Table
Pike Place Farmers' Market
84 Pine St.
Seattle, WA 98101
(800) 243-0852

Wide variety of baking and cooking equipment and books.

Unifine Milling Company
P.O. Box 565
Pullman, WA 99163
(509) 332-2607

Flourgirls whole wheat flour.

Washington State University Creamery
101 Food Quality Building
Pullman, WA 99164-6392
(509) 335-4014
(800) 457-5442

Cougar Gold, American Yellow Cheddar, and approximately 10 other cheeses. Call between 8:30 a.m. and 4:30 p.m. Mountain Time, Monday through Friday. No shipments during July and August.

Weber-Stephen Products Co.
200 East Daniels Rd.
Palatine, IL 60067-6266
(847) 934-5700

Outstanding selection of charcoal and gas grills and accessories.

White Mountain Farms, Inc.
8890 Lane 4 North
Mosca, CO 81146
(719) 378-2436
(719) 378-2429

Offers organically grown black quinoa, quinoa, quinoa flour, and several varieties of exotic potatoes.

Williams-Sonoma
P.O. Box 7456
San Francisco, CA 94120-7456
(800) 541-2233

Large selection of cookware, baking equipment, and specialty foods.

Credits for Photos and Quotes

Photos

Photos on pages ii, 9, 10, 27, 35, 45, 64, 93, 100, 105, 110, 122, 127, 131, 149, 176, 183, 193, 226, 235, and 247 reprinted with permission of The University of Montana, Mansfield Library.

Photos on pages 79 and 111 reprinted courtesy of Jo Rainbolt.

Quotes

Page 1: "In Search of the Oregon Trail." Produced and directed by Michael Farrell. Nebraska ETV Network and Oregon Public Broadcasting, 1996.

Page 6: Bryan, Lettice. *The Kentucky Housewife*. Columbia, SC: University of South Carolina Press, 1991.

Page 7: Marcy, Randolph. *The Prairie Traveler*. Bedford, MA: Applewood Books, 1859.

Page 8: Butruille, Susan G. *Women's Voices from the Western Frontier*. Boise, ID: Tamarack Books, Inc., 1995.

Page 13: Butruille, Susan G. *Women's Voices from the Western Frontier*. Boise, ID: Tamarack Books, Inc., 1995.

Page 15: Webber, Bert. *The Oregon Trail Diary of Twin Sisters, Cecelia Adams and Parthenia Blank in 1852*. Medford, OR: Webb Research Group, 1994. Telegram reprinted courtesy of Tony Grace.

Page 23: Butruille, Susan G. *Women's Voices from the Western Frontier*. Boise, ID: Tamarack Books, Inc., 1995.

Page 31: Webber, Bert. *The Oregon Trail Diary of Twin Sisters, Cecelia Adams and Parthenia Blank in 1852*. Medford, OR: Webb Research Group, 1994.

Page 33: Butruille, Susan G. *Women's Voices from the Western Frontier*. Boise, ID: Tamarack Books, Inc., 1995.

Page 47: Marcy, Randolph. *The Prairie Traveler*. Bedford, MA: Applewood Books, 1859.

Page 51: Gilliss, Julia. *So Far From Home: An Army Bride on the Western Frontier 1865–1869*. Eugene, OR: Oregon Historical Society Press, 1993.

Page 63: *A Country Kitchen*. Maynard, MA: Chandler Press, 1987.

Page 79: Author's interview with Tony Grace in May, 1992, in Hamilton, MT.

Page 85: Holmes, Kenneth L., ed. *Covered Wagon Women: Diaries and Letters from the Western Trails, 1840–1890*. vol. 10. Spokane, WA: Arthur H. Clark, 1991.

Page 89: Butruille, Susan G. *Women's Voices from the Oregon Trail: The Times That Tried Women's Souls and A Guide to Women's History Along the Oregon Trail*. 2nd ed. Boise, ID: Tamarack Books, 1994.

Page 95 (Top): Williams, Jacqueline. *Wagon Wheel Kitchens: Food on the Oregon Trail*. Lawrence, KS: University Press of Kansas,1993.

Page 95 (Bottom): Holmes, Kenneth L., ed. *Covered Wagon Women: Diaries and Letters from the Western Trails, 1840–1890*. vol. 7. Glendale, CA: Arthur H. Clark, 1991.

Page 96: Leslie, Eliza. *Directions for Cookery*. Philadelphia: Henry C. Baird, 1857.

Page 97: Author's interview with Tony Grace in May, 1992, in Hamilton, MT.

Page 99: Arnold, Sam. *Fryingpans West*. Denver: Arnold and Company, 1985.

Page 100: Author's interview with Tony Grace in May, 1992, in Hamilton, MT.

Pages 110, 111: Author's interview with Tony Grace in May, 1992, in Hamilton, MT.

Page 113: Gilliss, Julia. *So Far From Home: An Army Bride on the Western Frontier 1865–1869*. Eugene, OR: Oregon Historical Society Press, 1993.

Page 115: Author's interview with Tony Grace in May, 1992, in Hamilton, MT.

Page 117: Greenberg, Judith E. and Helen Carey McKeever, *A Pioneer Woman's Memoir*. New York: Franklin Watts, 1995.

Page 121: Author's interview with Tony Grace in May, 1992, in Hamilton, MT.

Page 122: Arnold, Samuel P. *Eating Up the Santa Fe Trail*. Niwot, CO: University Press of Colorado, 1990.

Page 127: Arnold, Samuel P. *Eating Up the Santa Fe Trail*. Niwot, CO: University Press of Colorado, 1990.

Page 135: Butruille, Susan G. *Women's Voices from the Oregon Trail: The Times That Tried Women's Souls and A Guide to Women's History Along the Oregon Trail*. 2nd ed. Boise, ID: Tamarack Books, 1994.

Page 147: Greenberg, Judith E. and Helen Carey McKeever. *A Pioneer Woman's Memoir*. New York: Franklin Watts, 1995.

Page 153: Williams, Jacqueline. *Wagon Wheel Kitchens: Food on the Oregon Trail*. Lawrence, KS: University Press of Kansas,1993.

Page 159: Butruille, Susan G. *Women's Voices from the Western Frontier*. Boise, ID: Tamarack Books, Inc., 1995.

Page 161: Gilliss, Julia. *So Far From Home: An Army Bride on the Western Frontier 1865–1869*. Eugene, OR: Oregon Historical Society Press, 1993.

Page 173: Gilliss, Julia. *So Far From Home: An Army Bride on the Western Frontier 1865–1869*. Eugene, OR: Oregon Historical Society Press, 1993.

Page 176: Butruille, Susan G. *Women's Voices from the Western Frontier*. Boise, ID: Tamarack Books, Inc., 1995.

Page 177: Gilliss, Julia. *So Far From Home: An Army Bride on the Western Frontier 1865–1869*. Eugene, OR: Oregon Historical Society Press, 1993.

Page 181: Gilliss, *Julia. So Far From Home: An Army Bride on the Western Frontier 1865–1869*. Eugene, OR: Oregon Historical Society Press, 1993.

Page 183: Gilliss, Julia. *So Far From Home: An Army Bride on the Western Frontier 1865–1869*. Eugene, OR: Oregon Historical Society Press, 1993.

Page 203: Greenberg, Judith E. and Helen Carey McKeever. *A Pioneer Woman's Memoir*. New York: Franklin Watts, 1995.

Page 215: Gilliss, Julia. *So Far From Home: An Army Bride on the Western Frontier 1865–1869*. Eugene, OR: Oregon Historical Society Press, 1993.

Page 218: Child, Mrs. *The American Frugal Housewife*. New York: Samuel S. and William Wood, 1844.

Page 219: Author's interview with Tony Grace in May, 1992, in Hamilton, MT.

Page 221: Parke, Charles Ross. *Dreams to Dust: A Diary of the California Gold Rush, 1849-1850*. Lincoln, NE: University of Nebraska Press, 1989.

Page 231: Bowen, Asta. *The Huckleberry Book*. Helena, MT: American Geographic Publishing, 1988.

Page 237: Butruille, Susan G. *Women's Voices from the Oregon Trail: The Times That Tried Women's Souls and A Guide to Women's History Along the Oregon Trail*. 2nd ed. Boise, ID: Tamarack Books, 1994.

Page 240: Butruille, Susan G. *Women's Voices from the Oregon Trail: The Times That Tried Women's Souls and A Guide to Women's History Along the Oregon Trail*. 2nd ed. Boise, ID: Tamarack Books, 1994.

Selected Bibliography

Arnold, Samuel P. *Eating Up the Santa Fe Trail*. Niwot, CO: University Press of Colorado, 1990.
Recipes, lore, and anecdotes, with an extensive bibliography.

————. *Fryingpans West*. Denver: Arnold and Company, 1985.
Historically accurate recipes and history of food and drink of the western frontier.

Arora, David. *Mushrooms Demystified*. rev. ed. Berkeley: Ten Speed Press, 1990.
Comprehensive guide to wild mushroom identification with delicious recipes.

Ash, John and Sid Goldstein. *American Game Cooking: A Contemporary Guide to Preparing Farm-Raised Game Birds & Meats*. New York: Addison-Wesley, 1993.
Covers all types of game, how to cook them, and what wines to serve with them; includes extensive list of sources.

Bertolli, Paul and Alice L. Waters. *Chez Panisse Cooking: New Tastes & Techniques*. New York: Random House, 1988.
Excellent general cookbook, with exemplary chapter on breads (including various sourdoughs).

Bittman, Mark. *Fish: The Complete Guide to Buying and Cooking*. New York: Macmillan, 1994.
Everything you need to know about fish from anchovies to wolffish, including how to clean and fillet a fish properly.

Butruille, Susan G. *Women's Voices from the Oregon Trail: The Times That Tried Women's Souls and A Guide to Women's History Along the Oregon Trail*. 2nd ed. Boise, ID: Tamarack Books, 1994.
Quotes from diaries relating what life was like on the trail; includes photos and an extensive bibliography.

————. *Women's Voices from the Western Frontier*. Boise, ID: Tamarack Books, 1995.
Women settlers' quotes about their new life in the West; includes photos and extensive bibliography.

Cox, Beverly and Martin Jacobs. *Spirit of the Harvest: North American Indian Cooking*. New York: Stewart Tabori & Chang, 1991.
Detailed history and survey of Native American cookery, with recipes and color photographs.

Gilliss, Julia. *So Far From Home: An Army Bride on the Western Frontier 1865-1869*. Portland, OR: Oregon Historical Society Press, 1993.
One pioneer woman's collection of letters.

Greenberg, Judith E. and Helen Carey McKeever. *A Pioneer Woman's Memoir*. New York: Franklin Watts, 1995.
Based on the journal of Arabella Clemens Fulton, who first settled in the Idaho Territory in 1864. Authors' historical information provides the framework for Fulton's recollections. Archival photos and sketches included.

Holmes, Kenneth L., ed. *Covered Wagon Women: Diaries and Letters from the Western Trails, 1840-1890*. Glendale, CA/Spokane, WA: Arthur H. Clark, 1983–1991.
Ten volumes in a series that is an indispensable source for historians.

Hooker, Richard J. *Food and Drink in America*. Indianapolis: Bobbs-Merrill, 1981.

An essential reference with a comprehensive bibliography.

Jamison, Cheryl A. and Bill Jamison. *Smoke & Spice: Cooking with Smoke, The Real Way to Barbecue on Your Charcoal Grill, Water Smoker, or Wood Burning Pit*. Boston, MA: Harvard Common Press, 1994.

A useful all-purpose guide to smoking with delicious recipes.

Knote, Charlie and Ruthie Knote. *Barbecuing & Sausage Making Secrets*. rev. ed. Cape Girardeau, MO: Culinary Institute of Smoke Cooking, 1993.

Detailed discussions of smokers and sausage formulas. To order, write The Culinary Institue of Smoke Cooking, 2323 Brookwood Dr., Box 163, Cape Girardeau, MO 63702-0163.

Leader, Daniel and Judith Blahnik. *Bread Alone: Bold Fresh Loaves from Your Own Hands*. New York: William Morrow, 1993.

Most of the recipes are for hearty whole-grain breads; includes excellent discussion of grains, fermentation, and various kinds of starters.

Lucchetti, Cathy. *Home on the Range: A Culinary History of the American West*. New York: Villard Books, 1993.

Hundreds of black-and-white archival photos along with a detailed, lively text summarizing the culinary history of a vast region.

Marcy, Randolph B. *The Prairie Traveler*. Bedford, MA: Applewood Books, 1988.

A facsimile of the handbook originally published in 1859. Includes information on routes, first aid, clothing, provisions, wagon maintenance, and much more. Used by many pioneers on their way west.

Niethammer, Carolyn. *American Indian Food & Lore*. New York: Simon & Schuster, 1974.

Describes dozens of plant foods used by Native Americans and how to cook with them. About 150 vegetarian recipes with large, clear pencil sketches of the plants described.

Oppenneer, Betsy. *The Bread Book*. New York: Harper Collins, 1994.

Yeast and quick breads for the home cook described by a professional baker in clear, no-nonsense language. Nice discussion of various starters.

Ortiz, Joe. *The Village Baker: Classic Regional Breads from Europe and America*. Berkeley: Ten Speed Press, 1993.

Insights from a master baker. Includes helpful photos and sketches. No quick breads.

Patent, Dorothy Hinshaw and Diane E. Bilderback. *The Harrowsmith Country Life Book of Garden Secrets*. Charlotte, VT: Camden House, 1991.

Describes organic vegetable gardening by climatic zones; especially helpful to gardeners in the Rocky Mountain West.

Rainbolt, Jo. *The Last Cowboy: Twilight Era of the Horseback Cowhand, 1900-1940*. Helena, MT: American & World Geographic Publishing, 1992.

Profiles the lives of seven cowboys, including Tony Grace.

Root, Waverley. *Food*. New York: Simon and Schuster, 1980.

Encyclopedic dictionary of the world's foods, with history, sketches, and photos. An invaluable reference.

Root, Waverley and Richard de Rochemont. *Eating in America: A History*. New York: Ecco Press, 1994.

A comprehensive social history of American gastronomy from the time of the earliest explorers to the present. An essential volume for serious cooks.

Sharpe, J. Ed and Thomas B. Underwood. *American Indian Cooking and Herb Lore*. Cherokee, NC: Cherokee Publications, 1973.

A 32-page booklet with recipes, illustrations, and stories. To order, write Cherokee Publications, P.O. Box 430, Cherokee, NC 28719, or call 704-488-8856.

Silverton, Nancy and Laurie Ochoa. *Nancy Silverton's Breads from the La Brea Bakery: Recipes for the Connoisseur*. New York: Random House, 1996.

Offers the most detailed and clear descriptions for making successful starters from wild yeasts, making terrific breads with the starters, and keeping the starters alive; for the absolutely devoted home bread makers.

Sunset editors. *The Sunset Cookbook of Breads*. Menlo Park, CA: Lane Book Company, 1963.

Excellent collection of yeast and quick breads, with an easy-to-follow description of making a milk-based wild yeast starter that really works.

The Web-Foot Cookbook. Portland, OR: W.B. Ayer, 1994.

A facsimile edition of the original, which was published by the First Presbyterian Church of Portland, Oregon, in 1885. This is perhaps the first cookbook to come out of the Pacific Northwest. Essential reading for food historians.

Webber, Bert. *The Oregon Trail Diary of Twin Sisters, Cecelia Adams and Parthenia Blank in 1852*. Medford, OR: Webb Research Group, 1994.

Two sisters' accounts of their wagon train journey. Illustrated with photographs and a map. To order, write Webb Research Group, Publishers, P.O. Box 314, Medford, OR 97501.

Williams, Jacqueline. *Wagon Wheel Kitchens: Food on the Oregon Trail*. Lawrence, KS: University Press of Kansas, 1993.

Vivid descriptions of life and cooking on the Oregon Trail. Lively prose and illustrations.

Wood, Rebecca. *Quinoa the Supergrain: Ancient Food for Today*. New York: Farrar, Strauss, & Giroux, 1989.

A history of quinoa with lots of recipes.

Zumbo, Jim. *Amazing Venison Recipes*. Cody, WY: Wapiti Valley Publishing, 1994.

Everything you need to know about venison, with recipes also for elk, moose, antelope, and other big-game animals. To order, write Wapiti Valley Publishing Co., P.O. Box 2390, Cody, WY 82414, or call 307-587-5486.